D1118580

CRIME OF THE CENTURY

The Kennedy Assassination from a Historian's Perspective

THE HARVESTER PRESS LTD.

CRIME OF THE CENTURY

THE KENNEDY ASSASSINATION FROM A HISTORIAN'S PERSPECTIVE

BY MICHAEL L. KURTZ

The Harvester Press Ltd.
16 Ship Street
Brighton
Sussex BN1 1AD
England

ISBN 0-7108-0471-7

PREFACE

THE ASSASSINATION of President John Fitzgerald Kennedy is one of those historical events that etch themselves forever in the mind. Few adults cannot recall precisely what they were doing when they first heard of the fateful shooting in Dallas. Kennedy's murder proved to be a stunning, shocking event that seemed to alter history with one blow. Today, many years later, the Kennedy assassination remains one of the great traumatic events of contemporary society.

Television brought the assassination and its aftermath vividly into the national consciousness. In their finest hours, the electronic news media captured the events unfolding in Dallas and Washington and transmitted them instantaneously to the American people. Far more graphically and realistically than the printed page, the video screen depicted some of the most unforgettable scenes in recent history: a tearful Walter Cronkite announcing the news of the president's death; Jacqueline Kennedy, her suit and stockings smeared with her husband's blood, disembarking from Air Force One; three-year-old "John-John" Kennedy saluting his father's flag-draped coffin; the haunting cadence of the muffled drums sounding the rhythm of the funeral cortege; Jack Ruby gunning down Lee Harvey Oswald.

The impact of the Kennedy assassination on American history was considerable. It plucked Lyndon Johnson from the obscurity of the vice-presidency and played a significant role in the Democratic party's sweep of the 1964 national elections. It reversed our Vietnam policy, from Kennedy's deescalation of United States involvement in the Indochina conflict to Johnson's escalation of it. It invigorated the seemingly defunct political career of Richard Nixon, for Barry Goldwater's disastrous defeat in 1964 prompted the Republican party to turn to Nixon as its standard-bearer in 1968. It fostered the legend of Camelot, a legend expounded in print by Arthur Schlesinger, Jr., and Theodore Sorensen and in politics by John Kennedy's brothers, Robert and Edward. Perhaps most significantly, the Kennedy assassination was the first of the explosive events of the 1960s—assassinations, riots, demonstrations—that rocked the nation's social and political structure and ushered in an age of cynicism and distrust.

Such an event deserves the serious and careful scrutiny of the scholar. Unfortunately, it has not received that scrutiny. For the most part, professional scholars have neglected the assassination, as if it never occurred. This lack of attention has created a vacuum filled by journalists, free-lance writers, and others, most of whom have examined the assassination more for its sensational than for its objective value. As a result, virtually all of the innumerable Kennedy assassination studies have displayed obvious bias and have lacked the careful analysis of objective evidence that characterizes the scholar.

This work examines the assassination of President Kennedy according to the available evidence. That evidence includes a variety of sources ranging from reliable documentary and scientific material to reckless and irresponsible speculation. For over a decade after the tragedy in Dallas, the federal government systematically withheld significant portions of the evidence from public scrutiny. In the past five years, however, the pressure of numerous Freedom of Information Act lawsuits resulted in the declassification of such important materials as the voluminous assassination files of the Federal Bureau of Investigation and the Central Intelligence Agency, as well as most of the previously classified Warren Commission documents.

Although some assassination evidence remains classified or otherwise unavailable for research, the evidence that is available, including the thirteen published volumes of the Select Committee on Assassinations of the House of Representatives, provides the raw material for a thorough historical investigation. In addition to the documentary sources, the author has conducted a fifteen-year research into the assassination. The secondary source materials consulted include the thousands of published accounts of the assassination. In addition, the author has interviewed scores of eyewitnesses and medical, ballistics, and scientific experts and has intensively examined a wide variety of films, sound and video tapes, photographs, and slides. In many instances, the persons interviewed and the materials analyzed had not been previously available to assassination researchers.

Like any important historical event, the Kennedy assassination cannot be explained with simplistic answers or with magical solutions to the myriad problems it poses. The evidence in this case offers a bewildering variety of possible and plausible explanations of the many puzzling events in it. Only after years of careful research and analysis has the author been able to sift through the maze of conflicting evidence and to interpret it in a reasonable manner.

Not all of the mysteries of the Kennedy assassination will be solved. Nevertheless, much of the evidence does lend itself to reasonable interpretation. The evidence, for example, clearly demonstrates that John Kennedy was killed as a result of a conspiracy and that, intentionally or unintentionally, the federal government assisted in concealing proof of that conspiracy. The evidence also indicates that the assassination was a cleverly planned and carefully executed operation. It also shows that Lee Harvey Oswald was not simply the "lone nut" that the federal authorities claimed he was.

Despite the expenditure of over ten million dollars of the taxpayers' money, the two official federal investigations, those of the Warren Commission and of the House Select Committee on Assassinations, failed to resolve the manifold questions raised by the assassination. Both investigations heightened the controversies over such matters as the source and direction of the shots and the existence of a conspiracy. Both inquiries proved seriously deficient in their failure to employ the methodology of the historian: the objective evaluation of the evidence according to the established standards of professional scholarship.

However flawed the federal investigations were, they do provide the raw materials for this book. After an opening chapter setting the background to this event, the book critically analyzes the Warren Commission and House Select Committee investigations, insofar as the available evidence permits such an analysis. The analysis is followed by an examination of the many questions raised by the assassination. The work closes with an explanation of how the assassination occurred and the nature and extent of the conspiracy involved.

Only those aspects of the Kennedy assassination that lend themselves to reasonable interpretation will be presented. However tempting it might be, speculation is not within the realm of the historian. Unlike most works on the assassination, which rely on flimsy or nonexistent evidence to "prove" their theories, this work concentrates on reliable primary source material. Only the closing chapter of this work, separated from the rest of the volume, presents an interpretation of the evidence to show how the assassination occurred. It is an original interpretation based on a carefully calculated scrutiny of the most reliable and convincing sources.

Given the available evidence, this work attempts to tell the story of the assassination of President Kennedy as thoroughly and objectively as possible. It is not merely a rehashing of the familiar critiques of the *Warren Report,* although it does present some of the most convincing arguments raised by the critics. This work offers much new evidence about the crime and provides an original and plausible interpretation of it. If this book succeeds in making the reader aware of the historical significance of the assassination of President Kennedy and in providing him with an appreciation of its magnitude and complexity, it will have served its purpose.

Michael L. Kurtz

7 May 1981

CONTENTS

ILLUSTRATIONS

Maps

CRIME OF THE CENTURY

The Kennedy Assassination from a Historian's Perspective

CHAPTER I

THREE MURDERS IN DALLAS

IT HAD RAINED earlier in the morning. But now, shortly before noon, as President John Fitzgerald Kennedy disembarked from Air Force One at Dallas's Love Field, the sun shone brilliantly through clear blue skies. Small gusts of wind disrupted an otherwise perfect autumn day, but the size and enthusiasm of the crowds that turned out to greet him demonstrated to Kennedy his popularity with the people of Texas.[1]

For President Kennedy, it had been a grueling two-day sojourn into Texas. Politics had motivated him to make this trip. Kennedy wanted to reconcile the two warring factions of Texas's Democratic party: one under Vice-President Lyndon Johnson and Governor John Connally, and a more liberal one under Senator Ralph Yarborough and Representative Henry Gonzalez. Keenly aware of his mediocre rating in the latest Gallup poll, Kennedy believed that Texas's twenty-four electoral votes would be critical in his bid for reelection in 1964. He had barely carried Texas against Richard Nixon in 1960, and the Republicans appeared likely to nominate Senator Barry Goldwater as their candidate for the 1964 contest. Since Goldwater was extremely popular in Texas, the Democrats needed to patch up their differences to confront the Republicans with a united organization. So eager was he to make a favorable impression on the Texans that Kennedy even made the unusual gesture of bringing his wife, Jacqueline, with him. The first day of the trip —visits to Houston and San Antonio on 21 November—had been very successful. Now, on 22 November 1963, after an overnight stay in Fort Worth and a brief flight to Dallas, Kennedy stepped into a waiting limousine, ready to take him on a motorcade through the Dallas business district and then to the city's Trade Mart for a speech.[2]

The motorcade had been carefully arranged to give the president maximum exposure to the public. It would proceed on the main street of downtown Dallas during the noon lunch hour, when tens of thousands of people would be on the streets. Leading the motorcade was an escort vehicle driven by Dallas Police Chief Jesse Curry, followed by several police motorcycles. Then came the presidential limousine, a massive black Lincoln convertible specially made to Secret Service specifications by the Ford Motor Company. Secret Service Agent William Greer drove the car. Next to him sat Agent Roy Kellerman, the head of the Secret Service's White House detail. In the midsection of the car, in folding jump seats, sat Governor and Mrs. Connally, the governor on the right side and his wife on the left. In the rear seat sat President Kennedy on the right and Mrs. Kennedy on the left. Behind the presidential limousine were, in order, a Secret Service car, a convertible carrying Vice-President and Mrs. Johnson, and another Secret Service car. The rest of the caravan of twenty-one vehicles included cars and busses transporting politicians, various members of the presidential entourage, and the press, all escorted by Dallas police officers on motorcycle.[3]

When the motorcade left the airport, the Secret Service decided not to use a clear, bullet-proof "bubbletop" shield to cover the limousine. Several times President Kennedy stopped the limousine and got out to shake the hands and greet crowds of well-wishers. As the motorcade slowly meandered through the Dallas business district on the appropriately named Main Street, it was apparent to all that his visit to Dallas was a rousing success. When the limousine turned onto Houston Street and entered Dealey Plaza, an open area on the outskirts of the downtown section, Mrs. Connally turned to the president and remarked, "You can't say that Dallas doesn't love you." The president replied, "That's obvious."[4]

As the caravan made the turn from Main Street onto Houston Street, the crowd had thinned noticeably. However, Kennedy continued to smile and wave to the people during the short, one-block trip on Houston Street. He kept up the friendly gestures after the vehicle made a left-hand turn onto Elm Street, a thoroughfare that led directly to the freeway on which the Trade Mart was located. This block-long stretch of Elm Street was flanked on one end by a seven-story red brick structure called the Texas School Book Depository building, and on the other end by a small hill covered with bushes and surrounded by a six-foot-high wooden fence.[5]

The sharp turn onto Elm Street caused driver Greer to slow the limousine to a snail's pace, and it took several seconds for the Lincoln to travel a hundred feet. At this point, clothing manufacturer Abraham Zapruder flicked the switch of his 8-millimeter Bell and Howell home movie camera, focused his telephoto lens on the president, and began filming. Fewer than three seconds elapsed when a sharp report reverberated throughout Dealey Plaza. Unaware that he was recording the most graphic and sensational piece of film in history, Zapruder maintained a steady focus on the limousine. Through the camera lens Zapruder saw President Kennedy grimace in pain as the limousine emerged from behind a street sign that had blocked his view of the car for one brief second. Several more reports followed, and Zapruder saw the president's head explode in a spray of red and his entire body thrust violently backward and to the left. Mesmerized by the carnage inflicted on the president he loved, Abraham Zapruder continued filming as Mrs. Kennedy crawled onto the trunk of the limousine, to be met by Secret Service Agent Clint Hill, who had sprung from the car behind the president. Zapruder did not stop the camera until he could no longer see the speeding Lincoln as it disappeared through an underpass leading to the freeway.[6]

Many of the spectators in Dealey Plaza witnessed these spectacular events and others not recorded by Zapruder's camera. Howard Leslie Brennan had taken time off from his construction job in order to see the president. Arriving at the corner of Elm and Houston about ten minutes before the motorcade, Brennan sat down on a concrete ledge directly opposite the Book Depository building. As he awaited the motorcade, Brennan glanced up and observed a man standing in the sixth-floor window at the southeast corner of the building. As the man withdrew from the window and returned to it several times,

Brennan noticed that he held a rifle. Hearing the motorcade, Brennan paid no more attention to the man in the window. Shortly after the Kennedy car turned onto Elm Street, Brennan heard a noise like a firecracker. He looked up at the sixth-floor window and saw the man aiming his rifle in the direction of President Kennedy. Then the man fired and paused a moment, as if he wanted to be sure he had hit his target. Fearing for his life, Brennan dove behind a concrete ledge and stayed there, hunched over, for several minutes. When he felt assured that it was safe to get up, Brennan ran to a nearby law enforcement officer and gave him a description of the rifleman.[7]

Amos Lee Euins, a fifteen-year-old boy, also saw the sixth-floor rifleman fire a shot at the president. Three people riding in the motorcade also noticed unusual happenings in the window. Robert Jackson, a photographer for the *Dallas Times-Herald,* saw a rifle in the window. The wife of the mayor of Dallas, Mrs. Earle Cabell, saw a pipelike object protruding from the window.[8]

Other persons witnessed strange occurrences elsewhere in the building. About ten minutes before the shooting, Arnold Rowland saw a man holding a rifle standing in the sixth-floor southwest corner window of the Book Depository. Carolyn Walther saw two men in a fifth-floor window; one of them held a gun. Several inmates watching the motorcade from the Dallas County jail on Houston Street also saw the gunman on the fifth floor.[9]

Earlier that day, Julia Ann Mercer was driving on Elm Street, and she saw a green truck parked on the side of the road, about one hundred fifty feet before the underpass. A man stepped out of the truck and, carrying an object that resembled a gun case, went up a hill and behind a wooden fence. This fenced, hilly area into which the man disappeared would shortly become one of the most famous pieces of real estate in America. It was called the Grassy Knoll.[10]

A railroad employee named Lee Bowers was stationed in a tower overlooking the train tracks behind the Grassy Knoll. Bowers saw two men behind the fence and observed a flash of light or smoke in the knoll during the shooting. Another railroad employee, J.C. Price, saw a man carrying what appeared to be a gun run from the Grassy Knoll immediately after the shots. Secret Service Agent Forrest Sorrels and Senator Ralph Yarborough detected the distinct smell of gunpowder as their cars sped past the Grassy Knoll after the shots.[11]

Motorcycle Police Officer Marrion L. Baker rode near the end of the motorcade and had just turned onto Houston Street when the shooting began. After the last shot, Baker raced to the corner of Elm and Houston, jumped from his motorcycle, and rushed past a crowd of spectators into the Texas School Book Depository building. He wanted to get to the roof in order to obtain a panoramic view of Dealey Plaza. Accompanied by Roy Truly, the building superintendent, Baker ran up the back stairs. When he reached the second floor landing, he observed a man standing in front of a Coke machine in a lunchroom. Baker ran into the room, drew his revolver, and ordered the man to approach. Truly came in and identified the man as one of his employees. Officer Baker replaced his gun and resumed his ascent to the roof. The man in the lunchroom purchased a Coke and slowly walked toward the front of the building. His name was Lee Harvey Oswald.[12]

In the meantime, about ten seconds after the shots, Secret Service Agent Greer accelerated the presidential limousine and followed the police chief's car onto a freeway at a speed of over sixty miles an hour. After climbing back into the rear seat of the limousine, Jacqueline Kennedy and Secret Service Agent Clint Hill made no attempt to readjust the stricken president, even though the impact of the bullet had knocked him face down on the rear seat, with his left foot dangling over the rear door of the car. Blood and brain tissue were splattered all over the rear seat and trunk of the vehicle.[13]

About five minutes later, the limousine arrived at Dallas's Parkland Memorial Hospital. The president and governor were removed from the limousine, placed on stretchers, and wheeled into emergency rooms on the first floor. Just as nurses finished removing Kennedy's clothing, Doctors James Carrico and Malcolm Perry arrived. They saw at once that he was beyond help. A huge, gaping hole on the right side of Kennedy's head bled profusely, and brain tissue slowly exuded from it onto the stretcher sheets and emergency room floor.[14]

As the surgeon in charge, Dr. Perry had to decide what steps to take. He knew that President Kennedy could not possibly survive the massive damage to his head. Since Kennedy was still technically alive (the doctors heard a feeble heartbeat and detected slight respiration), Perry ordered emergency life-saving measures to begin. The president was given an injection of hydrocortisone because of his history of adrenal insufficiency. Endotracheal tubes were placed in his chest to drain blood and mucous from his respiratory system.[15]

These and other measures were performed by the numerous physicians crowding into Trauma Room Number One. Malcolm Perry confined his activities to a tracheotomy—cutting a hole directly into the windpipe and then inserting a tube in order to provide a more direct air passage into and out of the lungs. As he was about to make his incision, Dr. Perry noticed a tiny hole immediately below the president's Adam's apple. Only an eighth of an inch in diameter, the hole in the neck was round, had a small ring of bruising around it, with blood slowly trickling out. Perry immediately recognized these signs of a bullet entrance hole but thought no more about it. His job was to assist the president's breathing, so he sliced through the hole in the neck, making it large enough to put the tube in. Since the bullet hole was in the exact spot that Dr. Perry wanted to make his tracheotomy incision, he simply extended the tiny hole to the large, jagged size of a tracheotomy.[16]

It was to no avail. Shortly after the doctors began working on Kennedy, the electrocardiogram recorded no heart activity. Several doctors feverishly pumped their fists on the president's sternum, but this closed cardiac massage failed to generate a heartbeat. Aware of Kennedy's Roman Catholic faith, hospital authorities had called Father Oscar Huber, whose parish included Parkland Hospital. As soon as he arrived at the hospital, the priest was ushered into the emergency room. He performed the last rites of the Church and, joined by Mrs. Kennedy, who knelt before her husband's stretcher, said the Act of Contrition, the Church's prayer for forgiveness of sin. After Father Huber left, Dr. Kemp Clark, a neurosurgeon, pronounced John Kennedy dead. The time was a few minutes before 1:00 P.M.[17]

After being told that Kennedy was dead, the new president, Lyndon Johnson, and his entourage left immediately for Air

Force One. Then presidential adviser Malcolm Kilduff informed the press that President Kennedy had died. Texas authorities moved to claim the body. Presidential assassination was not a federal crime (the law has since been changed) and therefore fell under the Texas state laws governing homicide. State law required an autopsy to be performed in all cases of violent death. But the slain president's entourage refused to permit the body to leave their possession. After a brief disagreement, the Texas officials relented. A local undertaker donated a coffin for the transportation of the corpse back to Washington. At about 2:15 P.M., the Kennedy party arrived at the airport. Mrs. Kennedy was called to the front cabin of Air Force One. She stood silently as Judge Sara Hughes administered the oath of office to Lyndon Baines Johnson as the thirty-sixth president of the United States.[18]

In Dealey Plaza, the final curtain had not yet fallen on the day's high drama. Dallas Police Officer Joe Marshall Smith directed traffic at the corner of Elm and Houston. Immediately after the shooting, Smith saw many people running up the embankment on the Grassy Knoll, and he ran over there to see what was happening. After scaling the wooden fence, Smith drew his revolver and began looking around the area. He noticed a man attempting to leave the parking lot behind the knoll. When Officer Smith accosted him, the man pulled out Secret Service credentials, so Smith let him go.[19]

About fifteen minutes after the assassination, Deputy Sheriff Roger Craig saw a man run from the rear of the Book Depository building. The man got into a light-colored Rambler station wagon driven by a dark-complected man. The vehicle proceeded down Elm Street, through the triple underpass, and onto the freeway. At the same time, other police officers combed the railroad yards next to the Grassy Knoll. They discovered three suspicious men hiding in a boxcar. The officers arrested the trio and led them off.[20]

Within minutes of the shooting, hundreds of law enforcement officials converged on Dealey Plaza. Some of the police questioned witnesses, one of whom was Howard Brennan. Brennan described the gunman he saw in the sixth-floor window as a slender white male about five feet ten inches tall and weighing one hundred sixty-five to one hundred seventy pounds. The description was immediately broadcast over the Dallas police radio. Another message sent out over that radio ordered all available policemen either to Dealey Plaza or to Parkland Hospital. The only exception was Officer Number 78, who was ordered to remain in his patrol car in the Oak Cliff residential section of Dallas, and to "be at large for any emergency that comes in." The officer was J.D. Tippit.[21]

Since Brennan had pointed out the Book Depository building as the source of the shots, the police began searching it floor by floor. A little after 1:00, Deputy Sheriff Luke Mooney pushed some stacks of boxes aside because they blocked the southeast corner of the building's sixth floor. As he approached the corner, Mooney discovered several cartridge cases lying on the floor near the left-hand window. He also saw chicken bones strewn all over the place. About ten minutes later, Deputy Sheriff Eugene Boone and Deputy Constable Seymour Weitzman found a rifle hidden under a stack of boxes near the stairway at the northwest corner of the sixth floor.[22]

The Dallas Police fingerprint expert, Lieutenant J.C. Day, arrived at the scene and photographed the cartridge cases and rifle. Then he dusted the rifle for prints and, finding none, handed the weapon to the Dallas homicide chief, Captain J. Will Fritz. Fritz opened the bolt of the rifle, and a live round of ammunition appeared in the firing chamber. Lieutenant Day went back to the southeast corner of the sixth floor and began dusting numerous book cartons surrounding the corner. He found prints on several of the cartons.[23]

Governor John Connally had also been wounded in the shooting. Like President Kennedy, he was placed on a stretcher and wheeled into an emergency treatment room. After nurses removed the governor's clothing, Dr. Robert Shaw, a thoracic surgeon, observed a large wound on the governor's chest, just below his right nipple. Shaw determined that Connally required immediate surgery, so he was taken, still on the original stretcher, to a second-floor operating room. There the governor was transferred to an operating table, and an orderly pushed his empty stretcher into a waiting elevator.[24]

Governor Connally had been wounded in the chest, wrist,

and thigh. Dr. Shaw operated on his chest, Dr. Charles Gregory on his wrist, and Dr. Thomas Shires on his thigh. Dr. Shaw found that a bullet had entered Connally's back, bounced against his fifth rib, and exited from his chest. The rib shattered from the impact, and flying bone fragments collapsed his right lung. Dr. Gregory found that a bullet had entered the underside of the right wrist and had fractured the radius, the large bone on the thumb side of the wrist. Dr. Gregory removed several small bullet fragments from the wrist. The bullet had then exited the wrist. Dr. Shires observed a tiny hole in Connally's thigh. Although X-rays revealed a bullet fragment located near the governor's thigh bone, Shires did not operate on the wound, since no serious damage had been caused. After repairing the governor's wounds, the three surgeons agreed that John Connally would fully recover.[25]

A little after 1:00, Hospital Engineer Darrell Tomlinson got into an elevator and noticed an empty stretcher in it. Unaware that it was Governor Connally's stretcher, Tomlinson removed it from the elevator and placed it against a wall in a corridor on the ground floor. He saw another stretcher already in the corridor, blocking the entrance to a men's bathroom. About forty-five minutes later, Tomlinson returned to the ground floor corridor. He saw the first stretcher blocking the corridor. Apparently, someone had used the men's room and had pushed this stretcher out of the way. Tomlinson pushed the stretcher back against the wall, next to the Connally one. But when the stretcher bumped against the wall, a bullet rolled out. Tomlinson immediately called O.P. Wright, the hospital's security director, who came and saw the bullet on the stretcher. Wright informed Secret Service Agent Richard Johnsen, who ordered Wright to bring the bullet to him. Wright did so, and Johnsen put the bullet in his pocket. A few minutes later, Agent Johnsen left the hospital with the slain president's entourage.[26]

Secret Service Agent Andrew Berger stood guard outside Trauma Room Number One. Not long after President Kennedy had been pronounced dead, Berger saw a tall man try to enter the room. Berger stopped him, and the man shouted that he was with the Federal Bureau of Investigation (FBI). Berger refused to admit him into the room, and the man tried to force his way in. He did not relent until Berger received help from another agent, who led the protesting individual away. A little later, Berger had to restrain another man from entering the room where Kennedy's corpse lay. This man claimed to be with the Central Intelligence Agency (CIA).[27]

Not far away from Trauma Room Number One, Scripps-Howard reporter Seth Kantor walked down the main hospital corridor. He recognized an old friend and shouted "Hello, Jack" to him. Wilma Tice also saw the man, whom she, too, knew as Jack. The well-dressed, stocky, middle-aged man whom Kantor and Tice saw at Parkland Hospital a little before 1:30 was named Jack Ruby.[28]

By the time of Kantor's and Tice's observation of Jack Ruby at Parkland Hospital, the news that President Kennedy was dead had been announced to the American people. The original news bulletins had been terse and stunning. The United Press International (UPI) teletype stated simply, "Kennedy . . . wounded; perhaps seriously; perhaps fatally; by assassin's bullet." Now, as flashes of the high-speed dash to Parkland Hospital and news leaks by nurses, doctors, and even Father Huber began to pile up on his desk, CBS announcer Walter Cronkite began to lose control. When confirmation of the president's death reached him, Cronkite's voice cracked, and he wept openly as he read the fateful news to a television audience that rapidly increased with each passing minute.[29]

Few people watch television in the middle of the day, but as news of the shooting in Dallas reached more and more people, the entire nation seemed to stop its ordinary activities and stare, spellbound and shocked, at the screen. With no official authorization, people stopped their normal duties. Stores closed; schools were dismissed; people simply went home early from work; many stopped what they were doing and headed directly for church.[30]

The news of the assassination stunned and shocked the American people every bit as much as did that of the Japanese attack on Pearl Harbor. For many, it was incredible that John Kennedy could be cut down in the prime of his life. Kennedy, to be sure, had not transformed America into another Camelot, as some later myth-makers would allege. Yet this young president had somehow touched a responsive chord in people's hearts. He brought a certain elegance and charm to the White House, an *élan vital* that excited and inspired them. Kennedy seemed to symbolize the promise, the vigor, and the dash that made America a special place to live. His call for a New Frontier, his challenge to the American people to roll up their sleeves and work for their country, and his confrontations with Castro and Krushchev signified a new age of greatness awaiting the nation. His death removed more than just a man; it took away from the American people that remarkable vision of national glory that John Kennedy had given them.[31]

Mrs. Robert Reid, a secretary in the Book Depository, watched the motorcade from the front steps of the building. After the shooting, she went back inside in order to avoid being shot herself. Not knowing what else to do, Mrs. Reid took the front stairs to the second floor and walked toward her desk. Just as she arrived at the desk, Mrs. Reid noticed Lee Harvey Oswald walking toward her. He was drinking a Coke. Mrs. Reid asked Oswald if he knew the president had been shot. Oswald muttered something she did not understand and proceeded very slowly toward the stairs leading down to the front door of the Depository Building. The time was 12:33.[32]

Seven minutes later, Cecil McWatters, a driver for the Dallas public transportation system, noticed a young man enter his bus about seven blocks away from the Depository building. The man took a transfer and sat down. Another passenger on the bus, Mary Bledsoe, recognized the man as one of her former tenants. Bledsoe slinked down in her seat so the young man would not see her. She owed him two dollars and disliked him intensely. She felt relieved when he got off the bus, apparently annoyed at the extremely slow progress the bus was making. Traffic congestion slowed it down as it approached Dealey Plaza.[33]

Several blocks away, William Whaley sat in his taxicab in front of the Greyhound bus terminal. A young man opened the front door on the passenger side. Simultaneously, an elderly lady attempted to enter the vehicle from the opposite side. The man offered to let her have the taxi, but she agreed to catch the cab parked behind Whaley's. Whaley drove his passenger to the 500 block of North Beckley Avenue, located in a residential area of Dallas several miles from Dealey Plaza. After the man paid his ninety-five-cent fare and got out of the cab, Whaley recorded the time of the start of the trip in his logbook as 12:30 P.M.[34]

Earlene Roberts worked as a housekeeper at 1026 North Beckley Avenue, a house converted into single rooms rented by young men. At about one o'clock, Mrs. Roberts saw one of the tenants, Lee Harvey Oswald, enter the house and hurry upstairs to his room. A minute or two later, she heard the "beep-beep" of an automobile horn outside the rooming house. Mrs. Roberts looked out the window and saw a Dallas police car parked in front of the house. Another minute or two later, Oswald came down the stairs and left through the front door. Mrs. Roberts again looked out the front window. She no longer saw the police car but observed Oswald standing at a bus stop. She noticed that he now wore a jacket (he wore none when he entered the house). The time was 1:03 or 1:04.[35]

Some time around 1:10 P.M., Helen Markham stood on a curb at the intersection of Tenth Street and Patton Avenue, a little less than a mile from the Beckley Street rooming house. Mrs. Markham looked down Tenth Street and saw a young man about half a block away. A police car that had been following the man caught up with him. The man stopped and walked to the side of the car, leaned against the window, and began chatting with the police officer. Markham believed they were having a friendly conversation. Suddenly, the policeman got out of the car and approached the young man. As the officer reached the left front wheel, the man pulled out a handgun and fired several shots. The policeman fell to the ground, and his assailant ran toward Helen Markham. Terrified, Markham screamed and covered her face with her hands. As the man sped past her, she spread her fingers and peeked at him.[36]

Farther down the street, Domingo Benavides drove his truck. As he came to within twenty-five feet of the police car, he also saw the man shoot the policeman. Benavides remained in his truck until a couple of minutes after the gunman disappeared around the block; then Benavides ran to the fallen officer. He tried to call for help over the car's police radio, but he could not figure out how to operate the microphone. At this point, T.F.

Bowley drove up to the scene. After parking his truck, he ran to the policeman and saw that he was beyond help. Noticing Benavides fumbling with the police radio, Bowley ran to assist him. Bowley took the microphone from Benavides and called for help to the police dispatcher, whose automatic timer recorded the time of Bowley's call as 1:16 P.M. Shortly afterward, an ambulance arrived and rushed the policeman to Parkland Hospital. It was too late, and Officer J.D. Tippit was pronounced dead on arrival.[37]

William Scoggin sat in his taxicab eating his lunch. Although he was just around the corner from the scene of the Tippit slaying, Scoggin did not see it because a bush obscured his view. But he did see a young man flee down the street. Others also saw the man running away. He headed down Jefferson Avenue, the main thoroughfare in the Oak Cliffs section of Dallas. A few blocks away, Johnny Calvin Brewer, the manager of Hardy's Shoe Store, noticed a young man dart into the store lobby. He appeared to be trying to avoid the police cars racing down the avenue. After the police cars passed, the man ran to the Texas theater, several stores away. Brewer had just heard the radio broadcasts about President Kennedy's assassination, and he wondered if the man had been involved. So he ran to the theater and informed its cashier, Julia Postal, who called the police. Several minutes later the Dallas Police surrounded the movie house and began a systematic search of the patrons inside. Brewer pointed out the man he had seen, and the police ordered him to rise. The man put up a brief scuffle but was overcome. The police led the handcuffed man to a police car waiting outside the theater.[38]

The individual arrested at the theater was a twenty-four-year-old employee of the Texas School Book Depository named Lee Harvey Oswald. At Dallas Police Headquarters, Oswald was photographed, fingerprinted, and booked on suspicion of murdering Officer Tippit. The police suspected Oswald because he had resisted arrest and because he had a .38 caliber revolver in his possession, the same caliber weapon used to shoot Tippit. Their suspicions became certainty when Helen Markham picked Oswald out of a lineup and positively identified him as the man she saw shoot Officer Tippit. Early in the evening of

22 November, Lee Harvey Oswald was formally charged with the murder of J.D. Tippit.[39]

Meanwhile, officials began checking on those employees of the Book Depository not present at a roster check held shortly after the discovery of the rifle in the building. One of the missing employees was Lee Harvey Oswald. Although Lee did not live with his wife, Marina, two detectives went to the home of Ruth Paine, with whom Marina lived. For two months, the Oswalds had lived apart. Lee lived at the North Beckley rooming house in Dallas, and Marina lived at the Paine house in Irving, a suburb of Dallas. Marina told the detectives that Lee owned a rifle. She led them to a garage and showed them the blanket in which Oswald wrapped the weapon. But when they unrolled the blanket, it was empty.[40]

As Air Force One headed back for Washington, Jacqueline Kennedy decided to have the autopsy on her husband's body performed at Bethesda Naval Hospital, since John Kennedy had served in the Navy during World War II. When the jet landed at Andrews Air Force Base, a waiting hearse took the coffin and drove it to the hospital. Located in Bethesda, Maryland, about thirty miles from Washington, the hospital was the official medical treatment center for members of the Navy. Now, the Navy's most distinguished alumnus was to receive the final manipulations humans get: autopsy and embalming.[41]

Notified that Bethesda was to be the location of the autopsy, Captain James H. Stover, the hospital director, made the necessary preparations. He ordered the hospital's chief of pathology, Commander James J. Humes, to head the autopsy team. To assist Humes, Captain Stover selected Navy Commander J. Thornton Boswell and Air Force Lieutenant-Colonel Pierre A. Finck. They proved to be poor selections. Humes and Boswell were hospital pathologists and had very little experience in doing autopsies on victims of violent death. Neither man qualified as a forensic pathologist. Doctor Finck did so qualify and, as the head of the Armed Forces Institute on Pathology, had some expertise in the field of wounds ballistics. However, Finck was in the Air Force, and the autopsy would be conducted under the authority of the Navy.[42]

After the body was X-rayed and photographed, the pathologists began their external examination of it. They immediately noticed a huge, gaping hole on the right side of the head, covering the area from the forehead back to the ear. It measured more than five inches in diameter. A very large flap of scalp and skull bone hung down over the right ear. The doctors also saw the wide tracheotomy incision that Dr. Perry had made in President Kennedy's neck. It was a wide, irregular cut that stretched almost across the front of the neck. The three physicians also observed severe swelling and bruising of the eyes, numerous lacerations crisscrossing the scalp, and clotted blood and dried brain tissue imbedded in the hair. After the body was turned over, Doctors Humes, Boswell, and Finck found two holes, one in the upper back and the other in the head.[43]

When Dr. Humes started to examine the head wound more closely, he discovered that the force of the bullet had been so devastating that the skull literally came apart in his hands. The resulting cavity was so large that he could lift the brain out without having to do any cutting away of the skull. The X-rays revealed many tiny bullet fragments scattered throughout the right half of the brain. Dr. Humes removed two of the largest fragments and gave them to FBI Agents Francis O'Neill and James Sibert, who were taking notes for a report on the autopsy ordered by FBI Director J. Edgar Hoover. The doctors could see that the right side of the brain suffered extensive damage, so much so, in fact, that over three-quarters of the right half of the brain was missing, apparently blasted out of the head by the exploding bullet.[44]

In the rear of the skull, just below the large prominent bone in the back of the head, Dr. Humes discovered a small oval hole, three-fifths by one-quarter of an inch in diameter. On the inside of the skull he saw a much larger hole. This proved that the bullet had entered the rear of the skull, causing a small wound of entrance. But as it passed through, the missile began to expand, producing a larger hole where it entered the brain cavity. These observations, coupled with the massive damage to the right front of the head, led the pathologists to their first conclusion. A bullet had entered the rear of John Kennedy's head, expanded rapidly as it drove through the brain, fragmented extensively, and exploded out of the right front of the head, blasting brain matter and skull bone out ahead of it. Clearly, this was the shot that killed the president.[45]

The doctors then turned their attention to the small opening in Kennedy's back. Located just below the junction of the shoulder and the neck, it had all the characteristics of a bullet entrance wound. The tiny round hole, only one-quarter by one-fifth of an inch in diameter, slanted inward, downward, and to the left, indicating that the assassin was above, behind, and to the right of President Kennedy when he fired that shot. The doctors wanted to dissect this wound, a standard pathological procedure for tracing a bullet track through the body. However, one of the high-ranking naval officials present at the autopsy ordered them not to dissect the back wound.[46]

Prohibited from dissecting the wound, Dr. Humes decided to probe it manually, so he inserted his finger into it. After he pushed his finger about two inches into the wound, Humes could probe no farther, for he could feel the end of the missile track. This posed a serious problem for the three pathologists. They found no exit hole in the front of the president's body. Yet the X-rays clearly showed that no bullet remained anywhere in the back, chest, or neck. Where did the bullet that entered President Kennedy's back go? At that time, an FBI agent entered the autopsy room and reported that a whole bullet had been discovered on a stretcher at Parkland Hospital. Assuming that the stretcher in question was the one used for the treatment of President Kennedy, the autopsy physicians speculated that a bullet had entered his back but had penetrated only a short distance into it. Since external closed chest cardiac massage had been performed as one of the emergency life-saving measures in Dallas, the pathologists guessed that the massaging caused Kennedy's back muscles to relax, thus forcing the bullet to squirt out of the hole in the back and onto the stretcher.[47]

Based on their observations of Kennedy's body, Doctors Humes, Boswell, and Finck concluded that two bullets struck the president, both fired from above and behind him. One bullet entered his upper back and caused little damage, from which Kennedy undoubtedly would have recovered. The other bullet, however, entered the rear of the skull and caused such massive destruction of the brain as it exploded out of the right front side of the head that it killed President Kennedy. Upon the completion of the autopsy near midnight, Doctors Boswell and Finck left. Doctor Humes, however, remained while a team of Washington undertakers prepared Kennedy's body for burial. Humes marveled at the skill of these craftsmen in using rubber, plastic, and mesh to restore Kennedy's shattered head to its normal appearance. The undertakers did not finish until 4:00 Saturday morning. Exhausted from a busy day at the hospital and from the grueling, nerve-wracking circumstances of the autopsy, Humes went home to get a much needed and deserved rest.[48]

In Dallas, Deputy Sheriff Roger Craig returned to police headquarters about 4:00 Friday afternoon, after helping comb the Depository building for clues. When he entered the third-floor office of Captain J. Will Fritz of the Homicide Bureau, Craig saw Fritz interrogating a young man. Immediately recognizing the man as the same person he saw flee the assassination scene only fifteen minutes after the shooting, Craig informed Captain Fritz. Fritz paid little attention to Craig's story. He was questioning the suspect, Lee Harvey Oswald, about the murder of Officer Tippit, not about the Kennedy slaying. But shortly thereafter, evidence began to accumulate that implicated Oswald in the Kennedy assassination as well. The rifle found on the sixth floor belonged to Oswald; his prints were found on boxes at the window; and eyewitness Howard Brennan selected Oswald from a lineup as the person most resembling the man he saw shoot the president.[49]

Not long before 9:00 P.M., Oswald was fingerprinted and given a paraffin test to determine whether he had fired a weapon recently. As he was led back and forth from Captain Fritz's office to lineup and identification rooms, Oswald was questioned by the news reporters jamming the corridors of police headquarters. To the question of whether he had shot President Kennedy, Oswald replied that he knew nothing of the assassination and had not been charged with that crime. He also complained that the police were denying him his legal rights, especially the right to a lawyer of his choice.[50]

At 11:26 P.M., Captain Fritz signed the legal complaint formally charging Lee Harvey Oswald with the murder of John F. Kennedy. Oswald, however, did not know of this second murder charge against him until 1:30 A.M., when he was arraigned before Justice of the Peace David Johnston. In the meantime, the police brought Lee Oswald downstairs for an extraordinary midnight press conference. Dallas Police Chief Jesse Curry and District Attorney Henry Wade finally yielded to the unrelenting demands of the newsmen and agreed to permit them to question Oswald. During the press conference, Wade mistakenly announced that Oswald belonged to the Free Cuba Committee. One of the people in the room, a man named Jack Ruby, corrected Wade and stated that Oswald really belonged to the Fair Play for Cuba Committee.[51]

The press conference lasted only a few minutes, during which Oswald repeated his earlier denial of any involvement in the assassination. When the conference was over, a policeman led Oswald into an elevator. A magazine photographer rode with them and talked with Oswald, who vehemently denied shooting Kennedy and asserted that he was a "patsy," taking the blame for others. Just before he entered his cell, Oswald told the photographer that the truth about the assassination "conspiracy" would be revealed at his trial.[52]

On Saturday, 23 November, Lee Harvey Oswald attempted to telephone a New York lawyer, John Abt. Long associated with left-wing causes, Abt had defended numerous Communists and had himself been identified as a member of the Communist group that had infiltrated various New Deal agencies in the 1930s. Oswald, however, could not reach Abt. The Dallas police did permit brief visits to Oswald by his wife, mother, and brother, and by the president of the Dallas Bar Association. Most of Lee's day consisted of long interrogation sessions, highlighted by his adamant denial of guilt for the murders of John Kennedy and J.D. Tippit.[53]

In Washington, Kennedy family members and government officials completed arrangements for the president's funeral. It was decided that he would have a formal state funeral, with burial in Arlington National Cemetery. Dignitaries and officials from around the country and around the world streamed into the nation's capital to pay respects to President Kennedy's family and to visit the new chief of state. Less than twenty-four hours after the assassination, the cold, unfeeling hand of government reached into the tragic, eventful day. For the transition of power took concrete form, as workmen removed John Kennedy's personal effects from the White House and replaced them with Lyndon Johnson's. Out of respect for Mrs. Kennedy, however, the Johnsons did not take immediate possession of the executive mansion. Instead, the new president worked his first full day as the nation's chief executive in the Executive Office Building across the street from the White House.[54]

About four o'clock Saturday morning, Doctor James Humes felt relieved as the hearse bearing John Kennedy's embalmed body and reconstructed head departed from Bethesda Naval Hospital. It had been a grueling night for Commander Humes, made all the more demanding on his professional skills by the prestigious nature of his autopsy victim and by all the high-ranking military and naval brass present to witness and supervise his work. Now that it was all over, Humes could relax. He had just one minor detail to complete before he could go home. He telephoned Dr. Malcolm Perry in Dallas, since Dr. Perry had been the surgeon in charge of President Kennedy's emergency treatment at Parkland Hospital.[55]

Dr. Perry's revelation that the president had a bullet hole in his throat must have astounded Dr. Humes. At the autopsy, the three pathologists observed only the large tracheotomy incision in the neck. The reason was simple. Dr. Perry had sliced right through the bullet hole as he made the tracheotomy. Thus, no bullet hole was visible by the time the autopsy began. But now, James Humes faced a serious dilemma. He and his colleagues had failed to include one of Kennedy's wounds in their autopsy findings. Dr. Perry's description of the wound as very small and round sounded like the description of an entrance wound. But with no exit wounds anywhere in the body and no bullets found still in the body, Humes was puzzled. It appeared that both the bullet that entered the president's back and the one that entered his throat had not exited, yet had somehow disappeared.[56]

After thinking about this, Dr. Humes telephoned Dr. Perry again to obtain a more precise description of the throat wound. During their conversation, Humes had a sudden inspiration and shouted, "so that's it!" He went home, attended a school function with his son, and slept for several hours. Then he took his original autopsy notes, stained with John Kennedy's blood, and burned them in his fireplace. Then he drew up a new autopsy protocol based on the new information he had gleaned from Dr. Perry. The new report stated that a bullet had entered Kennedy's neck and exited from his throat. Even though there was only slight medical evidence to confirm this, Dr. Humes concluded that it provided the only reasonable explanation for the wounds in Kennedy's body.[57]

Dallas Police Chief Jesse Curry decided that police headquarters did not provide sufficient security for his prisoner. Not only did newspaper reporters, photographers, television cameramen, and other representatives of the press and news media constantly swarm all over the building in their relentless attempts to secure interviews and bits of information, but Curry also received several threats on Oswald's life. Not the usual crank calls such sensational events always attract, these threats appeared real. The central lockup at the county jail possessed far more secure facilities for Oswald's detention. Therefore, Curry decided to transfer him on Sunday morning.[58]

Chief Curry and Captain Fritz arranged an elaborate transfer plan to insure Oswald's safety. An armored police truck would leave police headquarters and travel by prearranged route to the county jail. The truck would be a decoy, designed to lure any potential threats to Oswald's life away from the real route. Immediately after the armored truck left, Oswald would be placed in an unmarked car and whisked off to the jail by another route. It was a plan that demanded utmost secrecy for its successful fruition. But Curry and Fritz could not resist the temptation of more national publicity for the Dallas police. Therefore, they tipped the press of the transfer plan and told them to await Oswald's arrival in the basement of police headquarters shortly after eleven in the morning of Sunday, 24 November.[59]

Tens of millions of Americans watched on television as they saw John Fitzgerald Kennedy's flag-draped coffin in the rotunda of the Capitol. Then the networks suddenly switched to Dallas for a live viewing of Oswald's transfer. The viewers saw dozens of armed policemen waiting in the basement. Then they saw Lee Oswald, escorted by three police officers, enter the basement. Suddenly, at 11:20 A.M., the television cameras recorded one of the most shocking and dramatic scenes ever seen on live television. As the Oswald party advanced toward a waiting automobile, a short, stocky man dressed in a dark suit bolted out of the waiting crowd. With a revolver in his hand, the man rushed up to Oswald, pointed the weapon at him, and fired one shot into his abdomen. Oswald shrieked in pain and crumpled to the floor. The police recovered from their immediate shock and overcame Oswald's assassin. His name was Jack Ruby. Rushed to Parkland Memorial Hospital, Oswald underwent emergency surgery. The bullet entered his left side, shattering his spleen, damaging his kidney and liver, and puncturing his aorta. The resulting massive internal hemmorhaging proved fatal. A little after one in the afternoon, the Parkland surgeons pronounced Lee Harvey Oswald dead.[60]

On Monday, 25 November 1963, John F. Kennedy was buried in Arlington National Cemetery. His widow, Jacqueline, brought the long funeral rites to an end by lighting the flame that would burn over Kennedy's grave. On the same day, in Fort Worth, Texas, Lee Harvey Oswald was laid to rest. So few people were there that several newsmen volunteered to lower his coffin into the grave. In Dallas, the district attorney's office made preparations for the trial of Jack Ruby for the murder of Lee Harvey Oswald.[61]

CHAPTER 2

THE WARREN COMMISSION

WITHIN AN HOUR after the assassination, the FBI began investigating it. The accumulation of evidence against Oswald was so great that on 23 November 1963, FBI Director J. Edgar Hoover informed President Johnson that Oswald was the sole assassin. Deputy Attorney General Nicholas Katzenbach concurred with the FBI findings and believed that they should be made public in order to silence "speculation" that there was a conspiracy.[1]

On 25 November, President Johnson ordered the Justice Department and the FBI to conduct a "prompt and thorough" investigation of the assassination and of Ruby's murder of Oswald. Johnson stated that he wanted to "get by" with the FBI inquiry. But on 27 November, Senator Everett M. Dirksen called for a Senate Judiciary Committee investigation, and Texas Attorney General Waggoner Carr announced that a state court of inquiry would investigate the assassination.[2]

Upset by the "rash of investigations," Johnson rather reluctantly agreed to Katzenbach's recommendation that he appoint a presidential commission to probe the killings. In a memorandum to presidential advisor William Moyers, Katzenbach outlined his reasons for the suggestion: "the public must be satisfied that Oswald was the assassin; that he did not have confederates who are still at large; that the evidence was such that he would have been convicted at trial . . . [that] we need something to head off public speculation or congressional hearings of the wrong sort."[3]

Despite J. Edgar Hoover's warning that a presidential commission would turn out to be "a three-ring circus," President Johnson called on the chief justice of the United States, Earl

Warren, to head the commission. At first, Warren declined. But the president turned on the "LBJ treatment" and told Warren that unless public doubts about the assassination were assuaged, the United States might be forced into a nuclear war. Warren then agreed to chair the commission.[4]

On 29 November 1963, President Johnson issued Executive Order No. 11130 creating the President's Commission on the Assassination of President Kennedy. The commission, universally called the Warren Commission, comprised six men besides Chief Justice Warren. The six included two Republicans, Senator John Sherman Cooper and Representative Gerald Ford; two Democrats, Senator Richard Russell and Representative T. Hale Boggs; and two men who had distinguished records of government service, Allen Dulles, the former director of the CIA, and John McCloy, the ex-United States high commissioner for Germany. The purposes of the commission were to investigate all evidence about the deaths of John F. Kennedy and Lee Harvey Oswald and to report the commission's findings and conclusions to the president.[5]

Such were the origins of the Warren Commission, conceived because of the desire to allay public suspicions of conspiracy. In his memoirs, Lyndon Johnson admitted that he created the commission to assuage public suspicions about an assassination conspiracy. A member of the Warren Commission's legal staff verified the purposes of the commission in a memorandum recounting the initial staff meeting of the commission. Counsel Melvin Eisenberg wrote, "He [Warren] placed emphasis on . . . quenching rumors, and precluding further speculation such as that which has surrounded the death of Lincoln." Eisenberg, however, did go on to state that Chief Justice Warren also "emphasized that the Commission had to determine the truth, whatever that might be."[6]

Busy with other activities, the seven men who composed the Warren Commission devoted little time to the commission's daily operations. These they assigned to a staff headed by J. Lee Rankin. As the commission's chief counsel, Rankin selected the other members of the staff, directed their investigation, and acted as the Warren Commission liaison with such federal agencies as the CIA, the FBI, and the State Department. Rankin was also responsible for approving the final draft of the commission's report.[7]

Rankin designated six areas for the Warren Commission investigation: (1) basic facts of the assassination, (2) identity of the assassin, (3) Lee Harvey Oswald's background, (4) possible conspiratorial relationships, (5) Oswald's death, and (6) presidential protection. Each of these areas was to be examined by two commission junior counsels, who were directly responsible to one of Rankin's six senior counsels. In general, this arrangement worked well, but the evidence suggests that much of the commission's groundwork was laid by only a few of the junior counsels. For example, Arlen Specter, the junior counsel responsible for the medical and ballistics evidence, should have reported to senior counsel Francis Adams. In reality, Adams did little work, and, as Specter related, "I ended up as the only counsel in my area."[8]

Since President Johnson had designated the FBI as the primary investigatory agency, Rankin decided not to use independent investigators to probe the evidence. Instead, he relied on the FBI to do much of the necessary research. On 9 December 1963, the FBI submitted a five-hundred-page report of its findings and conclusions. This report remained the basis of the Warren Commission's work. From it, the commission derived all of its main findings and conclusions.[9]

The Warren Commission completed its staff organization on 10 January 1964 and began its investigation of the assassination shortly afterward. In February and March, the commission held hearings, at which ninety-four witnesses testified. From 14 March to 17 June, the commission staff examined evidence and took depositions of witnesses. In June, the first drafts of the six area staffs were circulated among the counsels. In August, the commission staff revised its chapters, and on 4 September, the galley proofs of the final draft were submitted to the commission and its staff. On 24 September 1964, the Warren Commission presented its report to President Johnson. Four days later, the *Warren Report* was released to the public, and the Warren Commission was dissolved. In November, the twenty-six supplemental volumes of commission hearings and exhibits were released.[10]

We shall now turn our attention to the manner in which the Warren Commission arrived at its main conclusions.

The commission's first area of investigation, "Basic Facts of the Assassination," called for an analysis of eyewitness testimony, medical and ballistics evidence, and the physical evidence at the scene of the crime. As a starting point for this phase of its assignment, the commission determined that "the shots which killed President Kennedy and wounded Governor Connally were fired from the sixth floor window at the southeast corner of the Texas School Book Depository." The Texas School Book Depository was a seven-story building located at the southeast corner of Dealey Plaza. Since the presidential limousine had already passed the Depository building when the shots were fired, they must have come from above and behind the vehicle.[11]

To support this finding, the commission relied first on eyewitnesses to the assassination, the most important of which was Howard Leslie Brennan. About ten minutes before the motorcade arrived, Brennan sat down on a concrete ledge directly opposite the south side of the Depository building. As he glanced around, while waiting for the motorcade, Brennan noticed a man in the sixth-floor southeast corner window. The man left the window and returned to it several times. The motorcade arrived and made the left turn from Houston onto Elm Street and proceeded away from Brennan. Then Brennan heard a sound like a firecracker. He looked up and recalled that "this man that I saw previous [in the sixth-floor window] was aiming for his last shot." The man rested the gun on his left shoulder, aimed, and fired. Then he drew the gun back to his side and stood there, Brennan stated, "as though to assure hisself [*sic*] that he hit his mark, and then he disappeared."[12]

Other witnesses confirmed Brennan's observation. Amos Lee Euins, a teenager, saw a "pipe thing sticking out the window." After the first shot, Euins looked up at the sixth-floor window and saw a man fire a shot from it. A photographer for the *Dallas Times-Herald,* Robert H. Jackson, looked up toward the Depository building immediately after the last shot was fired and saw a rifle slowly being drawn back into the sixth-floor window. Two other people, Malcolm O. Couch, a television cameraman, and

Mrs. Earle Cabell, the wife of the mayor of Dallas, both saw an object protruding from the sixth-floor window, but neither could be certain that it was a rifle or a rifle barrel.[13]

Although there were a few minor inconsistencies in the testimony of these witnesses, the commission accepted the general substance of their observations: a rifle was fired from the sixth-floor window of the Texas Book Depository building. The commission was particularly impressed by the fact that no other eyewitnesses saw a gun fired from anywhere else in Dealey Plaza.[14]

Eyewitness testimony by itself, of course, hardly proves that an event occurred. The Warren Commission possessed a substantial amount of other evidence that strongly reinforced the witnesses' recollection of what they had seen. Foremost among this evidence was the fact that three used cartridge cases had been discovered on the floor directly under the southeast corner window of the building. Another equally significant discovery on the sixth floor was that of a rifle, found hidden among book cartons in the northwest area of the sixth floor (the entire sixth floor was one large room). Two large bullet fragments were found in the front seat of the presidential limousine, and three tiny fragments were found under the seat occupied by Mrs. Connally. Finally, an intact bullet was discovered on a stretcher at Parkland Hospital. The commission subjected these items to ballistics and firearms analysis by experts in these fields.[15]

The results of the experts' examination of these items of physical evidence indicated that shots were indeed fired from the sixth-floor southeast corner window of the Depository building. The rifle was a bolt-action, clipfed, 6.5 mm. model 91/38 Mannlicher-Carcano rifle, manufactured in Italy in 1940. The experts determined that all three cartridge cases had been fired in that rifle, to the exclusion of all other weapons. They also determined that the two fragments found in the front seat of the limousine had been fired from that same rifle. The three tiny fragments located under Mrs. Connally's seat, however, were too small to permit positive identification of the weapon from which they had been fired. The bullet found on the hospital stretcher had also been fired from the Depository rifle.[16]

The commission now had persuasive evidence that shots were fired from the Depository window. Its next task was to determine whether any of those shots struck President Kennedy or Governor Connally. This determination was made through an analysis of the wounds inflicted on the two men. For this, the commission analyzed the medical reports of the physicians who treated Governor Connally and who attended President Kennedy at Parkland Hospital, as well as the autopsy report on the president. In addition, the commission heard testimony from the physicians and autopsy pathologists.

Governor Connally had three separate entrance wounds, one in the back, one in the wrist, and one in the thigh. Because of Connally's seated position at the time he was shot, his physicians concluded that all three wounds had been inflicted by bullets that entered from the rear. The doctors, however, could not surmise whether the governor was struck by only one bullet or by more than one. All three wounds aligned in such a way that they could have been caused by a single bullet or by three separate ones.[17]

The autopsy report on President Kennedy revealed that he was struck by two bullets, both of which entered from the rear. One shot entered his neck very near the junction of the shoulder and neck and exited from his throat just below the Adam's apple. The second bullet entered the rear of the president's head, fragmented extensively inside the skull, and exploded out of the head on the right side, slightly above and in front of the ear. This second bullet was the fatal one, for it caused extensive loss of skull and brain tissue and severely lacerated the brain on the right side. Based on this evidence, the autopsy pathologists concluded that John Kennedy died "as a result of two perforating gunshot wounds inflicted by high velocity projectiles . . . fired from a point behind and somewhat above the level of the deceased."[18]

The medical evidence clearly supported the eyewitness and ballistics evidence already gathered. The Warren Commission now had proof that shots were fired from the sixth-floor southeast corner window of the Book Depository building and that all bullet wounds were caused by rear-entering missiles. The commission did not stop here. It went on to conduct scientific tests to determine whether the trajectories of bullets fired from the sixth-floor window fit the trajectories of bullet wounds in Kennedy and Connally. The results of trajectory tests conducted by the FBI sustained the contention that all the wounds could have been caused by shots fired from the sixth-floor window.[19]

THE SINGLE-BULLET THEORY

One of the most significant pieces of evidence in the assassination was the Abraham Zapruder film. Zapruder was standing in an ideal location for a cameraman—on an elevated concrete abutment midway between the Depository building and the Grassy Knoll. In filming the presidential motorcade as it traveled down Elm Street, Abraham Zapruder recorded the reactions of President Kennedy and Governor Connally to their wounds. The resulting twenty-two seconds of film (8 mm., color, shot through a telephoto lens) would become one of the most famous and controversial films ever taken.

Those who view the film see the motorcade on Elm Street. President Kennedy is smiling and waving to the crowd of spectators. Then the limousine is blocked for a brief second by a street sign. As the vehicle emerges from behind the sign, John Kennedy grimaces in pain, and his arms bolt upward in an apparent attempt to guard his face. Then the president slowly slopes forward and to his left almost within the grasp of his wife, Jacqueline. The viewer is abruptly roused from this almost tranquil scene as he sees the president's head suddenly explode in a burst of red and pink. Then he sees John Kennedy violently flung backward and leftward until he bounces off the back of the rear seat and collapses. Then the shocked viewer watches as Jacqueline Kennedy climbs onto the limousine's trunk to be met by Secret Service Agent Clinton Hill, who jumps onto the trunk. The film ends with the limousine becoming a blur as it speeds off through the triple underpass at the west end of Dealey Plaza. The Zapruder film is an unforgettable experience, a shocking visual recording of the murder of John Fitzgerald Kennedy.[20]

Like all films, the Zapruder film is actually a series of still photographs, or frames, strung together in motion picture format. The Zapruder film, therefore, provides not only a continuous visual recording of the assassination but also a frame-by-frame chronicle of it. Each frame of the film is 1/18th of a second in duration. All together, there are almost four hundred frames of the film, or a total recorded time span of twenty-two seconds. For reference, each frame of the film is numbered. By correlating the Zapruder frames with certain landmarks in Dealey Plaza, one can determine the precise instant when an event occurred. For example, the fatal head shot occurs in frame Z313.

Arlen Specter, the commission's junior counsel responsible for the "Basic Facts of the Assassination" section of the investigation, noticed something in the Zapruder film that stunned him. President Kennedy first shows a reaction to being hit at frame Z225, and Governor Connally first reacts at frame Z236. Specter calculated that this entailed only 11/18ths of a second. The FBI, however, had already tested the Depository rifle and had determined that the bolt-action weapon could not fire two shots in less than 2.25 seconds. The obvious implication of the FBI data struck Specter. If Kennedy and Connally were struck only 11/18, or 0.7 seconds apart, the Depository rifle could not have been the only weapon used in the assassination. This, of course, meant that two assassins must have fired shots, and by definition, John Kennedy's murder would be the result of a conspiracy.[21]

Specter's startling discovery threatened to destroy the Warren Commission. It will be recalled that the commission was set up mainly to dispel public suspicions of a conspiracy in the assassination. Specter therefore carefully looked for some way to reconcile the evidence of the Zapruder film with the government's contention that there was only one assassin. Specter discovered that President Kennedy was most probably wounded before frame Z225 because that frame was the first one in which Kennedy's face is visible after the limousine emerges from behind the street sign. However, Kennedy could not have been struck earlier than frame Z210 because an oak tree blocked the assassin's view of the motorcade between frames Z166 and Z210.[22]

These facts permitted Specter to extend the moment of Kennedy's injury from frame Z225 back to frame Z210. Specter also decided that Governor Connally's reaction to being wounded becomes evident in frame Z238. He then calculated the time span between their woundings. Since Kennedy was hit no earlier than frame Z210 and Connally no later than frame Z238, the maximum possible time for the two shots was 238 minus 210, or 28 Zapruder frames. Since each frame of the film lasted 1/18 of a second, the time was 28/18ths or 1.556 seconds. The table below lists the appropriate data.

Zapruder Frames	*Event*
Z166–Z210	Oak Tree Blocks View of Car From Sixth-Floor Window
Z207–Z225	Car Behind Street Sign
Z225	Car Emerges From Behind Sign; Kennedy Hit
Z236–Z238	Connally Hit
Z210	Earliest Time of Hit on Kennedy
Z238	Latest Time of Hit on Connally

Specter had extended the total possible times for Kennedy and Connally to be struck by separate bullets to 1.6 seconds. But the FBI ballistics data still made the new time too short; the Depository rifle could not fire two shots in less than 2.25 seconds. Arlen Specter faced a question that threatened to prove a conspiracy. How could this rifle have wounded both Kennedy and Connally in only 1.6 seconds?

We do not know if Specter found the answer to that question in a flash of inspiration or by careful deduction, but we do know that he found his answer. Specter knew that the rifle was used in the assassination. He knew that the cartridge cases, the bullet fragments from the limousine, and the bullet from the hospital stretcher had all been fired in the rifle. He knew that the wounds on Kennedy and Connally were all inflicted by bullets fired from the rear of the limousine. And he knew that the trajectories of bullets fired from the sixth-floor window matched the angles of the entry wounds on the two men. He also knew that only one shot could have been fired from the rifle between Zapruder frames Z210 and Z238. Finally, he knew that the commission had no evidence whatsoever of a second gunman in Dealey Plaza.

Given this set of circumstances, the only logical explanation was that both Kennedy and Connally were struck by the same bullet. The process of elimination having exhausted all other alternatives, this was the conclusion Specter reached. Thus was born the "single-bullet theory," one of the most disputed aspects of the entire Kennedy assassination case. It was not conceived out of a desire to cover up evidence of a conspiracy, as some Warren Commission critics have charged. Rather, the theory was the only reasonable explanation for the facts Specter had at his disposal.[23]

The commission heard testimony from Dr. Alfred Olivier, who supervised certain wounds ballistics tests with the Mannlicher-Carcano rifle and ammunition. Dr. Olivier declared that this rifle and ammunition were quite capable of inflicting the wounds on Kennedy and Connally. The trajectory tests conducted by the FBI showed that Kennedy and Connally were aligned in such a manner that a single bullet could have passed through both men. Moreover, the autopsy revealed that a bullet had entered the rear of President Kennedy's neck and exited from the front of his throat at a downward angle. This raised an all-important question. If that bullet did not strike Connally, where did it go? None of the other occupants of the limousine were injured. There was no significant damage to the vehicle itself, damage that a bullet exiting from the president's throat would have caused, if that bullet had not struck Connally.[24]

The main impediment to Specter's single-bullet theory was the testimony of Governor Connally, corroborated by his wife. The governor unequivocally stated that he was struck by a separate bullet from the one that hit the president. In his testimony before the commission, Connally emphatically declared that he heard the first shot, turned around to see what had happened, and began to turn back around when he was struck by a bullet. The governor went on to inform the commission that since rifle bullets travel faster than the speed of sound, the first bullet had already struck the president when the sound of the shot reached his ears. Therefore, since the bullet that struck him impacted after he heard the first shot, he must have been hit by a second bullet.[25]

Governor Connally's testimony summarized the original official versions of the assassination. The Secret Service, for example, surmised that the first shot hit Kennedy in the neck, the second hit Connally in the back, and the third hit Kennedy in the head. The FBI Supplemental Report of 9 December 1963 also concluded that separate bullets hit the men. The Warren Commission itself originally assumed that the president and governor had been hit by separate bullets. Senior commission counsel Melvin A. Eisenberg expressed this in a commission memorandum of 22 April 1964. Another memorandum, from junior counsel David Belin to J. Lee Rankin, also speculated that all three shots struck: the first hitting Kennedy; the second, Connally; and the third, Kennedy.[26]

Despite these initial assumptions, and despite Governor Connally's testimony, the Warren Commission concluded that "there is very persuasive evidence from the experts to indicate that the same bullet which pierced the President's throat also caused Governor Connally's wounds." There was simply no other feasible way to explain the medical, ballistics, and photographic evidence.[27]

According to the Warren Commission, the basic facts of the assassination were as follows. Three shots were fired from a 6.5 mm. Mannlicher-Carcano rifle from the sixth-floor southeast corner window of the Texas School Book Depository. One of the three shots missed. The first of the two shots that hit struck President Kennedy in the lower rear neck and exited from his throat. This same bullet entered Governor Connally's back, passed through his chest, drilled through his wrist, and lodged in his thigh. The second of the bullets to hit its mark entered the rear of President Kennedy's head and blasted out the right front side of the skull, causing massive and fatal destruction.

THE ASSASSIN

Having proved to its satisfaction that all the shots were fired from the sixth-floor southeast corner window of the Texas School Book Depository building, the Warren Commission proceeded to its second area of concern, the identity of the assassin. The commission's identification of Lee Harvey Oswald stemmed from the very large accumulation of evidence against him.

The commission's first category of evidence incriminating Oswald was his ownership and possession of the assassination weapon, the rifle found on the sixth floor of the Depository building. Because of the serial number C2766 stamped on the rifle, the FBI traced the weapon to Klein's Sporting Goods, a Chicago company specializing in mail-order sales of weapons. Klein's reported that it had shipped the rifle to A. Hidell in Dallas, Texas, on 20 March 1963. The company also produced a filled-in coupon from a Klein's magazine advertisement and a money order for $21.45, the total cost of the rifle. Even though these documents all contained the name A. Hidell, experts established that they were all written by Lee Harvey Oswald. Further investigation revealed that Oswald had frequently used the aliases A. Hidell and Alex Hidell.[28]

When the rifle was discovered, the Dallas police fingerprint expert, Lieutenant J.C. Day, examined the weapon and found only one identifiable print, a right hand palmprint located on the underside of the rifle barrel. After dusting the print with powder, Day "lifted" it from the barrel by using a piece of tape, and three fingerprint experts positively identified the palmprint as Lee Harvey Oswald's. The FBI also discovered several blue, black, and orange cotton fibers caught in a crack between the metal plate on the butt end of the rifle and the wooden butt itself. These fibers matched cotton fibers from the shirt Oswald wore when he was arrested. However, since other items had identical fibers, the FBI fiber expert, Paul M. Stombaugh, concluded that the rifle fibers "could have come" from Oswald's shirt.[29]

Another article linking Oswald with the rifle was a photograph of Oswald holding the rifle. Oswald's wife, Marina, testified that she took the photograph in the back yard of their Dallas home in April 1963, not long after Oswald obtained the weapon. Careful examination by the FBI disclosed that the negative matched the photograph in every detail, that the photograph was taken with Oswald's camera, and that the rifle in the photograph was probably identical to the one found on the sixth floor.[30]

Finally, Marina Oswald testified that she often saw and heard Oswald practicing operating the bolt action of the rifle. When shown the Depository rifle, Marina exclaimed that it was "the fateful rifle of Lee Oswald." She also informed the commission that in October and November 1963, while she lived with her friend Ruth Paine, that the rifle was wrapped in a blanket roll lying in the Paine garage. About three hours after the assassination, two law enforcement officials arrived at the Paine home. Marina informed them that her husband owned a rifle and led them to the garage. When they opened the blanket roll, however, it was empty.[31]

The establishment of Oswald's ownership of the murder weapon was reinforced by the commission's contention that he brought the rifle into the Depository building on the morning of 22 November. Lee and Marina were estranged, and they lived apart, Marina with Ruth Paine in Irving and Lee in a rooming house in Dallas. From time to time, Lee visited Marina. Since he did not own a car, Oswald usually rode home with a fellow worker, Buell Wesley Frazier. Frazier lived with his sister, Lillie Mae Randall, at her home in Irving, only a block away from Ruth Paine's house. The following day, Oswald would ride back to work with Frazier. Both men worked at the Texas School Book Despository.[32]

On Thursday, 21 November, Oswald rode to Irving with Frazier. Since Oswald had always traveled with him only on weekends, Frazier asked why he was going on a weekday. Oswald replied that he was going to get some curtain rods. The following morning, Lillie Mae Randall saw Oswald approach her carport. He was carrying a package in a brown paper sack. Frazier saw Oswald put the package on the back seat of the car, and he asked him what it contained. Oswald replied "curtain rods." When they arrived in the company parking lot, Oswald retrieved the package from the car and walked quickly toward the Depository building, leaving Frazier behind. It was the first time that Oswald had not waited and walked alongside Frazier to work.[33]

The Warren Commission concluded that Oswald fabricated the curtain rod story. His landlady testified that Oswald's room already had curtains. A long paper sack, constructed out of wrapping paper and tape from the Depository's shipping department, was found on the floor next to the sixth-floor window. The sack contained a fingerprint and palmprint of Oswald's. The commission determined that Oswald retrieved the rifle from the blanket in the Paine garage, disassembled it, and carried it in the paper sack. Since the disassembled rifle was 35 inches long, Oswald could not procure a ready-made container for it. Therefore, he must have put the homemade sack together, the commission decided. The sack found on the sixth floor measured 38 inches long, the perfect size to hold the rifle. The bag also contained fibers that matched fibers from the blanket. Since the bag and blanket never came into contact with each other, the rifle must have picked up fibers from the blanket and transferred them to the bag. Thus, the Warren Commission had substantial reason to conclude that Lee Harvey Oswald put the rifle in the paper sack and carried it into the Depository building on the morning of 22 November 1963.[34]

The third link in the commission's chain of evidence against Oswald was that he was present at the window from which the shots were fired. To substantiate this allegation, the commission relied first on fingerprint evidence. Oswald's prints were on the bag found next to the window, although, of course, he may have made these prints somewhere else. Three of Oswald's prints were uncovered on book cartons adjacent to the window. Since Oswald worked at the Depository and specifically used the sixth floor as one of his main working areas, the commission only gave this matter "probative value" in deciding whether or not Oswald was present at the window at the time of the assassination. The commission also gave some weight to the testimony of Charles Givens, a Depository employee. Givens saw Oswald on the sixth floor at 11:55 A.M., thirty-five minutes before the shooting. No one else saw Oswald until the time of the shooting itself.[35]

In addition to this very strong evidence, the commission relied heavily on the testimony of eyewitness Howard Brennan, who stated that the man he saw fire the rifle from the sixth-floor window was Lee Harvey Oswald. On the evening of 22 November 1963, Brennan selected Oswald from a police lineup as the man bearing the closest resemblance to the rifleman he had observed. The reason he failed to make a positive identification, Brennan maintained, was that he believed the assassination was "a Communist activity, and I felt like there hadn't been more than one eyewitness, and . . . my family or I, either one, might not be safe." By the time of his appearance before the commission, in March 1964, Brennan was certain that Oswald was the man he saw.[36]

The commission also discovered that Oswald's actions immediately subsequent to the assassination were consistent with his having been at the sixth-floor window at the time of the shooting. As indicated in the first chapter, officer Marrion Baker encountered Oswald in a second-floor lunchroom approximately one and a half minutes after the shots. The commission retraced Oswald's movements and had Officer Baker retrace his. The reconstruction demonstrated that Oswald could have descended to the lunchroom before Baker would have reached it.[37]

At approximately 1:15 P.M., forty-five minutes after the assassination, Dallas Police Officer J.D. Tippit was shot to death. The Warren Commission found Lee Harvey Oswald guilty of that crime as well. In determining Oswald's implication in the Tippit killing, the commission first traced Oswald's movements from the Depository building to the scene of Tippit's murder, over three miles away. Then it analyzed the medical, ballistics, and eyewitness evidence in the Tippit case.

According to the commission, Oswald left the Depository at 12:33. He walked seven blocks and caught a bus driven by Cecil McWatters. One of the passengers in the bus was Mrs. Mary Bledsoe, a former landlady of Oswald's. Mrs. Bledsoe recognized Oswald and so testified to the commission. Further evidence that Oswald was on the bus was found in a bus transfer removed from one of Oswald's pockets at the time of his arrest. The transfer, punched with the distinctive marks of McWatters' puncher, revealed that it was issued on the afternoon of 22 November.[38]

As the bus approached Dealey Plaza, it became ensnared in the heavy traffic jam that was developing. Oswald left the bus and walked several blocks to a Greyhound Bus station, arriving there at 12:48. He then got into a taxi driven by William Whaley. The cab drove him to the 500 or 700 block of North Beckley Avenue, near his rooming house. The cab driver, Whaley, positively identified Oswald as the man who took his cab. The commission's reconstruction of the taxi ride showed that the 2½-mile drive took about six minutes. This made Oswald leaving the cab at 12:54.[39]

The address of the rooming house where Oswald boarded was 1026 North Beckley Avenue. It took Oswald about six minutes to walk the distance from the place where the cab discharged him (Whaley couldn't remember if it was the 500 or 700 block) to the rooming house. In any event, Mrs. Earlene Roberts, the housekeeper, saw Oswald enter the rooming house about 1:00 P.M. He went to his room and, now wearing a jacket, left about 1:03 to 1:04 P.M.[40]

The next place Oswald was seen was the corner of Tenth Street and Patton Avenue shortly before the Tippit murder. This is almost a mile from the rooming house. Since the Tippit murder occurred at 1:15, Oswald must have walked the distance in eleven or twelve minutes. Warren Commission junior counsel David Belin walked the distance and demonstrated that Oswald could have accomplished the feat if he walked at a brisk pace.[41]

Helen Markham stood at the corner of Tenth and Patton. As she looked down Tenth Street, she saw a police car stop a man. The man walked to the right window and began talking to the policeman inside. The policeman got out of the car, and as he approached the front of the vehicle, the man pulled out a gun and shot him. The man ran back toward Patton Avenue in Mrs. Markham's direction and then headed away from her. That afternoon, Helen Markham picked Lee Harvey Oswald out of a lineup as the man she saw shoot the policeman. She reaffirmed her positive identification of Oswald before the commission.

Another eyewitness was Domingo Benavides, only fifteen feet away from the scene of the crime. Benavides, however, could not positively identify Oswald as Tippit's killer. Numerous other eyewitnesses also testified that they saw Oswald fleeing the scene of the Tippit murder. Thus, the commission had very strong eyewitness evidence against Oswald.[42]

The ballistics evidence consisted of a .38 Special Smith and Wesson revolver found in Oswald's possession at the time of his arrest, four bullets removed from Tippit's body, and four cartridge cases found near the scene of the shooting. Four experts determined that the four cartridge cases were fired from Oswald's revolver. They could not, however, positively identify the source of the bullets removed from Tippit's body because the bullets were too mutilated for the necessary scientific tests.[43]

A total of nine eyewitnesses identified Oswald as the man

who shot Tippit or as the man who fled from the scene. The cartridge cases found there were fired from Oswald's revolver, to the exclusion of all other weapons. That revolver was in Oswald's possession when he was arrested shortly after the murder. Oswald's jacket was found a couple of blocks from the crime scene. To the Warren Commission, this evidence overwhelmingly proved that Lee Harvey Oswald killed J.D. Tippit.[44]

To buttress this evidence thus far accumulated against Oswald, the commission used the police interrogation sessions against Oswald. During his confinement at Dallas police headquarters, Oswald lied to police about numerous things, including his ownership of the rifle and the curtain rod story he told to Frazier. The commission also used Oswald's unsuccessful attempt to shoot former United States Army Major General Edwin A. Walker on 10 April 1963. Even though the attempt on Walker's life took place over seven months before the assassination, the commission believed that the Walker attempt demonstrated Oswald's "disposition to take human life."[45]

Having demonstrated Oswald's guilt, the Warren Commission turned to the matter of conspiracy, both in the assassination of President Kennedy and in the murder of Oswald. After carefully investigating the backgrounds of Lee Harvey Oswald and Jack Ruby, the commission determined that there was no evidence of a conspiracy involving either man. Oswald's action resulted from a long-standing resentment toward those in authority. Assassinating the president was, for him, a means of recognition, an event that would give him the prominence he deserved. Deeply sympathetic toward Jacqueline Kennedy and wanting to spare her the ordeal of a trial, Ruby killed Oswald.[46]

The publication of the *Warren Report* in September 1964 met with critical acclaim from the press and news media. The Warren Commission was almost universally praised for its diligence and for its definitive account of the assassination. Within a few months, however, numerous critics challenged the commission's findings and generated widespread public disbelief in its sole-assassin thesis. In the light of the controversy it has provoked, the *Warren Report* demands an objective analysis to determine the validity of its conclusions. We shall now turn to that analysis.

CHAPTER 3

THE SHOTS

IN ORDER to pinpoint the location of the assassin, the Warren Commission first considered evidence supplied by various eyewitnesses in Dealey Plaza. According to the commission, "Witnesses at the scene of the assassination saw a rifle being fired from the sixth floor window of the Depository Building, and some witnesses saw a rifle in the window immediately after the shots were fired."[1]

The commission's statement incorporated only a small portion of the eyewitness evidence. Two people did see a rifle fired from the window, and two other persons saw a rifle in the window right after the shooting. However, many witnesses, including trained law enforcement personnel, heard shots fired from the Grassy Knoll. Several witnesses observed gunmen in other windows of the Depository building. If the eyewitness testimony should be accepted as reliable evidence, as the commission suggested, then that evidence indicates shots from more than one direction.

Several witnesses saw a gun barrel in the sixth-floor window of the Depository building, and one witness believed he saw a rifle being fired from the window. Dallas newsman Robert Jackson, for example, saw a rifle in the window immediately after the shots were fired. Amos Lee Euins, a fifteen-year-old boy saw a man fire a rifle from the window, although Euins could not determine whether it was a white man or a Negro.[2]

The most persuasive of the eyewitnesses, Howard Leslie Brennan, swore that the man he saw fire from the window was "standing up." Photographs of the building taken seconds before and after the shots reveal the window open only one foot from the bottom. Since an individual standing up and firing, as Brennan testified, would have been compelled either to fire through glass or to shoot with the rifle at knee height, the commission conceded that "although Brennan testified that the man in the window was standing when he fired the shots, most probably he was either sitting or kneeling."[3]

The commission relied heavily on Brennan's testimony, since he was the only eyewitness who saw Lee Harvey Oswald fire the shots. According to the commission, Brennan described the man to the Dallas police, who then broadcast a description of the suspect at 12:45 P.M., fifteen minutes after the assassination. Since Brennan was the only witness who saw the actual gunman, his description must have been the basis for the police broadcast. Yet the commission failed to explain how Brennan could have estimated the height, weight, age, and physical build of the man over one hundred feet away, "sitting or kneeling" behind a concrete ledge and a double thickness of glass.[4]

The commission further failed to investigate Brennan's testimony that he gave his description to Secret Service Agent Forrest V. Sorrels, about ten minutes after the last shot. Since Sorrels did not arrive back at the scene until twenty to twenty-five minutes later, Brennan's memory seems faulty. Sorrels, moreover, himself testified that while riding in the motorcade he had a clear view of the sixth-floor window of the building and saw no one there. Thus, the commission chose to ignore the testimony of Sorrels, a professionally trained observer, which clearly exculpated Oswald and instead chose to believe the testimony of Brennan, which contains many contradictions.[5]

In its statement about witnesses, the commission chose to ignore the testimony of other witnesses. For example, of seventy-five eyewitnesses who reported hearing shots, thirty-nine believed that at least one shot came from the vicinity of the Grassy Knoll, a bushy embankment on the southwestern corner of Dealey Plaza. These witnesses included such trained observers as Dallas Police Chief Jesse Curry, motorcycle escort Patrolman Bobby W. Hargis, riding directly behind and to the left of the presidential limousine, Deputy Sheriff Seymour Weitzman, and Secret Service Agent Forrest Sorrels.[6]

One eyewitness, Arnold Rowland, who had better than 20/20 vision, while Brennan needed corrective eyeglasses, saw a man with a rifle in the far south*west* corner window of the sixth floor about ten minutes before the shots. The commission stated that when Rowland told his wife about the rifleman, "she looked back more than once at the Depository building and saw no person looking out of any window on the sixth floor." She also said that "'At times my husband is prone to exaggerate.'"[7]

The commission's statement is misleading and inaccurate. If Mrs. Rowland saw no one on the sixth floor, she rebutted not only Arnold Rowland's testimony but also Howard Brennan's. In addition, the phrase "prone to exaggerate" was used in an entirely different context. She swore to the commission that her husband, a mediocre student, exaggerated only about his report card grades, and not to "what he saw in the building at the time."[8]

The commission's tendency to accept evidence that supported the lone-assassin thesis and to reject that which contradicted it seems to be confirmed by the fact that Brennan failed to select Oswald from a police lineup. After changing his mind three times, Brennan then swore to the commission that the gunman was Oswald. Characterized by the commission as "an accurate observer," Brennan made numerous mistakes in his account of the shooting. The commission also stated categorically that Brennan "saw a rifle being fired." This is contradicted by Brennan's answer of "No" to commission member John McCloy's question, "Did you see the rifle discharge, did you see the recoil or the flash?" The Mannlicher-Carcano rifle allegedly used by Oswald emits smoke and has a recoil.[9]

The commission also failed to give serious consideration to other evidence indicating a source of the shots from a location other than the Book Depository building. Three witnesses saw strange men at the Grassy Knoll before and shortly after the assassination. One witness, J.C. Price, saw a man fleeing the scene with what may have been a gun in his hand.[10]

Patrolman J.M. Smith, who had been standing in front of the Depository building at the time of the shooting, thought the shots came from behind the wooden fence on the Grassy Knoll. When he arrived in the parking lot behind the fence, Smith smelled gunpowder and accosted a man who flashed false Secret Service credentials to him. Another law enforcement officer, Constable Seymour Weitzman, scaled the wall adjacent to the Grassy Knoll immediately after the shots. He too saw "Secret Service" men there and noticed "numerous kinds of footprints that did not make sense because they were going in different directions." The commission failed to consider the sinister circumstances of Smith's and Weitzman's confrontations with Secret Service men immediately after the shots were fired. According to the *Warren Report* itself, the Secret Service agents "remained at their posts during the race to the hospital. *None stayed at the scene of the shooting.* . . . Forrest V. Sorrels was the first Secret Service agent to return to the scene of the assassination, approximately 20 to 25 minutes after the shots were fired."[11]

James Worrell saw a man resembling Lee Oswald run out of the back door of the Depository shortly after the shooting. Richard Carr saw a man answering a similar description enter a Rambler station wagon driven by a Negro. Marvin Robinson saw a Rambler station wagon stop next to the Depository building and then saw a white man enter the vehicle. Deputy Sheriff Roger Craig also saw a man enter a Rambler station wagon driven by a "dark complected white male." Later, Craig identified the person entering the car as Lee Harvey Oswald.[12]

Robert Hughes took an 8 mm. film which shows the Depository building within five seconds of the first shot. The Hughes film shows a figure that appears to be a person in the sixth-floor southeast window. It also shows a second figure only about ten feet away at the second pair of windows from the southeast corner of the sixth floor. The commission determined that the figure was not a person, but boxes and cartons. In November 1975, however, CBS News used the facilities of the Itek Corporation, a photographic interpretation center, and ascertained that the figure in the corner window was a man. No mention was made of the second person in the same room. This second figure looks much more like a person than the figure in the far southeast window.[13]

The figure in the far southeast window, moreover, is wearing a light-colored (possibly pink or tan) shirt. According to the commission, Oswald was wearing a dark, rust-colored shirt. In addition, the shadows from the boxes or cartons stacked near the window could not have, as the commission contended, left images higher than the window, for the sun shone directly into it, thereby casting shadows behind, rather than in front of the boxes. Who these two figures are has never been determined.[14]

From the foregoing examples, it should be clear that the Warren Commission failed to evaluate properly the eyewitness evidence. While Brennan and other witnesses did see a gunman or a gun in the sixth-floor southeast window of the Texas School Book Depository building, other witnesses saw equally suspicious things elsewhere in Dealey Plaza. By citing only the testimony of those witnesses who tended to support its preconceptions, the commission provided a misleading and inaccurate account to its readers.

THE RIFLE AND THE BULLETS

The second statement by the commission to substantiate its contention that the shots were fired from the sixth-floor southeast window of the Depository is "The nearly whole bullet found on Governor Connally's stretcher at Parkland Memorial Hospital and the two bullet fragments found in the front seat of the Presidential limousine were fired from the 6.5 millimeter Mannlicher-Carcano rifle found on the sixth floor of the Depository Building to the exclusion of all other weapons." This statement is somewhat misleading. A bullet was indeed found on a stretcher at the hospital. It is, however, extremely unlikely that the bullet was fired from the Mannlicher-Carcano at President Kennedy, and the evidence demonstrates that it probably did not come from Governor Connally's stretcher.[15]

When the limousine arrived at Parkland Hospital, Governor Connally was placed on a stretcher and rolled into Trauma Room Number Two in the emergency ward of the hospital. After being examined by doctors, the governor, still on the stretcher, was taken to a second-floor operating room. There he was removed from the stretcher and placed on an operating cart. An orderly, R.J. Jimison, then rolled the stretcher onto an elevator, leaving it unattended.[16]

Senior Hospital Engineer Darrell Tomlinson discovered the stretcher in the elevator and placed it next to a stretcher located in a corridor on the ground floor. Tomlinson left the stretcher unattended for almost forty-five minutes. The commission states that "a few minutes later he [Tomlinson] bumped one of the stretchers against a wall and a bullet rolled out." Since Tomlinson rolled the stretcher into the corridor at about 1:12 P.M. and since he did not discover the bullet until 1:45 to 1:50 P.M., the "few minutes" noted by the commission were actually closer to three-quarters of an hour.[17]

After going about his duties, Tomlinson returned to the first-floor corridor. The original stretcher, which according to the commission was "wholly unconnected with the care of Governor Connally," was pushed out from the wall where it had been blocking the entrance to a men's room. Tomlinson pushed the stretcher back against the wall. As he testified before the commission, "I bumped the wall and a spent cartridge or bullet rolled out that apparently had been lodged under the edge of the mat."[18]

Thus, Tomlinson discovered the bullet on the stretcher that had no connection with the assassination. It is worth noting that the commission had already determined that the bullet was found on Connally's stretcher even before Tomlinson was interviewed. On 16 March 1964, when Dr. James J. Humes, the chief autopsy surgeon, testified, Commissioner Allen Dulles stated that he thought the bullet had been found on the stretcher of President Kennedy. "In response, Commission Counsel Arlen Specter stated: 'There has been other evidence, Mr. Dulles . . . we shall produce later, subject to sequential proof, evidence that the stretcher on which this bullet was found was the stretcher of Governor Connally.'"[19]

Since Specter did not question Tomlinson until 20 March 1964, one wonders where Specter had his "evidence." Since no "sequential proof" was ever produced that the bullet came from Connally's stretcher, Tomlinson, the person who found the bullet, was the only source of information about the projectile's location. Originally certain that the bullet came from the stretcher that had no connection with the case, Tomlinson finally admitted that the bullet may have come from the Connally stretcher, after being subjected to a series of leading questions by Specter. Tomlinson later told a private researcher that he had been "unhappy" with Specter's line of questioning. The commission, however, was quite happy and ascertained that "although Tomlinson was not certain whether the bullet came from the Connally stretcher or the adjacent one, the Commission has concluded that the bullet came from Governor Connally's stretcher."[20]

The commission, moreover, failed to demonstrate that the bullet found on the stretcher was indeed the bullet commonly referred to as Commission Exhibit 399. Neither Tomlinson nor the man to whom he handed the bullet, O.P. Wright, personnel director of security at the hospital, would identify Bullet 399 as the one found on the stretcher. In November 1966, Wright was interviewed by *Life* researcher Josiah Thompson. He told Thompson, in the presence of two witnesses, that Bullet 399 was definitely not the one handed him by Tomlinson. Wright procured a pointed .30 caliber bullet and told Thompson that the bullet resembled it.[21]

Wright's revelation to Thompson suggests that after he turned the bullet over to a Secret Service agent, it was switched for Bullet 399, ballistically demonstrated to have been fired from Oswald's rifle. Even if it turns out that Bullet 399 was the stretcher bullet, the commission neither proved that the bullet was found on Connally's stretcher nor that the bullet had ever caused any of the wounds in either President Kennedy or Governor Connally.[22]

Since the stretcher had been left unattended in the corridor, within easy access to the hordes of people in the hospital during that hectic time, the possibility that it was planted on the stretcher cannot be dismissed. The commission assumed that Bullet 399 was a genuine assassination bullet and never seriously investigated the possibility of a plant.

The commission did not even attempt to establish the chain of evidence linking Bullet 399 to the one found by Tomlinson. After Tomlinson told him of the stretcher bullet, Wright ordered him to leave it there undisturbed. He contacted the FBI, and they were uninterested. He then contacted a Secret Service agent, who refused to view the bullet on the stretcher. Wright then picked the bullet up and brought it to Secret Service Agent Richard Johnsen. Johnsen said, "O.K." and without marking or identifying it in any way, then put the bullet in his coat pocket. The bullet then was handed over to Chief James Rowley of the Secret Service, who handed it to Elmer Todd of the FBI, who gave it to FBI firearms expert Robert Frazier.[23]

The commission made no comments nor did it try to investigate such curious and haphazard ways of handling critical evidence. In a court of law, Bullet 399 would not even be admitted as evidence. The bullet was not photographed in place on the stretcher. Neither Johnsen nor Rowley marked the bullet for the purpose of identification. Tomlinson and Wright, the only two witnesses who saw the bullet on the stretcher, would not identify Commission Exhibit 399 as that bullet, nor would Johnsen and Rowley.[24]

Two sizable portions of bullets were, however, found in the limousine. One fragment, discovered on the seat beside the driver, was 44.6 grains in weight and consisted of the nose portion of a bullet. The other fragment, found on the right side of the front seat, weighed 21 grains and consisted of the base portion of a bullet. Three tiny fragments between .7 and .9 grains each were also discovered underneath the left jump.[25]

One of the strongest pieces of evidence substantiating the Warren Commission's thesis was that the two large fragments were positively identified as having been fired from the Mannlicher-Carcano rifle found on the sixth floor of the Depository building. Critics of the commission have either omitted entirely or glossed over this very strong evidence against Oswald. Furthermore, while the three small fragments could not be positively proven to have come from Oswald's rifle, they were found to be similar in metallic composition to the two large ones.[26]

The only possible explanation for discovery of fragments in the limousine other than that they were fired into it is that they were deliberately planted there by one of the conspirators. Wedded to the lone-assassin hypothesis, the commission never seriously considered the possibility that the fragments may have been planted in the limousine. There are several possibilities.

Confusion and chaos reigned at the hospital from the limousine's arrival there at 12:35 until its departure at 2:00. Hundreds of people rushed to the hospital after hearing of the shooting. At the emergency entrance, several hundred people had easy access to the presidential limousine.[27]

Two witnesses testified that they saw Jack Ruby in the lobby of the hospital. The commission discounted this, claiming that since Ruby arrived at his Carousel Club at 1:45, and one of the witnesses, newspaper reporter Seth Kantor, saw him at 1:30, he did not have time to drive to the night club in fifteen minutes. "At a normal driving speed under normal conditions," the commission declared "the trip can be made in 9 to 10 minutes. However, it is likely that congested traffic conditions on November 22 would have extended the driving time." As will be seen later, the commission made no allowance for "congested traffic conditions" when it traced Oswald's route after leaving the Depository building. Indeed, it even reduced the test time for Oswald's cab to drive from downtown Dallas, a few blocks from the assassination scene. Thus, Oswald's speed was accelerated by 50 percent, while Ruby's was reduced 50 percent.[28]

Other, even more unusual, events occurred at the hospital during the ninety minutes the presidential party was there. Secret Service Agent Andrew Berger reported that an unidentified white male attempted to enter the emergency room in which the president was being treated. The man claimed to be "FBI" and had to be forcibly restrained from entering the room. Agent Berger also recounted the appearance of "an unidentified CIA agent" in the hospital corridor about thirty minutes after the assassination.[29]

A letter to the Warren Commission by James Rowley, head of the Secret Service, revealed that a "Political Cuban" of "disruptive influence" was employed at Parkland Hospital. The source of Rowley's information was Father Walter McChann, spiritual advisor to the Cuban refugee community in Dallas. Despite the known contacts between Oswald and Cuban groups, and the mysterious appearance of the stretcher bullet, the commission never attempted to interview Father McChann nor to identify the Cuban. Nor, for that matter, did it try to learn the identities of the "FBI" and "CIA" agents at the hospital.[30]

Thus, although ballistics tests demonstrated beyond question that Bullet 399 and the two large fragments found in the front seat were fired from Oswald's rifle, it failed to prove that they were fired from the rifle into the limousine. This does not, of course, mean that the bullet and fragments were planted. It does, however, indicate the necessity for tracing them from the rifle to their locations at the time of discovery. This the commission did not do. The question is still unanswered to this day as to whether or not the bullet and fragments were genuinely involved in the assassination.[31]

To further substantiate its contention that the shots were fired from the sixth-floor southeast window of the Texas School Book Depository building, the commission stated, "The three used cartridge cases found near the window on the sixth floor at the southeast corner of the building were fired from the same rifle which fired the above-described bullet and fragments; to the exclusion of all other weapons." Three cartridge cases were found on the sixth floor, two directly under the southeast corner window, the third 5 feet west and 2 feet behind the others. Two of the cases, Commission Exhibits 544 and 545, had marks "produced by the chamber of Oswald's rifle." One had marks produced by the magazine follower; the other had marks produced by the bolt of Oswald's rifle. Both cases had markings that showed they had been loaded into a rifle at least twice.[32]

The third cartridge case, Commission Exhibit 543, contained a dent in the opening so large that it could not have held a bullet in it. This cartridge case could not have received the dent after the assassination, since it was very carefully handled so that it would not be damaged. Moreover, the Dallas police retained possession of it until 28 November, five days after Commission Exhibit 544 and 545 were turned over to the FBI.[33]

The existence of the three cartridge cases was the main reason the commission concluded that the three shots were fired. As the *Report* states, "the most convincing evidence relating to the number of shots was provided by the presence on the sixth floor of three cartridge cases which were demonstrated to have been fired by the same rifle that fired the bullets which caused the wounds." It conceded that conflicting eyewitness testimony may have colored the popular impression that three shots were fired. It also conceded that only two shots may have been fired. "Nevertheless," the commission asserted, "the preponderance of the evidence, in particular the three spent cartridges, led the Commission to conclude that there were three shots fired."[34]

In its discussion of the cartridge cases, the commission never questioned the unusual circumstances surrounding this evidence. For example, the fact that of the three cases, only one, Commission Exhibit 544, had markings produced by the bolt of

Oswald's rifle. The other two had markings produced by the magazine follower. The magazine follower marks only the last cartridge in the clip. The last cartridge could not have been either Commission Exhibit 543 or 545, as a live bullet was later found in the firing chamber.[35]

In a letter to the Warren Commission of 2 June 1964, J. Edgar Hoover noted that Commission Exhibit 543 (FBI Number C6), the case with the dent, had "three sets of marks on the base of this cartridge case which were not found [on the others]." The case, according to Hoover, had also been loaded into and extracted from a weapon three times. The only marks linking the case to Oswald's rifle were marks from the magazine follower. As noted above, Case 543 could not have obtained the marks from the magazine follower on 22 November, since the last round in the clip must have been the unfired one in the chamber. Furthermore, Commission Exhibit 543 lacks the characteristic indentation on the side made by the firing chamber of Oswald's rifle.[36]

Dr. E. Forrest Chapman, forensic pathologist, who in 1973 was given access to the assassination materials in the National Archives, noted that Case 543 was probably "dry loaded" into a rifle. Since the dent was too large for the case to have contained a bullet on November 22, it was never fired from Oswald's rifle. The empty case, however, for some unknown reason could have been loaded into a rifle, the trigger pulled, and the bolt operated. Dr. Chapman discovered this phenomenon through experiments of his own.[37]

Dr. Chapman also noted that Case 543 had a deeper and more concave indentation on its base, at the primer, where the firing pin strikes the case. Only empty cases exhibit such characteristics. The FBI also reproduced this effect. Commission Exhibit 557 is a test cartridge case, fired empty from Oswald's rifle by the FBI for ballistics comparison purposes. It, too, contains the dent in the lip and deep primer impression similar to Case 543.[38]

Thus, the evidence proves conclusively that Commission Exhibit 543 could not have been fired from Oswald's rifle. Since Commission Exhibits 544 and 545 bear no markings from the firing pin of Oswald's rifle, the evidence proves only that they both had been loaded into the firing chamber and that Case 544 was ejected through the bolt action, but that Case 545 was not.

The commission apparently assumed that Case 543 received its dent in the process of being ejected from the rifle and falling to the floor. The case, however, is made of solid brass and would not dent in the ejection process. The only way for the dent to have been made in the case after firing a bullet from it was for Oswald to have somehow beaten a dent in it, for example, with a hammer. This is impossible since Oswald simply did not have the time, every second of his movements after the shooting being accounted for.[39]

The commission failed to account for the fact that all three cartridges had previously been loaded into a weapon, not necessarily Oswald's. It did speculate that examination of the cartridge cases established that they had been previously loaded and ejected from the assassination rifle, which would indicate that Oswald practiced operating the bolt. This is hypothesis and speculation. According to FBI Director Hoover, the cases had previously been loaded and ejected from some rifle, which may or may not have been Oswald's. Furthermore, according to Hoover, only one of the three cartridge cases, Commission Exhibit 544 (FBI Number C7), had marks "identified as having been produced by contact with the bolt of C14 [the FBI number for the rifle]."[40]

If anything, Hoover's statement means that both Case 543 and 545 had not been ejected from the rifle, since they were not marked with the bolt of the weapon. It is unlikely that Oswald would have practiced operating the bolt. It is usually practiced on with the rifle empty of cartridges, especially those used in such an important task as assassinating a president.[41]

The commission held a series of tests to determine whether the location of the cartridge cases at the time of discovery was consistent with their having been fired from the rifle. The results of the ejection tests were that "the cartridge cases were ejected to the right of and at roughly a right angle to the rifle." They found that the "assassin" firing from that window and ejecting the cartridge cases would see the cases fly backward, hit the boxes behind him, ricochet off the boxes, and "came to rest to the west of the window." Two of the three cases, however, came to rest not west of the window, but directly underneath it, indicating that they were ejected when the gunman was in some position other than firing out of the window, or that someone placed them there. Only one case (we do not know which one) was discovered west of the southeast corner window.[42]

The commission employed the evidence of the cartridge cases to substantiate its conclusion that the shots were fired from the sixth-floor southeast window of the Texas School Book Depository building. It assumed that the cartridge cases had been fired from the rifle. The evidence did not support that conclusion beyond doubt. A reasonable conclusion based on this evidence follows.

Of the three cartridge cases, one, Commission Exhibit 543, can be positively eliminated. The dent in its lip was too deep to permit a bullet to fit inside the case. It also lacked the characteristic indentation made by the chamber of Oswald's rifle on all other cases and bullets. Since Commission Exhibit 543 did not contain a bullet on November 22, and since it was never inside the firing chamber of Oswald's rifle (at least with a bullet in it), the only reasonable conclusion is that it played no role in the assassination.

Commission Exhibit 545 had been inside the firing chamber. However, it lacked the markings of the bolt of Oswald's rifle. Since its primer cap bore the impression of a firing pin, and since it did not have a dent similar to that of Case 543, we can conclude one of two things: Case 545 was indeed fired from Oswald's rifle and somehow managed to be ejected without being marked by the bolt, or it was fired from the other rifle into which it had been previously loaded and ejected. In either case, there is no evidence that this cartridge was fired from Oswald's rifle on the day of the assassination.

Commission Exhibit 544 bore the markings of the firing chamber and of the bolt of Oswald's rifle, and its primer held an impression similar to that made by Oswald's rifle's firing pin. Since the two metal fragments found in the front seat of the presidential limousine were positively identified as having been fired from Oswald's rifle, we can reasonably speculate that there is very strong evidence to believe that Case 544 contained a bullet fired at President Kennedy. However, the possibility that the fragments could have been planted in the limousine, the strange markings on case 544, indicating that it, too, had been previously loaded and ejected from another rifle, and the confusion as to which of the three cartridge cases was found west of the window give rise to serious doubts as to whether such a speculation is valid.

Thus, there is strong and compelling evidence that only one of the three cartridge cases, Commission Exhibit 544, could possibly have played a role in the assassination. Both Case 543 and Case 545 could not have done so, for reasons cited above. This substantiates the fact that only one of the three cases was discovered in a location consistent with the ejection pattern of Oswald's rifle. Commission Exhibits 543 and 545 must, therefore, have been placed there by someone. None of the three cases bore fingerprints of any kind, indicating that Oswald may not have handled them (Oswald left many other prints elsewhere). Since an absolute minimum of two shots were fired, most probably four or five, and since only one of the three cartridges could possibly have figured in the assassination, shots must have been fired from elsewhere.

From the foregoing examples, it should be clear that the Warren Commission failed properly to evaluate the evidence before it. The commission assumed that Lee Harvey Oswald fired the shots from the sixth-floor southeast window of the Book Depository building. It used evidence that supported this conclusion and rejected that which refuted it. While there was, indeed, hard physical, ballistics, and eyewitness evidence to substantiate the commission's conclusions in part, the historian cannot accept them as definitive. Other evidence clearly points to other places in Dealey Plaza as possible sources of the gunfire.

CHAPTER 4

THE SHOTS IN THE BACK

The nature of the bullet wounds suffered by President Kennedy and Governor Connally and the location of the car at the time of the shots establish that the bullets were fired from above and behind the Presidential limousine, striking the President and the Governor as follows:

(1) President Kennedy was first struck by a bullet which entered at the back of his neck and exited through the lower front portion of his neck, causing a wound which would not necessarily have been lethal. The President was struck a second time by a bullet which entered the right-rear portion of his head, causing a massive and fatal wound.

(2) Governor Connally was struck by a bullet which entered on the right side of his back and traveled downward through the right side of his chest, exiting below his right nipple. This bullet then passed through his right wrist and entered his left thigh, where it caused a superficial wound.[1]

OF ALL THE CONTROVERSY surrounding the Warren Commission and its conclusions, none has generated more heated debate than that concerning the medical evidence. The above statements form the *Warren Report*'s synopsis of the wounds inflicted on President Kennedy and Governor Connally. They are cited in the *Report*'s conclusions as part of the evidence for the assertion that all shots were fired from the sixth-floor southeast corner window of the Texas School Book Depository building.

The bases for the commission's medical evidence were the testimony and medical reports of the Dallas doctors who treated the president and of the autopsy surgeons, the president's and governor's clothing, films of the assassination, trajectory tests conducted by the FBI, and wounds ballistics tests conducted by the Army. Considering the testimony and evidence before it, the commission arrived at a reasonable conclusion. As we shall see, however, much of the medical evidence was never shown to the commission, and the panel was given misleading information by Arlen Specter, the legal counsel in charge of the medical and ballistics evidence.[2]

THE SINGLE-BULLET THEORY

According to the Warren Commission, "it is not necessary to determine just which shot hit Governor Connally." This, however, is not true. It is, in fact, essential to determine which shot struck Governor Connally, for that determination forms a vital link in the chain of evidence indicating the number of assassins.[3]

The critics of the Warren Commission rarely agreed with the commission about anything. One aspect of the medical and ballistics evidence that has generated the most controversy is the single-bullet theory. As discussed in Chapter Two, the theory maintains that a bullet from the rifle of Lee Harvey Oswald struck President Kennedy in the back of the neck and exited from his throat just below the Adam's apple. That same bullet entered Governor Connally's back, exited from his chest, went completely through his right wrist, and lodged in his left thigh. Because Oswald could not fire his bolt-action rifle fast enough to wound Kennedy and Connally with separate shots, the single-bullet theory is essential to the Warren Commission's lone-assassin thesis.[4]

Because the Zapruder film showed Kennedy reacting in pain to a shot in frame Z225, the shot must have been fired prior to that frame. The shot could not have been fired before frame Z210, however, because an oak tree blocked Oswald's view of the limousine before that frame. As the commission observed, "Even the most proficient marksman" could not have fired through the leaves of the tree and hit the president. Therefore, Kennedy must have been struck between frames Z210 and Z225.[5]

Governor Connally, however, appears to be uninjured in frame Z225. In that and in the succeeding ten frames, Connally shows no indication of pain or any other sign of being wounded.

1. *Zapruder Frame Z189.* Kennedy and Connally at the time of the first shot.

His response to the wounds inflicted on him first becomes evident in frames Z236–238, when the film shows his cheek puffing, his hair flying upward, his right shoulder slumping sharply downward, and his face grimacing in pain.[6]

The visual evidence of the Zapruder film, then, contradicts the single-bullet theory. The film shows Kennedy wounded no later than frame Z225 and Connally no earlier than frame Z236. After viewing the film, Governor Connally and the physicians who treated his wounds agreed that the president and the governor were struck by separate bullets.[7]

To the Warren Commission, this evidence posed a serious problem. If Kennedy and Connally were indeed struck by separate bullets, those bullets could not both have been fired by Lee Harvey Oswald. To resolve the issue, the commission simply concluded that Governor Connally experienced a delayed reaction to his wounds.[8]

So convincing is the film of two separate shots that the original Secret Service and FBI accounts of the assassination stated that the two men were struck by separate bullets. A 28 November 1963 memorandum of the Secret Service states that "President Kennedy . . . was shot. Immediately thereafter Governor Connally . . . was shot." An FBI Summary Report of the assassination stated that "two bullets struck President Kennedy, and one wounded Governor Connally." Even the Warren Commission itself at first accepted as fact the contention that separate shots struck Kennedy and Connally. A 30 January 1964 memorandum from commission staff lawyer David Belin to Commission Chief Counsel J. Lee Rankin states, "In determining the accuracy of Oswald we have three major possibilities: Oswald was shooting at Connally and missed two out of three shots, the two misses striking Kennedy; Oswald was shooting at both Kennedy and Connally and all three shots struck their intended targets; Oswald was shooting only at Kennedy and the second bullet missed its intended target and hit Connally instead." Another commission memorandum by counsel Melvin Eisenberg reveals that as late as 22 April 1964, five months after the assassination, the commission was still satisfied that separate shots hit Kennedy and Connally.[9]

The results of ballistics tests on Oswald's rifle, however, re-

2. *Zapruder Frame Z225.* Kennedy reacts to back wound; Connally begins reaction to his wounds.

vealed that Oswald did not have time to fire two shots and hit Kennedy and Connally separately. According to FBI ballistics expert Robert Frazier, the minimum time for firing two shots with Oswald's rifle is 2.25 seconds. Since President Kennedy was shot no earlier than frame Z210 (because of the oak tree shielding him) and Governor Connally no later than frame Z238 (according to the testimony of Connally's physicians), it is possible to calculate the maximum possible time between the wounding of the two men. Since each frame of the film is 1/18th of a second and since a maximum of 28 frames elapsed (between Z210 and Z238), the maximum possible time is 28/18ths seconds or 1.556 seconds. Therefore, since the minimum time for firing two separate shots from Oswald's rifle is greater than the maximum time between the wounding of the two men, two alternatives are possible. First, the two men were struck by the same bullet. Second, they were struck by separate bullets and thus by two assassins.[10]

Both the Warren Commission and its critics, however, have overlooked a vital fact that demonstrates that the single-bullet theory is not necessarily an integral aspect of the commission's lone-assassin thesis. That theory relies on FBI tests that showed that an oak tree blocked Oswald's view of the presidential limousine between frames 166 and 210 of the Zapruder film. Those tests were conducted on 24 May 1964, at a time when foliage on the tree was probably different from that on 22 November 1963. There is, of course, no way of determining the precise foliage conditions of the two days. But the possibility exists that there was less foliage in late November than in late May. Furthermore, the wind was blowing at the time of the assassination and not during the tests. The wind could have caused small branches at the top of the tree to move, possibly entirely out of Oswald's line of fire during the brief time of the shooting.[11]

By analyzing photographs, FBI photographer Lyndal Shaneyfelt determined that the oak tree blocked Oswald's view of the limousine. An FBI photographer took photographs of a reenactment limousine from a camera "whose lens recorded the view through the telescopic sight of the C2766 Mannlicher-Carcano rifle." The camera rested on a tripod; the photographer knelt at the extreme eastern end of the window. Presumably, he duplicated Oswald's position at the time of the shots.[12]

However, we do not know Oswald's exact firing position. The Warren Commission contended that Oswald either sat or knelt at the eastern end of the window and used stacks of boxes as a gun rest, but no one knows the precise arrangement and location of the boxes. The commission itself published four official yet contradictory versions of the boxes. The first shows three boxes resting on the eastern edge of the window, stacked at right angles to each other. The second shows the top box lying at a very sharp angle, on both the window sill and sash. The third shows three boxes located farther to the west than those in the first two "official" arrangements. Two of these boxes are touching each other; the third leans entirely on the window sill. The final position shows the boxes much farther to the west than in the previous three versions. Since the commission itself did not know which of the four arrangements of boxes, if any, that Oswald used, nor whether he was kneeling or sitting when firing, the photographs cannot duplicate his view of the limousine. A *Life* magazine photograph of Elm Street, taken a few hours after the shooting, clearly demonstrates how an "assassin," resting his rifle on the boxes depicted in the photograph, could have fired without hitting the oak tree. Furthermore, a recently discovered photograph, taken less than two minutes after the shooting, reveals that someone had already moved the boxes.[13]

The FBI tests, therefore, were invalid. The leaves of the tree were probably different on the two days. The wind was blowing during the assassination and not during the tests. And there is no way of determining the exact position of Oswald during the shooting. Because of the uncertainty about whether or not the oak tree did block Oswald's view of the limousine between frames Z166 and Z210 of the Zapruder film, the question of whether the single-bullet theory is, in fact, essential to the Warren Commission's lone-assassin thesis must remain unanswered.[14]

If the first shot was fired at frame Z166, Oswald would have had four seconds in which to fire a separate shot at Connally. Even if the first shot came as late as frame Z196, there was still sufficient time for a second shot to be fired at frame Z238.

3. *Philip Willis Slide #5.* Erect position of JFK (arrow) at instant of first shot.

There is evidence to indicate the possibility of a shot's being fired at frame Z189. A slide of the motorcade taken by Philip A. Willis coincides with frame Z202 of the Zapruder film. Willis believed that the sound of the first shot caused him to squeeze the shutter of the camera. Since bullets travel faster than sound, it is apparent that the shot must have been fired before Willis snapped the picture, i.e., before frame Z202. Extensive analysis of the Zapruder film by optics expert Robert Groden shows the president apparently reacting to a bullet wound as early as frame Z189.[15]

Critics of the *Warren Report* who have pointed out deficiencies in the single-bullet theory, have thus failed to demonstrate the validity of their arguments. Assuming that the FBI photographs of the oak tree were valid, the critics used evidence in a manner not acceptable to the historian. Because some "evidence" gathered by the Warren Commission suited their theories, they unquestioningly accepted and used it. The evidence on the single-bullet theory, however, is inconclusive. Since there is no objective method of duplicating the precise conditions prevailing on the day of the assassination, we can only conclude that Lee Harvey Oswald *may* have had sufficient time to wound President Kennedy and Governor Connally with separate bullets. The single-bullet theory, therefore, is not necessarily essential to any of the conclusions of the Warren Commission.

THE FIRST SHOT

Although the precise instant of the first shot is not known, we do know that it struck President Kennedy in the upper back. The autopsy disclosed a bullet hole, approximately 7 x 4 mm., located 14 cm. from the tip of the right acromium process and 14 cm. below the tip of the right mastoid process. This wound, according to the autopsy, was "presumably of entry." Examination of the president's thoracic cavity revealed bruising of the muscles on the right side of the neck and of the trachea, and bruising of the tip of the right lung. These factors led the autopsy pathologists to conclude that a bullet entered the upper back and passed through the neck. No exit wound was visible, since a large tracheotomy incision in the throat obscured any evidence of other

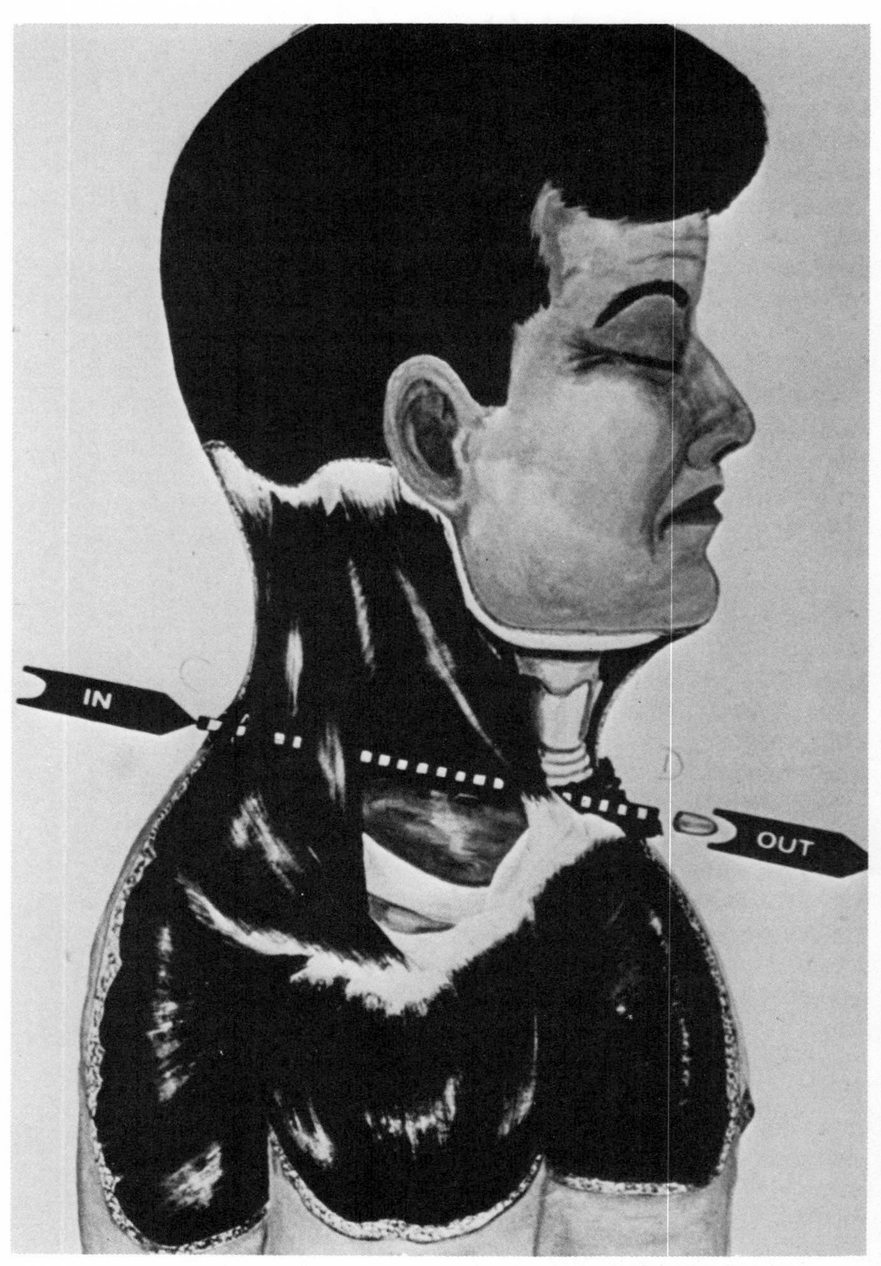

4. *Commission Exhibit 385.* Warren Commission version of first shot.

wounds. However, upon learning from Dr. Malcolm Perry of Parkland Hospital in Dallas that the tracheotomy was cut through an existing wound, the autopsy pathologists termed the original throat wound "presumably of exit." They therefore concluded that President Kennedy was first struck by a bullet that entered the rear of the upper back and exited "through the anterior surface of the neck."[16]

There are very serious discrepancies between this version of the president's wounds and what the evidence discloses. First, the autopsy failed to indicate the precise location of the wound in the president's back. The measurements of 14 cm. from the tips of the right acromium and mastoid processes depend upon such variables as the length of the president's neck, the width of his shoulders, and the position of the head and shoulders when the measurements were taken. Such standard and inflexible points of reference as the top of the skull and the midline of the body were not used.[17]

Later attempts to locate the wound have been equally imprecise. A panel of pathologists and a radiologist appointed by Attorney General Ramsey Clark to examine the Kennedy autopsy photographs and X-rays in 1968 located the wound 15 cm. from the right acromial process, 5 cm. lateral to the mid-dorsal line, and 14 cm. below the right mastoid process, and 5.5 cm. below a "transverse fold in the skin of the neck." These measurements are equally imprecise, since the location of the fold in the skin of the neck is not given. Dr. John Lattimer, who also viewed the autopsy materials, located the wound as "just below the junction of neck and back" and 5 cm. below the "transverse double fold in the skin at the junction of the neck and back." Forensic Pathologist Cyril Wecht located the wound as 4 to 4.5 cm. from the midline of the back and 5.7 cm. below the lowest crease in the neck. These observations of the autopsy photographs generally agree that the wound is very high in the upper back.[18]

Although the autopsy photographs verify the autopsy's general location of the back wound, other evidence disputes it. The Ramsey Clark panel observed that the photographs show that "obviously the cutaneous wound in the back was too small to permit the insertion of a finger." Yet the chief autopsy pathologist, Dr. J.J. Humes, testified before the Warren Commission

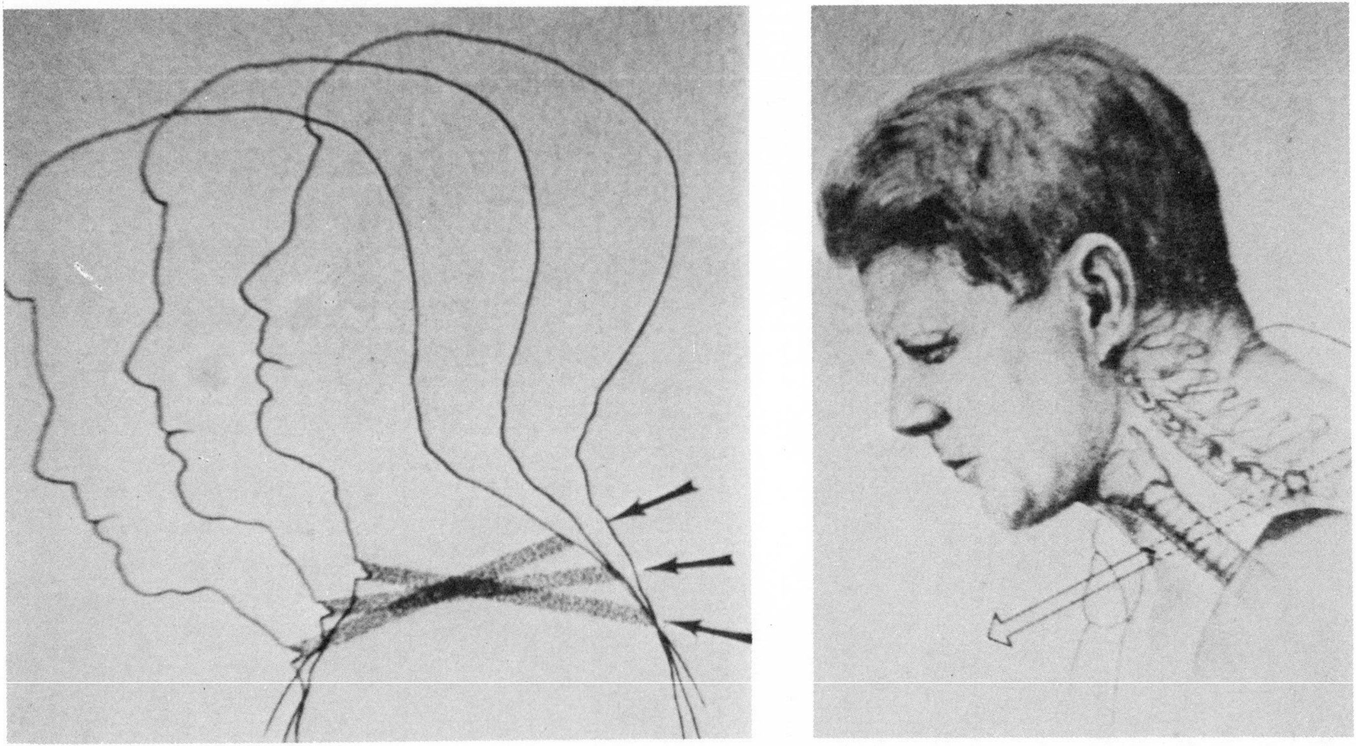

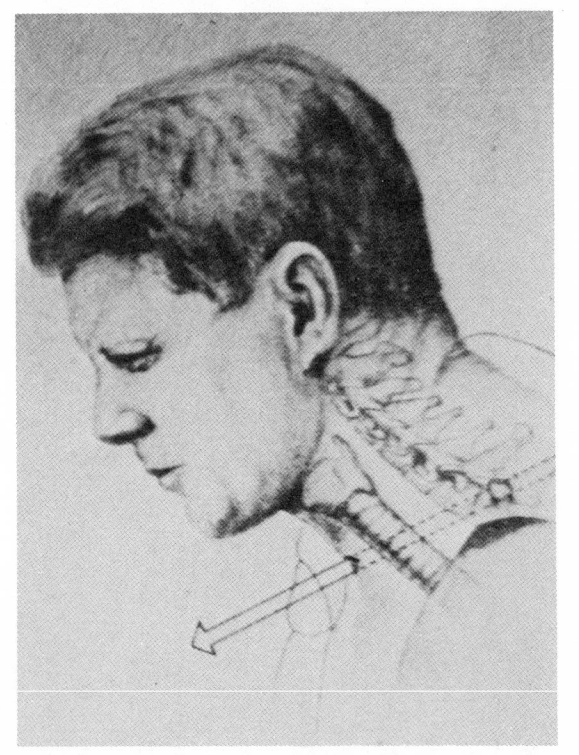

5. *HSCA Drawing.* House Select Committee's version of first shot. The Forensic Pathology Panel distorted JFK's position to make it appear that the bullet went through his neck.

that he had indeed inserted a finger into the wound. Two FBI eyewitnesses to the autopsy reported that the "opening was probed by Dr. HUMES with the finger."[19]

The photographs therefore appear to depict a wound different from that described in the autopsy. If, according to three eminent forensic pathologists, the wound shown in the autopsy photographs was too small to permit the insertion of a finger, then Dr. Humes must have probed a different wound.

The second discrepancy is the fact that both the shirt and coat worn by President Kennedy have bullet holes almost six inches below the top of the collar. This is substantially below the base of the neck-upper back area where the commission, the autopsy, and the photographs depict the hole. Defenders of the *Warren Report* claim that the shirt and coat were bunched up over the president's neck when he was shot. A photograph of the president, taken a few minutes before he was shot, does show the coat bunched up over his back and shoulders. Yet the photograph clearly shows that a bullet traveling at a downward angle would have made at least two holes in the coat, whereas the garment contains only one. Furthermore, the picture also clearly shows that the shirt is not bunched up.[20]

All photographs taken during the approximate time of the first shot (Zapruder frames Z166 to Z225) show the coat and shirt resting in normal position on the president's back. The Willis slide, for example, shows this clearly. At about frame Z233 of the Zapruder film, the president's shirt and coat do begin to bunch up, as he raises his elbows high with his hands facing his throat. The bunching up, however, occurs *after* the first shot was fired, at a time when Oswald could not have had sufficient time to fire a second shot. President Kennedy is clearly wincing in pain in frame Z225, when the shirt and coat are still in normal position. These observations give rise to several possibilities.[21]

It is possible that the unbuttoned suit coat may have risen four or five inches as the president was waving to the crowd. This is not true of the shirt. The shirt was a well-fitted dress shirt; all the buttons, including the collar button, are buttoned. Unless the president's tailor was unusually careless and made his customized shirts four sizes too large, it can reasonably be presumed that the garment fit its owner (all photographs of the

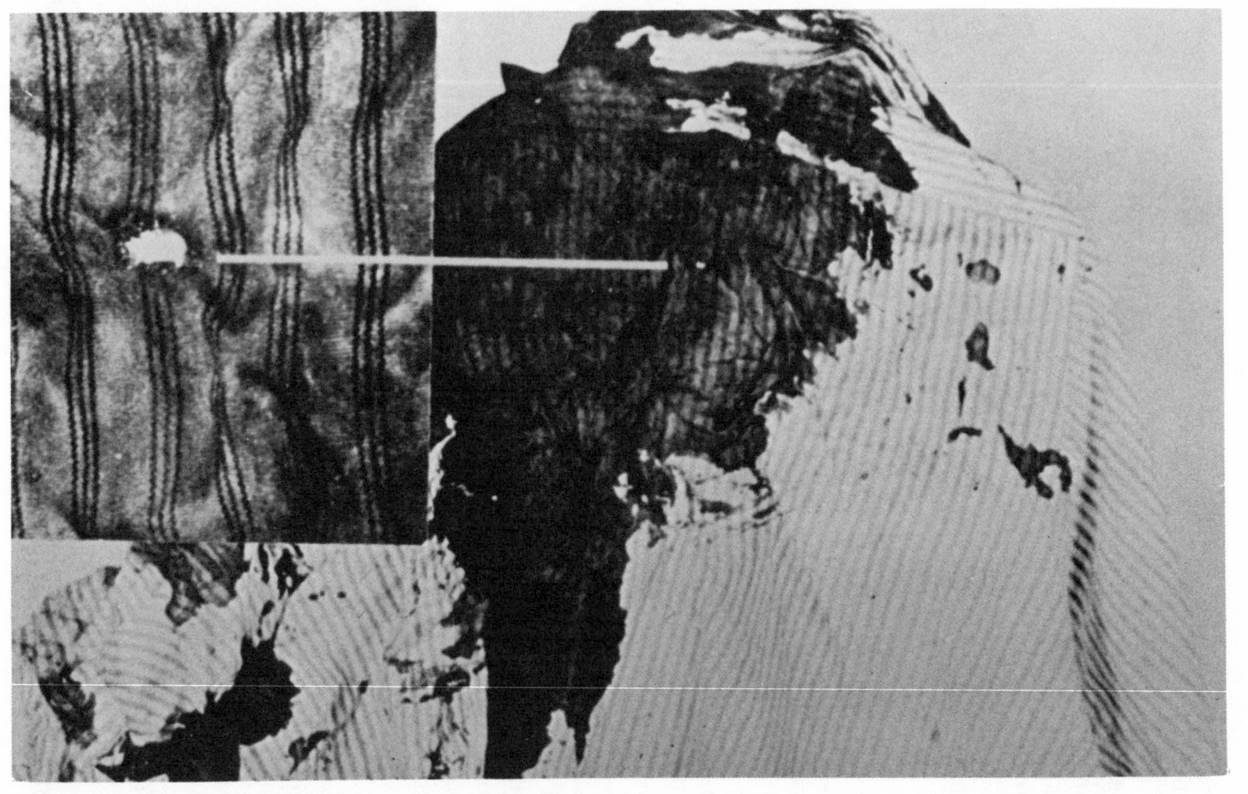

6. *FBI Exhibit #60*. Kennedy's shirt, showing the true location of the bullet hole in the back.

assassination confirm this). Since the shirt was tucked in the pants and held in place by the buttons and tie, it could not have risen six inches above his shoulders. Furthermore, any "bunching up" of the shirt and coat would have resulted in two holes in each garment. Only one bullet hole was made in each, however. Therefore, there is no explanation for the existence of bullet holes in both the shirt and coat unless the holes corresponded to one in the back about 4 to 6 inches (10 to 15 cm.) below the base of the neck.[22]

There is substantial evidence to suggest that the president was indeed shot in the back, well below the location stated by the Warren Commission. Several eyewitnesses to the autopsy testified that there was a back wound. Secret Service Agent Clint Hill recalled that he "observed a wound about six inches down from the neckline on the back just to the right of the spinal column." FBI Agents Francis O'Neill and James Sibert, present at the autopsy, saw "a bullet hole which was below the shoulders and two inches to the right of the middle line of the spinal column." An eyewitness to the autopsy, never questioned by the Warren Commission, has confirmed to the author the location of the bullet hole "about six inches below the base of the neck, to the right of the spinal column."[23]

There is medical corroboration for the eyewitness observations. The official autopsy diagram of the body locates the wound in the back about 15 cm. below the base of the neck. There are two death certificates of President Kennedy. One, signed by a Dallas justice of the peace, locates the wound "near the center of the body and just above the right shoulder," a location which confirms the Warren Commission version of the wound. This death certificate, however, was written two weeks after the assassination. It lists Dr. Malcom [*sic*] Perry as the source of information about the wounds. Dr. Malcolm Perry, however, never saw the back of the president's body and therefore could not have informed the justice of the peace about a wound there.[24]

The second death certificate, and the official one, was written by Admiral George Burkley, the president's personal physician. Present both at Parkland Hospital in Dallas and at the autopsy, Admiral Burkley had the opportunity to see more of the body than anyone else. According to this death certificate, the president received a wound "in the posterior back at about the level of the third thoracic vertebra." Burkley's location of the wound corresponds exactly with the holes in the shirt and coat, the autopsy diagram of the body, and the eyewitness observations.[25]

Even more persuasive evidence of the existence of a bullet hole in the president's back is from a declassified transcript of a Warren Commission meeting held 27 January 1964. This meeting occurred two months after the assassination, and the commission members had the full autopsy report available. Yet J. Lee Rankin, chief counsel to the Warren Commission, informed the members "it seems quite apparent now, since we have the picture of where the bullet entered in the back, that the bullet entered below the shoulder blade to the right of the backbone. . . ." One week earlier, Rankin was asked by Commissioner John McCloy whether the photographs of the president's body were available to the commission, and Rankin replied that they were.[26]

The picture of where the bullet entered in the back "below the shoulder blade" clearly conflicts with the autopsy photographs now in the National Archives. The picture which Rankin referred to has been replaced by one which depicts a bullet hole high in the upper back, just below the base of the neck.

THE THROAT WOUND

When President Kennedy was first brought into Parkland Hospital about five minutes after the shooting, several Dallas physicians noticed a tiny wound in his throat, just below the Adam's apple. The Dallas doctors were unanimous in their description of the wound. It was very small, 3 to 5 mm. in diameter, round, clean, and with some bleeding and bruising of the tissue around it. The initial impression of the Dallas doctors was that it was an entrance wound. Dr. Charles J. Carrico, for example, called it a "small penetrating wound" of the throat. Dr. Ronald C. Jones described "a small hole in anterior midline of the neck thought to be a bullet entrance wound."[27]

Contemporary press accounts quoted the Dallas physicians as believing that this hole was an entrance wound. Dr. Robert

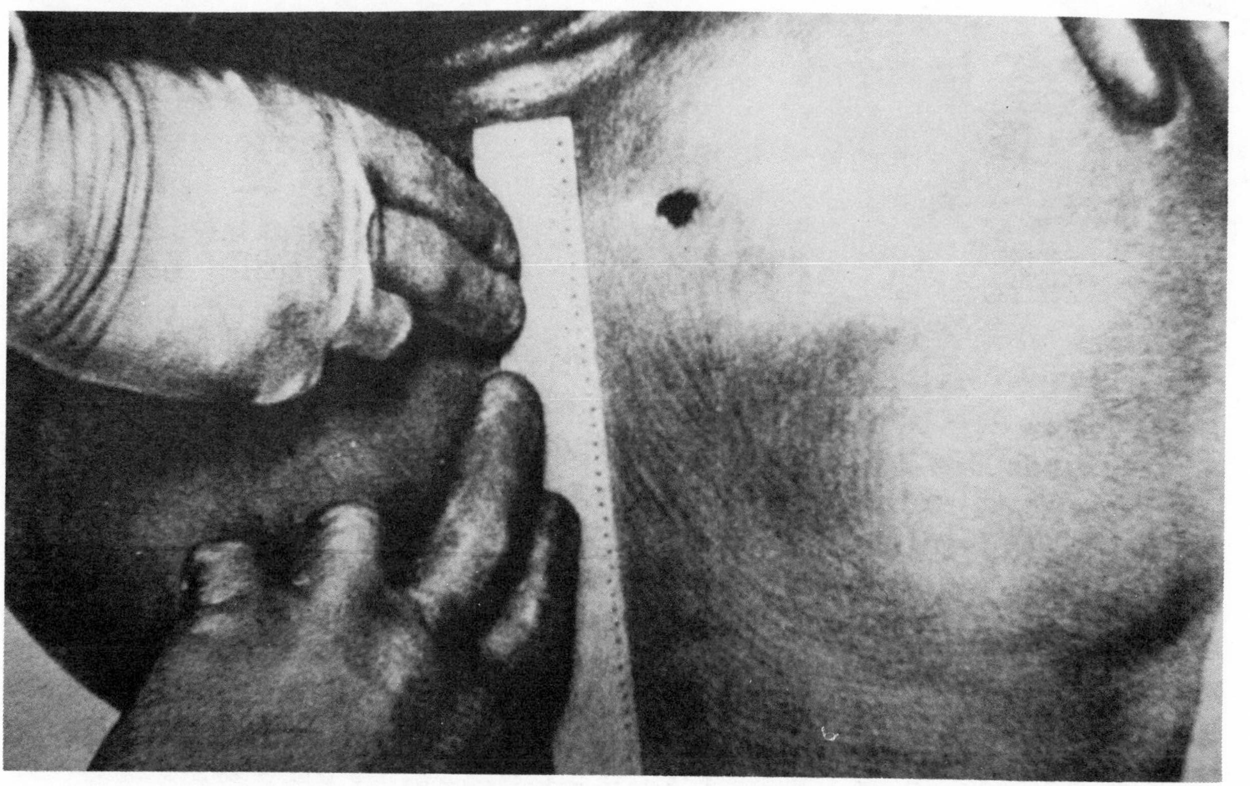

7. *HSCA Drawing.* Copied from an autopsy photograph, this drawing shows the hole in the back.

McClelland was quoted as stating that the wound "had the appearance of the usual entrance wound of a bullet." Dr. Malcolm Perry was reported as stating that "a bullet struck him in front as he faced the assailant." A *Life* issue of 29 November 1963 cites a Dallas doctor as the source of its statement that the bullet entered the president's throat from the front and *then lodged in his body*. Dr. Kemp Clark observed that a bullet struck the president in the throat, "ranged downward in his chest and did not exit." So sure was the Secret Service that the president was struck in the throat from the front that on 5 December 1963, two weeks after the assassination and the autopsy, the agency conducted tests in Dallas to determine how a bullet struck the president in front if it was fired from behind.[28]

The autopsy, however, disclosed no evidence of an entrance wound in the throat. The wound had been totally obliterated by a tracheotomy incision performed by Dallas physicians in a desperate attempt to save the president's life. The autopsy surgeons failed to fit the edges of the tracheotomy together and thus to reconstruct the original margins of the wound. Unaware of the existence of a bullet wound in the throat, the autopsy pathologists were puzzled because there was no exit hole for the bullet that entered the president's back. Instead of following proper pathological procedure and dissecting the wound, they resorted to speculation. According to both the *Warren Report* and the official FBI account of the autopsy, the pathologists theorized that external cardiac massage performed on the president in Dallas caused the bullet that entered his back to fall out of the entrance hole in the back. On 23 November 1963, Dr. Humes, the chief autopsy pathologist, called Dr. Malcolm Perry, the Dallas surgeon who had performed the tracheotomy. Dr. Humes was astounded to learn that the tracheotomy was made through a wound in the throat. After burning his original autopsy notes, Dr. Humes wrote a new version which presumed that the throat wound was the exit hole of the bullet which entered the back. The final, undated version of the autopsy refers to the hole in the back as "presumably of entry" and to the hole in the throat as "presumably of exit."[29]

The *Warren Report* states that after the speculation that the bullet had fallen out of the body, the autopsy surgeons "determined that the bullet passed between two large strap muscles and bruised them without leaving any channel, since the bullet merely passed between them." This is false. The bullet wound was not dissected, even though dissection is the only certain means of tracking a bullet's path through the body. At the trial of Clay Shaw in 1969, one of the autopsy pathologists, Dr. Pierre Finck, admitted that the autopsy team was ordered by a general or admiral not to dissect the back wound. Since no dissection took place, it is obvious that no bullet track was ever revealed at the autopsy.[30]

Even though the wound was not dissected, the body was opened up during the autopsy. The autopsy pathologists noticed bruising of the strap muscles on the right side of the neck and also on the very top of the right lung. This led to the unproven assumption that the bruising was caused by the bullet as it passed from the back through the upper thoracic cavity and exited out of the throat.[31]

The Ramsey Clark panel stated that "there is a track between the two cutaneous wounds as indicated by subcutaneous emphysema and small metallic fragments on the X-rays and the contusion of the apex of the right lung and the laceration of the trachea described in the Autopsy Report." Dr. John Lattimer answered the question of whether there was evidence of a bullet track between the wounds of the back and front of the neck. The answer is yes, he reported, but it is based on the "*circumstantial* evidence" that the metal fragments in the neck, the air in the tissues, the lack of visible fractures, the report of a bruise on the apex, of the pleura, and the hole in the trachea, all "lined-up" or "fitted together" to indicate that a bullet had passed between the two holes.[32]

As Dr. Lattimer noted, this is circumstantial evidence and not demonstrable proof of a bullet track. Only dissection of the wound through the body would provide conclusive evidence of the exact path of the bullet. Furthermore, the air in the tissues, the bruising, the laceration are no more indicative of a bullet's going from back to front than they are of a bullet's going from front to back. The fact that the hole in the front of the throat was only half as large as the hole in the back suggested either that they were both entrance wounds or that the hole in the throat was the wound of entrance and that in the back was the exit hole.

The *Warren Report* falsely asserted that experiments performed by Army wound ballistics experts "showed that under simulated conditions entry and exit wounds [made by bullets fired from Oswald's rifle] are very similar in appearance." Shots from Oswald's rifle were indeed fired through a simulated "neck" covered with animal skin. "The exit holes," the *Report* claimed, "appeared similar to the descriptions given by Drs. Perry and Carrico of the hole in the front of the President's neck." The doctors testified that the wound in the throat was 3 to 5 mm. in diameter, round, and clean. The wounds ballistics tests performed by the Army experts, however, proved that exit holes caused by Oswald's rifle did not even resemble the doctors' description of the actual wound. The exit holes in the tests were all elongated or oval shaped instead of round; all had sharp edges; and all measured 10 to 15 mm. in diameter, more than twice as large as the corresponding entrance holes.[33]

The possibility that the hole in the president's back was an exit hole for the frontal throat wound was never seriously explored by the Warren Commission. Because the back wound was small, 6 to 8 mm. in diameter, had a ring of abrasion around it, and the tissues were pushed inward, it has been presumed to be an entrance wound. The size is indeed much closer to an entrance than to an exit wound, yet it is twice as large as the throat wound, which is assumed to be a hole of exit. The ring of abrasion invariably occurs with an entrance wound, but it can also be present with an exit wound. There was also such a ring around the hole in the throat. This was not reported by the Warren Commission. But Dr. Perry informed a private researcher that the wound did indeed have bruising around it. The fact that the autopsy photographs show the tissue to be pushed inward is in itself meaningless. It should be recalled that Dr. Humes stuck his finger into the wound. If he did so before the autopsy photographs were taken, then that explains the appearance of the tissues. In any case, there is no evidence of the exact condition of the hole at the time of the shooting.[34]

This possibility is not a probability. In all likelihood, the back wound is one of entrance. In the supplementary autopsy report,

Dr. Humes stated that histological sections taken from the wound in the back reveal "loss of continuity of the epidermis with coagulation necrosis of the tissues at the wound margins." This is certain pathological evidence of a wound of entrance. Yet these slides, as well as others taken during the autopsy, are now missing and have never been studied by competent forensic pathologists.[35]

There is no certain evidence, then, that the hole in the president's throat was one of entrance or exit. Unfortunately, the autopsy pathologists failed to take tissue sections from this wound. The Zapruder film does not reveal a hole in the throat, although from frames Z225 through Z265, President Kennedy can be seen grimacing in pain and attempting to clutch his throat. The very tiny size of the hole, the opinions of the Dallas doctors, the lack of any traces of metal on the front of the president's shirt collar and tie, the ring of abrasion around the wound, the attempt by the president to grab his throat, all argue persuasively that this could have been, a wound of entrance, caused by a bullet fired from in front of President Kennedy.

Dr. John Lattimer speculated that the tight-fitting collar around the president's neck caused his skin to stretch taut and thus kept from stretching when the bullet exited. A thoracic surgeon, with extensive experience in treating gunshot wounds of the neck, has refuted Lattimer's contention. The surgeon noted that the very fact that the skin was stretched would have caused a much more explosive type of injury to the neck, if the bullet exited there. This is because the force of the bullet would have pushed tissues outward with great force, thus tearing the skin apart and causing a very large wound of exit.[36]

An examination of the president's clothing revealed small holes in the rear of the shirt and jacket, fibers pushed inward, and metallic residue around the edges of the holes. There were small slits on the front of the shirt and on the left side of the tie knot. The slits on either side of the shirt, below the neck button and buttonhole respectively, do not correspond with each other, nor are they of the same size. The FBI falsely reported to the Warren Commission that "the hole" [*sic*] "has the characteristic of an exit hole for a projectile." Both openings are slits, rather than holes. One is about twice as long as the other. The fibers of the shirt are not projected outward. The nick on the left side of the tie knot could not have been made by a bullet exiting on the right center of the throat. The clothing holes thus do not prove that a bullet exited from the throat, nor do they lend any support to the theory that the shot was fired from behind.[37]

BULLET 399

The Warren Commission stated that a single bullet, Commission Exhibit 399, struck Governor Connally on the right side of his back, entered the chest, and shattered his fifth rib. After emerging from his chest just below the right nipple, the bullet entered his right wrist, striking and causing a compound fracture of the radius. Bullet 399 exited from his wrist and entered his left thigh, where it lodged deep enough to deposit a fragment in the femur. In Chapter Three, we have already noted the mysterious circumstances surrounding the alleged discovery of Bullet 399 on Governor Connally's stretcher. We shall now examine the medical and ballistics evidence to see if this bullet could have caused the governor's wounds.[38]

Bullet 399 is a copper-jacketed Mannlicher-Carcano 6.5 mm. bullet. The copper jacketing is completely intact. Only the very base of the bullet contains any deformities. The base is slightly squeezed and flattened. About 1.5 to 2.5 grains of lead are missing from the lead core at the bottom of the missile. The bullet was ballistically traced to Oswald's rifle. The grooves and lines on the copper jacketing, caused by the interior of the rifle barrel, are completely intact, even under microscopic examination.[39]

The Warren Commission's claim that Bullet 399 caused seven different wounds on President Kennedy and Governor Connally, severely damaged two bones, and emerged virtually intact, losing only 1.5 to 2.5 grains of its original weight, has led numerous critics to dispute the claim. The critics contend that no bullet could possibly have caused such damage and emerge intact.[40]

The evidence demonstrates that it is extremely unlikely, but not impossible, for Bullet 399 to have caused all of Governor Connally's wounds. In order to determine the ability of bullets from Oswald's rifle to cause wounds similar to those of the gov-

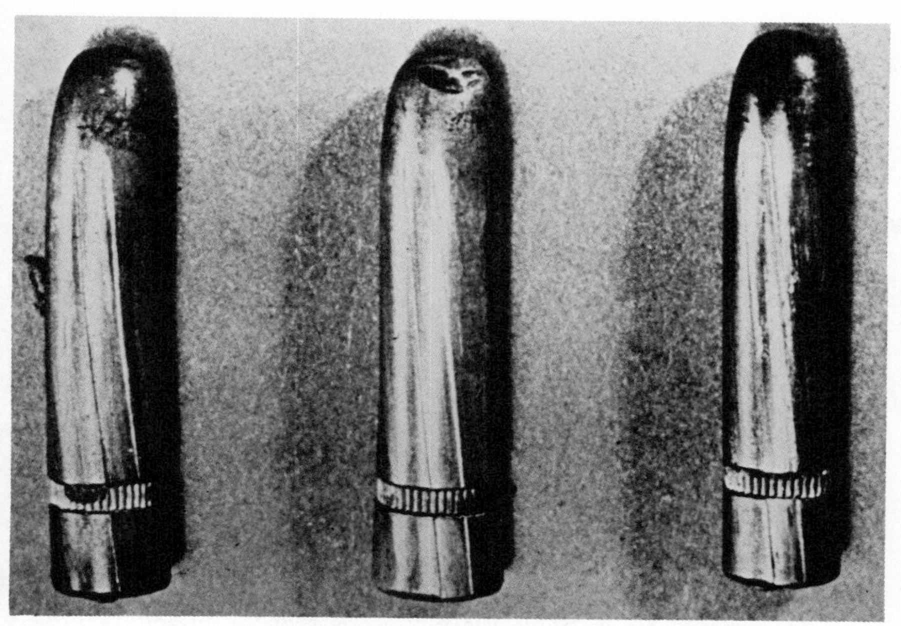

8. *Commission Exhibit 399.* Bullet 399 (middle), probably planted on the stretcher.

ernor, the Warren Commission hired a team of expert wounds ballistics scientists headed by Dr. Alfred Olivier. The scientists shot an animal with Oswald's rifle. The shots reproduced chest and wrist wounds very similar to those of Governor Connally. The bullets which caused the wounds, however, were considerably flattened and deformed, as contrasted with the nearly pristine Bullet 399.[41]

Of ten shots fired through cadavers' wrists, only one was shown to the commission staff. The final results of the wounds ballistics tests conducted by Dr. Olivier and his research team were not published until March 1965, six months *after* the *Warren Report* claimed that "the results of the wounds ballistics tests support the conclusions of Governor Connally's doctors that all his wounds were caused by one bullet."[42]

These test results were classified and not made available until March 1973. The report includes photographs of four bullets fired from Oswald's rifle into cadavers' wrists. Each of the bullets suffered severe mutilation, the noses of the bullets being flattened, twisted, and torn apart. No photographs of the other six bullets are available, and only one of the ten test bullets is in the Kennedy assassination materials in the National Archives. None of the bullets fired through a substance simulating President Kennedy's neck are available, and only one bullet fired through a rib is available, and it is severely mutilated.[43]

Even though the wounds ballistics evidence is incomplete, the results released hardly support the Warren Commission's contention that all the governor's wounds were caused by one bullet. Of the four ballistics experts employed by the commission to test Oswald's rifle, only one, Dr. Alfred Olivier, supported the commission. The other three experts, Dr. Arthur Dziemian, Dr. Joseph Dolce, and Dr. Frederick Light, were "very strongly of the opinion that Connally had been hit by two different bullets, principally on the ground that the bullet recovered from Connally's stretcher could not have broken his radius without having suffered more distortion." Even though this quotation is from a "Memorandum for the Record" written by one of its counsels, the commission chose not to publish it in its report. The commission instead twisted Dr. Dziemian's and Dr. Light's conclusions to make it appear that the two wounds ballistics experts believed that one bullet caused all of Governor Connally's wounds.[44]

Dr. John Lattimer has performed numerous experiments to test the commission's thesis about Bullet 399. Dr. Lattimer believes that Bullet 399 entered the rear of President Kennedy's neck and grazed his spine at the sixth or seventh cervical vertebra, thus causing the bullet to begin tumbling as it exited the front of the president's throat. The bullet, according to Dr. Lattimer, struck Governor Connally in the back as it tumbled, so that the side, or long part, rather than the tip of the missile entered the back. This accounts for the large and elongated entrance hole in Connally's back. The bullet continued tumbling over until by the time it exited the governor's chest, the base of the bullet was in front. It was the base which entered Connally's wrist and smashed his radius. Then as the still tumbling bullet exited from the wrist, it turned around and entered the thigh.[45]

Lattimer's theory about Bullet 399 does not take into account the fact that there is no evidence that this bullet entered President Kennedy's neck, nor, as has been discussed above, that it exited from his throat. The large and elongated entrance hole in Governor Connally's back does not necessarily have to have been caused by a tumbling bullet or by a bullet which previously struck someone else. Other types of ammunition than 6.5 mm. Mannlicher-Carcano can cause different kinds of entrance wounds. One of the Warren Commission's own tests, with Roberts .257 soft-nosed hunting ammunition, for example, shows this bullet could have caused an entrance wound similar to that in the governor's back.[46]

The fact that bullet fragments were found in Governor Connally's chest, wrist, and thigh bone also casts doubt upon the contention that Bullet 399 caused these wounds. We know that at least one, and probably more fragments, were removed from Connally's chest. The commission mentioned only one chest fragment. But the official report of the surgeon who operated on Governor Connally noted "several bits of metal" and that three small fragments were removed from the wrist, and one was seen in X-rays of the thigh.[47]

Dr. Lattimer believes that the fragments removed from the governor's body can be accounted for even if they came from

Bullet 399. He squeezed a Carcano bullet similar to Bullet 399 until 2 grains of lead protruded from the base. These 2 grains were then sliced into 41 fragments, proof, Lattimer contends, that Bullet 399 could have deposited fragments in Connally and still emerge virtually intact. Lattimer's experiment, however, is meaningless. It is theoretically possible to slice two grains of lead into one million fragments. The critical aspect is the relative size of the fragments. Lattimer's fragments averaged .05 grains each. The three fragments from Connally's wrist weighed about .5 grains each, or ten times larger. Lattimer placed several of his fragments on his wrist and thigh and X-rayed them. The X-rays do indeed resemble the Connally X-rays. However, Lattimer's X-rays are frontal projections only. He gives no evidence that the lateral projections were similar.[48]

The information about the Connally fragments is incomplete. The most thorough information about fragments is that of the thigh fragment. X-rays reveal that this fragment measures 1.5 x 3 mm. on the lateral projection and 1.2 x 2.5 mm. on the frontal projection. There is no place on Bullet 399 from which such an extensive fragment could have come. The copper jacketing of Bullet 399 is completely intact. The only part of the bullet missing any of its original contents is the base. There is a hole in the base about 1 x 3 x 1 mm. in size. This hole was made, not by lead pouring out during the bullet's course through the body, but by FBI ballistics expert Robert Frazier, who cut lead from the base for ballistics testing. At the trial of Clay Shaw, Frazier testified that he did, indeed, remove lead from the base of Bullet 399. Frazier did not state how much lead was removed. We do know that he sliced a piece off the nose of the bullet. That slice and the hole in the base are remarkably similar. The edges of the hole in the base even have sharp nicks, most probably made by Frazier's knife. This information that Frazier was responsible for the hole in the base has been overlooked by the commission's defenders, such as Dr. Lattimer. Unaware that Frazier made the hole, they assumed that it was caused by the path of the bullet through Kennedy and Connally. The fact that Frazier removed the lead proves that the bullet was virtually intact *after* being fired and that almost no weight was missing from it. Therefore, Bullet 399 could not have left fragments anywhere in his body.[49]

The lack of deformity to Bullet 399, however, is not necessarily an indication that it could not have caused the wounds on the governor. A shooting incident occurred in Tangipahoa Parish, Louisiana, in June 1976, an incident which strongly reinforces the Warren Commission's claims about Bullet 399. A man was shot with a .25 caliber copper-jacketed bullet. The bullet penetrated through his wrist and caused a compound fracture of the right radius. The bullet entered the victim's chest, breaking his right sixth rib, and was deflected upward and backward until it struck and broke his scapula. The bullet bounced upward and smashed against the man's clavicle, severely fracturing it. The bullet then was deflected downward along the spinal column and broke four different vertebrae before finally coming to rest in the neural canal. This bullet caused far more severe damage to bone structure than Bullet 399 allegedly did to Governor Connally. Yet its copper jacketing is intact, and no more than .7 grains of lead are missing from its base. This case belies the assertions by such Warren Commission critics as Milton Helpern and Cyril Wecht that bullets cannot strike bone and emerge unscathed. The case, on the other hand, does not prove the commission's thesis. Although copper-jacketed, this .25-caliber bullet is not the same as a 6.5 mm. Carcano slug. It was fired from a pistol, whereas Bullet 399 came from a rifle. And the rifling grooves from the barrel of the pistol have been broken up on this bullet. The grooves on Bullet 399 are completely intact.[50]

Forensic Pathologist Cyril Wecht examined the Kennedy autopsy photographs and X-rays. He calculated the angle of the bullet that entered the rear of the back and presumably exited through the "exit" hole in the throat. Dr. Wecht estimated the angles of the bullet path as 11.5 degrees downward and 17.5 degrees right to left. Both of these angles are incompatible with a shot fired from the sixth-floor southeast corner window of the Texas School Book Depository building. They are also incompatible with a bullet exiting Kennedy's throat and striking Governor Connally. The governor was struck on the right side of his back between the shoulder blade and the armpit. Since he was sitting directly in front of President Kennedy, a bullet traveling downward and right to left could not have struck Governor Connally unless the bullet made a right and then a left angle turn in mid-air. Dr. Wecht calculated that the bullet which exited the president's throat (an unproven assumption) would have passed over Mrs. Connally's right shoulder and over the left shoulder of the driver of the limousine, Secret Service Agent William Greer, and then would have struck the grass on the north side of Elm Street. Wecht believes that based on his computation of the angles of the bullet wounds in President Kennedy and Governor Connally, that the shots were fired from a lower floor of the Book Depository building and from the roof of the Dal-Tex building.[51]

Wecht's theory is valid only if the precise instant in which the president and governor were struck is known. Both Kennedy and Connally were smiling, waving, and turning their heads just before the first shot was fired. We do not know when that shot struck and thus cannot duplicate the conditions necessary for measuring the exact angles. Governor Connally's doctors measured the angle of the wound through his chest as 25 degrees. This measurement was based upon the assumption that the governor was sitting erect when struck. Since it is possible that Connally had a delayed reaction to his wounds, we do not know his exact position. A slight forward or backward or twisting movement by Governor Connally would have caused the 25 degree calculation to be seriously inaccurate.[52]

Even though precise angles of the bullet wounds are not known, Dr. Wecht's contention that a bullet fired from the sixth-floor southeast corner window of the Depository building and passing through President Kennedy's neck could not have hit Connally of the right side of his back is strongly supported by the known facts. Except for eighteen frames (or one second), the Zapruder film clearly shows Governor Connally to be seated directly in front of President Kennedy. If a bullet fired from the sixth-floor window entered the rear of Kennedy's neck and exited from the front of his throat, it would have traveled at a right-to-left angle to strike Connally. Since the entrance hole on Governor Connally's back was to the right of the alleged exit hole of the bullet from Kennedy's throat, that same bullet could not have struck the governor. Only during that one second, when the street sign blocked Zapruder's view of the limousine, could Connally have been struck by the same bullet. That is possible only under the extremely unlikely circumstance that the governor jumped out of his seat, moved four feet to his left, squatted down, received a shot in the back, then returned to his original position—all within one second.

SUMMARY

The medical evidence about the back wound on President Kennedy and the wounds on Governor Connally is inconclusive. The president was definitely struck high on the upper back by a bullet fired from the rear. Whether this bullet was fired from the sixth-floor southeast corner window of the Texas School Book Depository building has never been demonstrated. The failure of the autopsy pathologists to dissect this wound to trace its path through the body precludes any definitive statement about a path. Not only were the autopsy pathologists unsure about whether the bullet penetrated through the body, they were not even sure that the hole was an entrance wound and termed it "presumably of entry."

The hole in the front of the president's throat, as described by the Dallas physicians who saw it, could have been an entrance wound. Not only was it less than half as large as the entrance wound on the back, it was even smaller than the diameter of bullets from Oswald's rifle. Wounds ballistics tests performed for the commission showed that exit wounds caused by bullets from Oswald's rifle were over twice as large as entrance wounds. The other logical explanation for the wound in the throat is that it was caused by a fragment from the head wound. The commission's contention that it was an exit wound remains a highly unlikely possibility.

Governor Connally's wounds may or may not have been caused by the same bullet. The evidence is not conclusive on that point. The evidence does, however, strongly indicate that Bullet 399 did not cause any of those wounds. The intact condition of Bullet 399, the fact that bullet fragments were found in all of the wounds on Governor Connally, the wounds ballistics tests conducted for the commission, all militate strongly against the commission's assertion that Bullet 399 caused all the governor's wounds. Even Governor Connally's doctors all believed that Bullet 399 could not have caused his wounds.

As we have seen, the single-bullet theory, long supported as a prerequisite to the lone-assassin thesis, is not necessarily an essential aspect of the commission's case. The impossibility of duplicating the exact conditions under which Oswald fired precludes any definitive statement about how much time Oswald had in which to fire. There is a strong possibility that he had more than sufficient time to fire two separate shots at President Kennedy and Governor Connally.

The Warren Commission failed to demonstrate that any of the shots were fired from the sixth-floor window. At least two shots were fired from the rear. The angles of the shots do indicate a source of the firing as other than the sixth floor of the Depository building. If the Kennedy throat wound was an entrance wound, as the evidence suggests it was, that shot was fired from in front of the president.

CHAPTER 5

THE HEAD SHOTS

JOHN KENNEDY was killed by one or more shots to his head. That shot, or shots, blasted out over 70 percent of the brain and skull on the right side of his head. There is enormous controversy over whether the shots were from behind or from in front, and whether he was hit in the head one or more times.

The Warren Commission relied on the autopsy report, which stated that a bullet, fired from above, behind, and to the right of the limousine, struck President Kennedy in the rear of the head. This bullet entered the head and drove forward through the right side of the brain, depositing bullet fragments throughout the area. The bullet exploded inside the head, causing massive brain and skull destruction before it exited through a huge, gaping hole on the right front portion of the skull.[1]

At the autopsy, the pathologists noticed a small elliptical hole, 6 x 15 mm., with a ring of abrasion around it in the rear of the head. The hole penetrated into the scalp and skull, growing increasingly larger the deeper it became. This produced a "beveling" effect, indicating that the missile which entered the rear of the head expanded rapidly as it penetrated into the cranium. The interior of the head was characterized by massive destruction of brain and skull tissue along the right side of the head. Numerous fragments of bone and metal were dispersed throughout the area. The skull was extensively fractured all over. On the right side of the head was a huge hole, 13 cm. in diameter, through which both brain matter and skull bone had exuded. These observations led the autopsy surgeons to conclude that a bullet had entered the rear of the president's head and had exited through the right front portion of his skull, killing him.[2]

The nature of the head wounds, the physical circumstances

9. *Zapruder Frame Z312*. JFK's position the instant before the first head shot.

of the gunfire, the autopsy itself, and examinations of the autopsy photographs and X-rays of the body have led numerous critics to believe that the president was killed by a shot fired from a rifle or rifles other than the 6.5 Mannlicher-Carcano owned by Lee Harvey Oswald. In order to discuss the theories about the head wounds, it is necessary to examine each of the above categories in detail.

The autopsy report provided only sketchy information about the head wounds. For example, it failed to locate with precision the entrance wound in the rear of the head. The location of that wound, as noted in the autopsy report, was "2.5 cm. laterally to the right and slightly above the external occipital protuberance." The report also failed to locate with any precision the bullet fragments in the head, the nature of the skull damage, and the various areas of damage to the brain. Various drawings prepared for the Warren Commission, under the direct supervision of the autopsy pathologists, also proved confusing and contradictory. For example, Commission Exhibit 397 is an autopsy face sheet drawn by Dr. Humes with the body in his presence. It locates the entrance wound in the lower rear of the head and notes that the bullet traveled to the *left* after it entered. Commission Exhibit 385, however, notes the direction of the bullet to the *right.*[3]

Much more complete information is provided in the report by a panel of pathologists and a radiologist appointed by Attorney General Ramsey Clark to review the autopsy photographs and X-rays in the National Archives. The Clark Panel Report very strongly supported the autopsy and Warren Commission's contention that the president was killed by a single shot fired from behind. Yet the Clark Panel Report of the photographs and X-rays reveals many serious discrepancies between its review of the autopsy materials and the autopsy itself.

The Clark panel noted that no X-rays of the lower arms, wrists, hands, lower legs, feet, and ankles exist. Yet the autopsy noted that "Roentgenograms [X-rays] are made of the entire body." In his testimony before the Warren Commission, Dr. Humes stated "we then completed the X-Ray examination by X-Raying the President's body *in toto,* and those X-Rays are available." Thus, several X-rays are now missing.[4]

10. *Zapruder Frame Z315*. JFK's violent backward movement after the head shot.

In its inventory of the materials in the National Archives, the Clark panel noted that no photographs of the body from the rib cage down now exist. Only seven photographs of the brain exist, and all were taken from above or below the organ. No photographs of the sides of the brain, nor of the front and back exist. Only three X-rays of the skull were made, one from the front and two from the left. No X-rays of the top of the skull are available. No X-rays were made of the brain after it was removed from the body. No X-rays were made from the sides of the neck and chest, only ones from the front.[5]

The importance of this inventory is that the lack of many photographs and X-rays means that what is left can provide only an incomplete and possibly misleading picture of the wounds. For example, the X-rays of the side of the skull apparently show a straight line of bullet fragments running from the rear to the front of the head. But the X-rays of the front of the skull shows that the "line" of fragmentation is illusory. In reality, the fragments are scattered in different levels and planes of the brain.[6]

The detailed descriptions of the photographs contain several noteworthy observations. Photographs of the back of the head reveal that the contours of this area "have been grossly distorted by extensive fragmentation of the underlying calvarium [skull]." This is in the area of the entrance wound in the rear of the head. The extensive fragmentation of the skull is not characteristic of copper-jacketed Mannlicher-Carcano ammunition. This type of ammunition almost invariably penetrates directly through bone without causing fragmentation.[7]

Photographs of the frontal region of the skull reveal that "there was no exiting bullet defect in the supra-orbital region of the skull." Both Dr. John Lattimer and Dr. Werner Spitz, however, both of whom have studied the autopsy materials and support the Warren Commission, believe that a bullet did exit from the supra-orbital region of the skull.[8]

Photographs of the top of the brain show a "broad canal running generally in a postero-anterior direction and to the right of the midline." Why this canal runs from back to front and not simultaneously front to back is not answered by the panel. It is indicative neither of a bullet path from the front nor from the back. These photographs also disclose a 13 x 20 mm. structure

11. *Zapruder Frame Z321.* JFK thrown against rear seat of limousine. Note the large wound on the right side of the head.

in the base of the canal on the right side. Its identity was not established by the panel. According to Dr. John Lattimer, it is "rolled-up meninges." Dr. Cyril Wecht believes it may be a bullet fragment, a brain tumor, or hemmorhagic tissue. The autopsy made no mention of this object in the brain. The autopsy pathologists' failure to examine and identify it was a serious omission.[9]

The Clark panel reported that its observations of the photographs of the head "indicate that the back of the head was struck by a single bullet traveling at high velocity." This information scarcely supports the Warren Commission, for Oswald's rifle had a low velocity.[10]

The X-rays of the skull reveal massive multiple fractures of the skull on both the right and left sides. There is extensive fragmentation of the bone, and several pieces of the skull are missing. This type of damage is not produced by ammunition like that allegedly used by Oswald. Copper-jacketed bullets commonly penetrate straight through objects, leaving only small tracks and causing little in the way of bone fractures. Wounds ballistics tests performed for the commission confirmed this. Bullets from Oswald's rifle, from a .257 Roberts soft-point hunting rifle, and from a United States Army M-14 rifle were fired into blocks of gelatin covered with masonite. The Mannlicher-Carcano went straight through the gelatin, leaving a tiny track and causing little damage to the substance. The soft-point hunting bullet expanded rapidly upon entering and caused considerably more damage. The M-14 caused more destruction than the others. Rather than confirm the commission's thesis about Oswald's rifle causing all of the president's wounds, these tests indicated strongly that it was not capable of inflicting the type of damage that President Kennedy's head received.[11]

The skull X-rays also depicted extensive bullet fragmentation within the skull. This type of fragmentation is not typical of full-jacketed military ammunition. That ammunition was specifically designed to remain intact when passing through a body. Lead, or hollow-point, ammunition is the type that causes fragmentation. The fragments are distributed throughout the right half of the brain. On the lateral X-rays of the skull, they appear to lie in a line running from the large hole in the

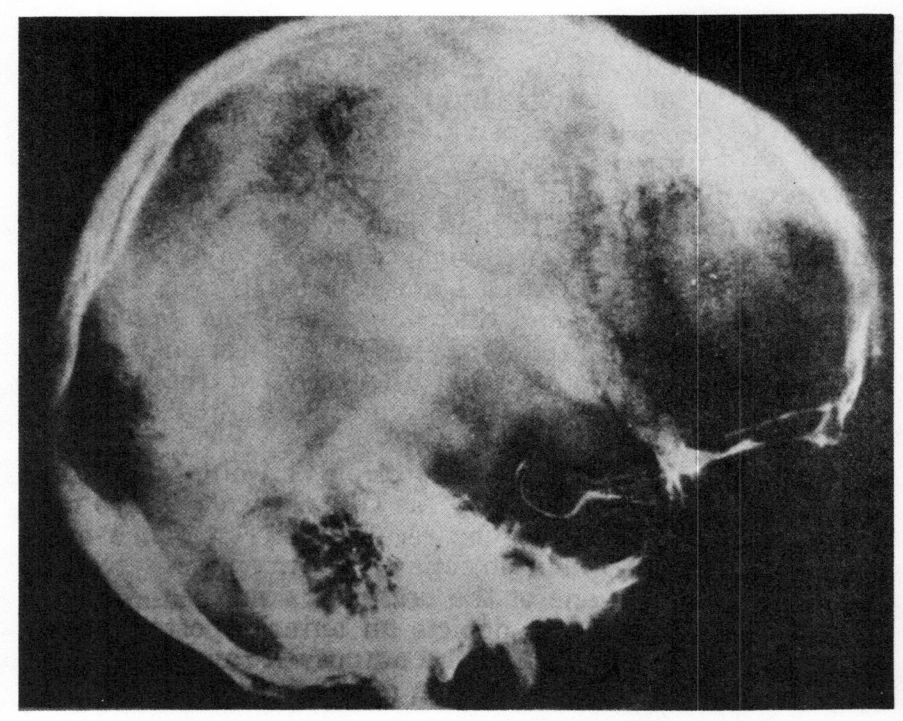

12. *JFK Skull X-ray.* Normal skull X-ray (right side view).

right side of the head backward to the middle rear of the right side of the brain. No fragments are visible in the area from the entrance hole in the rear to 4 inches in front of that hole. The Clark panel assumed that this fragmentation was caused by the bullet that entered the rear of the head. Yet, the distribution of the fragments is the usual pattern of a "dum-dum" bullet fired from the right front. "Dum-dum" bullets frequently explode upon impact and will cause extensive fragmentation at, or very near, the large, explosive wound of entry. The vast majority of the fragments in President Kennedy's head are located very near the large, gaping 13 cm. hole in the right side of the head.[12]

The X-rays also reveal a hole 8 mm. in diameter located 100 mm. above the external occipital protuberance (the bony knob in the back of the head). This conflicts with the autopsy report's location of a 6 x 15 mm. hole "slightly above the external occipital protuberance." The autopsy's location would place this hole in the middle of the head, whereas the Clark panel's location is at the top of the head. The Clark panel also noticed no bullet fragments on the left side of the brain. Dr. Cyril Wecht, however, did notice several small bullet fragments in that area. The lack of fragments on the left side, however, does not disprove the contention that a bullet was fired from the right front. "Dum-dum" bullets, for example, frequently will leave fragments only in the immediate area of entrance, since they explode upon impact, rather than penetrate into the skull.[13]

Thus, the Clark panel did not confirm the medical conclusions of the *Warren Report,* although, of course, it did not disprove those conclusions either. Another medical expert who has studied the autopsy photographs and X-rays is Dr. John K. Lattimer. Chairman of the Department of Urology at Columbia Presbyterian Hospital in New York City, Dr. Lattimer has published numerous articles based on his observations of the autopsy materials as well as on many wounds ballistics experiments that he has conducted. In all of his papers, Dr. Lattimer has steadfastly and consistently supported the Warren Commission's lone-assassin thesis. Critics of the commission have either overlooked his work or have dismissed it on the grounds that he is a urologist and thus not qualified to pass expert judgment on the Kennedy assasination evidence. Dr. Lattimer, how-

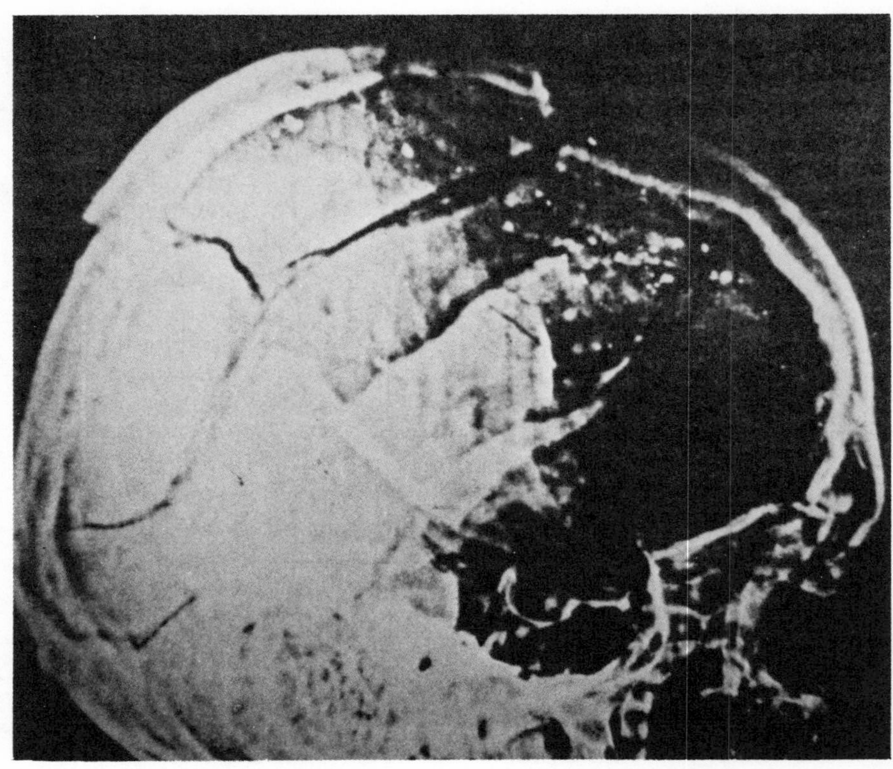

13. *JFK Skull X-ray.* Computer-enhanced autopsy X-ray of JFK skull. Note the large area of missing skull and the bullet fragments scattered along the right side of the head.

ever, has extensive experience in wounds and ballistics, serving as a surgeon in Europe during World War II and as a firearms range officer. His scientific papers collectively provide the strongest support for the *Warren Report* and therefore deserve careful analysis.[14]

Lattimer's first observation is of a 6 x 8 mm. wound in the back, which is a wound of entrance. The downward angle of the bullet through the body, however, was aproximately 40 degrees, as noted in one of Lattimer's diagrams. This angle is incompatible with a shot fired from the sixth-floor southeast corner window of the Texas School Book Depository building. The angle of a bullet fired from that window was measured by the FBI as 17 degrees. The only possible explanation for Lattimer's steep angle is that the president was leaning decidedly forward when shot. However, films, slides, and photographs of the assassination show him sitting erect, as does Lattimer's own sketch of the bullet path. We do not, however, know the precise instant of the first shot, and there is a slim possibility that the angle of the shot through his neck was as steep as Dr. Lattimer calculated.[15]

The next category which Dr. Lattimer discusses is the bullet fragmentation in the head. Like the Clark panel, Dr. Lattimer observed that the majority of the fragments lay toward the front of the head on the right side. Even though the largest cluster of fragments was in the front third of the head, they were, Lattimer noted, "arranged roughly in a line which, if extended posteriorly, would pass through the wound of entry. . . ." This "imaginary line" was consistent only with a bullet's entering the rear of the head and exiting from the right front side and was "compatible with no other direction." Lattimer's conjectures are based solely on the presumption that the bullet that struck the president in the rear of the head did fragmentize extensively during its path through the brain. The "line" of bullet fragments is no more consistent with a rear-entering bullet than with one entering from the front. A "dum-dum" bullet, for example, fired from the front, would fragmentize extensively upon impact, depositing most of its fragments in the right front of the head, as were the fragments in John Kennedy's head. The pattern of bullet fragmentation thus does not lend itself to definitive analysis. It is compatible with either a front- or rear-entering shot.[16]

The size and number of the bullet fragments in the head does raise serious reservations about the Warren Commission's assumption that they all came from one of Oswald's bullets. Two very large fragments were found on the front seat of the presidential limousine. They could only have come from the fatal head shot, if the Warren Commission's version of the assassination is the correct one. Obviously, they could not have come from the intact Bullet 399, nor from the shot which missed. These two fragments total 65 grains, or 40.6 percent of the total (160 grain) weight of a pristine Mannlicher-Carcano bullet. Three much smaller fragments, totaling approximately 2 grains, were found underneath Mrs. Connally's seat. The total weight of the limousine fragments was 67 grains, or 41.8 percent of the total weight of a pristine Mannlicher-Carcano bullet. The fragments inside the head must be added to the limousine fragments in order to determine whether they are greater or less than the total size and weight of a bullet from Oswald's rifle.[17]

Unfortunately, we do not have complete information on any of the head fragments. We know only the weight of the limousine fragments and only one or two dimensions of the head fragments. Based on the incomplete information, several tentative observations can be made. These observations are, of course, subject to revision if more complete information can ever be obtained.

There were 35 to 40 metal fragments in the head. The largest was a 6.5 mm. fragment embedded in the skull directly in front of the wound of entry in the rear of the head. The next largest fragment was a 7 x 3 mm. piece located in the right frontal sinus. Another fragment 1 x 2 mm. was located near this one. About six fragments between 1 mm. and 3 mm. in diameter were embeddded in the skull and in brain tissue near the very large hole in the right side of the head. Three 1 mm. fragments were embedded in a flap of skull which hung over the right ear. About a dozen fragments, 1 mm. to 2 mm. in diameter, were embedded in a piece of skull that had been blasted out of President Kennedy's head. Finally, there was a cluster of nineteen tiny fragments, "each about the size of a grain of sand," located near the front of the brain.[18]

Since we do not know all three dimensions of any of these fragments, it is impossible to add them together. One dimension of these adds up to over 67 mm. A pristine Mannlicher-Carcano bullet is 30 mm. long, 6.5 mm. wide at its base and for most (25 mm.) of its length, and tapers to a 1 mm. width at its nose. The limousine and head fragments collectively account for almost an entire Carcano bullet.[19]

It is impossible to provide more than a tentative analysis of the information about the fragments. The known fragments both inside and outside the head total more than two-thirds of an intact Mannlicher-Carcano bullet. This does not account for the fact that a sizable number of fragments exploded completely out of the head and were propelled out of the limousine on to the street. The Zapruder film clearly shows the fragments blowing out of the head. The Ramsey Clark panel states specifically that most of the bullet that struck the president "emerged from the head." Dr. Lattimer estimated that 95 grains of the bullet which struck the head "apparently went completely over the windshield to strike the street further along." His calculation is based on the fact that 65 grains of the bullet were recovered. This calculation, however, is based entirely upon the total weight of the limousine fragments. He does not include the weight of the two fragments recovered from the head nor those remaining in the head.[20]

Dr. Lattimer estimated that 70 percent of the right half of the brain as well as 50 percent of the right half of the skull was missing. Over thirty-five fragments, many over 1 mm. in diameter, two over 6 mm., remained in that portion of the brain and skull which did not explode out of the head. It is not unreasonable to postulate that at least as many fragments must have blown out of the head as remained in it.[21]

Wounds ballistics experiments conducted for the Warren Commission by Dr. Alfred Olivier confirmed this. A bullet from Oswald's rifle fired into a test skull fragmented extensively, ejecting over thirty fragments outside the skull. Two very large fragments composing approximately 70 percent of the test bullet were found outside the skull. Twenty-nine smaller fragments, some as large as 6 mm. in diameter, were also discovered outside the test skull. Collectively, these fragments total about 95 percent of the total size of the test bullet. Dr. Lattimer also performed ballistics tests that verified the fact that most of the intact size and weight of Mannlicher-Carcano bullets were blown out of the skulls.[22]

The results of these tests indicate that the total number of known and unknown fragments add up to substantially more than one of Oswald's bullets. The bullet fragments remaining in the brain plus those in the skull plus those removed from the brain plus the limousine fragments plus those never recovered strongly suggest that more than one bullet struck President Kennedy in the head. Through correspondence with the author, Dr. Cyril Wecht, a world-renowned forensic pathologist, agreed that, based on his observation of the Kennedy autopsy photographs and X-rays, the amount of fragmentation apparently rules out only one bullet's striking the head.[23]

The wounds ballistics experiments conducted by Dr. Lattimer provide little support for the Warren Commission. Dr. Lattimer fired shots from a Mannlicher-Carcano rifle at test skulls packed with a substance designed to simulate the scalp. The wounds inflicted on the skull were strikingly similar to those inflicted on President Kennedy's. Massive fractures of the skull, with extensive shattering of the front segments, produced very similar wounds.[24]

X-rays of Lattimer's skulls, however, revealed no bullet fragments, not even at the wound of entry in the rear top of the head. As mentioned above, the X-rays of President Kennedy's skull showed a very large fragment (6.5 mm.) embedded in the skull directly in front of the wound of entry. The Kennedy skull X-rays also depicted three fragments in a piece of the right parietal bone, as well as six fragments in the right occipital bone, and about a dozen fragments in one of the pieces of frontal bone. Thus, the experiments do not conclusively demonstrate that Mannlicher-Carcano bullets can produce the type of damage inflicted on the president.[25]

Further evidence on the autopsy photographs and X-rays has been provided by Dr. Cyril Wecht. While generally agreeing with the observations of the Clark panel and Dr. Lattimer, Dr. Wecht made three highly significant notations that raise serious questions. First, he observed several small bullet fragments on the left side of the brain. The existence of these fragments is denied by the Clark panel and by Dr. Lattimer. Since they would indicate a possible right front location as the source of a shot, it is curious that only Dr. Wecht, who disagrees with the Warren Commission, notes the existence of these left-side fragments, while its defenders do not.[26]

Dr. Wecht also saw in color photographs of the back of the head a small flap of skin or tissue near the hairline at the base of the skull and slightly to the left of the midline. It may possibly be a small wound of exit from a bullet fragment exiting the rear of the head. None of the other doctors even mentioned this damage on the left rear of the head.[27]

It should be noted that Dr. Wecht, along with every other doctor who examined the autopsy materials in the National Archives, agrees that the available medical evidence indicates only one shot, fired from the right rear, struck the president in the head. This provides very strong support for the Warren Commission's contention that all the shots were fired from the sixth-floor southeast corner window of the Texas School Book Depository building. In addition to the Clark panel, Dr. Lattimer, and Dr. Wecht, the other physicians who have examined the autopsy materials include Dr. E. Forrest Chapman, a forensic pathologist; a panel of neurosurgeons, wounds ballistics experts, and forensic pathologist Werner Spitz, appointed by the Rockefeller Commission in 1975, and Dr. James Weston, president of the American Academy of Forensic Sciences.[28]

Dr. Wecht's third observation, however, demonstrates that not even a prestigious array of men of medicine can definitively prove that the *Warren Report* is correct. "Because of the extensive loss of skull," Dr. Wecht stated, "it cannot be absolutely ascertained that no more than one bullet struck the President's head, at least from the available autopsy photographs and X-Rays." And, as Dr. Wecht told a researcher, "the fractured calvarium [skull], the hemmorhagic brain, and the bullet fragmentation are no more indicative of a shot fired from the rear than of one fired from the front."[29]

Dr. Wecht was the first physician to discover that many vital pieces of medical evidence have mysteriously disappeared from the autopsy materials in the National Archives. President Kennedy's brain, for example, was removed during the autopsy and placed in a formalin solution to allow it to harden before the organ was examined at the supplemental autopsy. This is standard pathological procedure in cases of gunshot wounds of the head. At the supplemental autopsy, the standard procedure is to slice the brain into coronal sections in order for the pathologist to calculate the precise path(s) of the bullet(s) through the head. The supplemental autopsy report, however, contains the curious remark that "in the interests of preserving the specimen, coronal sections are not made." Why there was an "interest" in preserving the brain of President Kennedy is not mentioned, nor has this morbid interest ever been explained. In any event, the brain was not dissected, the only certain means of determining the precise bullet track(s). The brain, however, has disappeared. It was not included in the materials presented to the National Archives when that agency was made the official depository of the autopsy evidence.[30]

Also missing from the National Archives are all microscopic slides of tissue sections taken from the margins of the wounds of entrance in the back and head, as well as from various areas of the brain. These slides are extremely important, for they can give a trained pathologist certain clues about wounds of entrance and exit. All photographs of the brain taken at the supplemental autopsy are also missing. The available photographs depict only the top and bottom of the brain. The supplemental photographs could be of great help in giving a more complete picture. Finally, photographs taken of the interior of the chest cavity are also missing. These could help in determining the track of the bullet through the chest. It is also worth noting that one roll of negatives, black and white, taken during the autopsy was deliberately unraveled and exposed to the light, thus ruining the film. What these photographs would have depicted is, of course, unknown, but such deliberate destruction of vital evidence was not even mentioned by the Warren Commission.[31]

The missing materials preclude any positive statements about absolute conclusions reached through an analysis of the autopsy evidence. The lack of the brain, the tissue slides, and the photographs noted above make it impossible for anyone to state conclusively what the autopsy evidence shows.

THE HEAD MOVEMENT

The single most important piece of evidence about the assassination of John Kennedy is the Zapruder film. After the first shot in frames Z189–238, President Kennedy is seen to bend his head and body forward and to the left, in the direction of his wife. Jacqueline Kennedy turns to her husband and moves her arms toward him. The scenes in frames Z240 through Z312 of the film can almost be described as reassuring. The president is within inches of being cradled in his wife' arms and brought to the security of her lap. Then, without warning, in frame 313 his head explodes in a brilliant spray of pink and red. The viewer, lulled into a false sense of security, gasps in shock as he sees John Kennedy's brains literally blasted out of his skull.[32]

In less than one-half second (frames Z313 through Z321), President Kennedy's head is thrown violently backward and leftward until it bounces off the rear seat and falls into his wife's lap. The helplessness, the violence, the horror, and the shock of seeing the Zapruder film for the first time are unforgettable experiences for the viewer.[33]

The movement of the president's head has caused numerous critics of the *Warren Report* to assert that only a shot fired from the right front could have caused that movement. These critics claim that Newton's Second Law of Motion states that the momentum and velocity of an object is in inverse proportion to the object striking it. Thus, the backward movement of the president's head could not have been caused by a bullet striking it from the rear. That movement must have been caused by one striking it from in front.[34]

Intensive scientific analysis of the Zapruder film by a team of *Life* researchers, as well as by the Itek Corporation, reveals that the head actually undergoes a double movement. The optically enhanced computer analysis by Itek demonstrated that in frames Z312 through Z313, President Kennedy's head flies rapidly forward. This forward head movement is not apparent to the viewer of the film because the head moves faster than the speed of the film and camera. In frame 314 the head reverses direction and moves rapidly backward until it hits the rear seat in frames Z321.[35]

Numerous attempts to explain the head movement have been offered both by those who support the Warren Commission and by those who oppose it. Foremost among the supporters is physicist Luis Alvarez, who has conducted experiments with melons in order to explain the backward head movement. Alvarez fired bullets at melons wrapped with tape. Each time, the melon was propelled backward in the direction of the rifle. According to Alvarez, the law of conservation of momentum applies. As the bullet enters the melon, the kinetic energy of the bullet is released forcing the mass of melon pulp ahead of the bullet. The expulsion of this mass causes a retrograde recoil, releasing over twice as much backward energy as the force of the incoming bullet. The result is a "jet effect." The spray of melon tissue forward is like the thrust of jet engines. The melons will therefore be propelled in the reverse direction of the pulp. In the case of President Kennedy, the massive forward expulsion of brain matter created an identical "jet effect," forcing the head rapidly backward, in the direction of the rifle.[36]

Alvarez's theory received strong support from wounds ballistics experiments conducted by Dr. John Lattimer. After firing shots from a Mannlicher-Carcano rifle similar to Oswald's at melons, Dr. Lattimer fired shots at skulls packed with melon contents and with "more accurate simulations of fresh brain tissue." The skulls always flew backward toward the rifle. In each experiment, the "brain tissue" exploded out of the front of the head, causing the "jet effect" backward movement of the skull. This movement was intensified by a neurological spasmodic stiffening of the actual head and body, giving greater impulse to the backward movement. The experiments led Dr. Lattimer to conclude that "the backwards and sideways lurch of President Kennedy's head toward the shooter . . . was to be expected from a bullet striking his head from the rear."[37]

The Alvarez-Lattimer "jet effect" theory fails to confirm the Warren Commission's conclusions. Neither theory explains both the forward *and* backward movement of the president's head. Neither explains why the explosion of tissue out of the head would have a greater impact than a bullet striking the head at 2,000 feet per second. The brain tissue, moreover, did not fly forward but backward. Both motorcycle police officers riding to the left rear of the limousine were splattered with brain tissue. Pieces of the president's skull were found on the ground to the left rear of the limousine. The melons used by Alvarez and the skulls used by Lattimer were resting on pedestals. President Kennedy's head, of course, was attached to his neck, and not only the head but the entire body moved forward and backward. Both Alvarez and Lattimer fired from much closer distances than the 265-foot distance between the sixth-floor window of the Book Depository building and President Kennedy's head. Finally, Lattimer's skulls were thrown backward and to the right, in the same direction as the gun. President Kennedy's head, however, was thrown backward and to the left, in the opposite direction from the Book Depository building.[38]

Another explanation for the head movement was provided by a panel of experts appointed by the Rockefeller Commission to examine the autopsy materials, the Zapruder film, and other assassination evidence. Three of the experts, neuropathologist Richard Lindenburg, forensic pathologist Werner Spitz, and radiologist Fred Hodges, reported that the movement of the president's head was not caused by a shot fired from the right front. Rather, it was "caused by violent straightening and stiffening of the entire body as a result of a seizure like neuromuscular reaction to major damage inflicted to nerve centers in the brain." The Zapruder film, however, clearly shows the president's body did not undergo a "violent straightening and stiffening." It remained quite limp throughout its backward flight.[39]

The most plausible explanation for the forward and backward movement of the head and body is that of a double impact on the head, one shot fired from the rear, and the other from the front. The author has interviewed numerous physicians and veterans who served in Italy during World War II. He has also interviewed several veterans of the Italian Army who used Mannlicher-Carcano rifles and copper-jacketed ammunition. Collectively, these people have seen several thousand gunshot wounds inflicted by Mannlicher-Carcano rifles. Their unanimous experience has been that the type of head wounds suffered by President Kennedy, as well as the double movement of his head, could not possibly have been caused solely by Oswald's rifle.[40]

World War II films of men being shot in the head by Mannlicher-Carcano rifles reveal absolutely no massive explosion of brain tissue and also show quite graphically that the men invariably fell in the same direction as the trajectory of the bullets that struck them. Autopsy photographs and X-rays of some of the victims of Mannlicher-Carcano-inflicted head wounds also showed no bullet fragmentation, no serious disruption of brain tissue, and very small exit wounds. A ballistics expert who served in the small arms ballistics division of the United States Eighth Army Ordnance Department in Italy during the war confirmed the above observations in his extensive analysis of Mannlicher-Carcano rifles and ammunition.[41]

This does not disprove the "jet effect" or neuromuscular reaction theories. It is possible that Oswald may have used hollow-point rather than fully jacketed ammunition for the head shot. This is only a possibility, and an unlikely one. The most likely possibility is that a bullet, fired from the right rear, struck President Kennedy in the rear of the head and caused a forward motion. Almost simultaneously, a bullet most probably a "dum-dum," fired from the right front, struck him above the right ear and caused him and the brain tissue to fly rapidly backward and to the left.

NEUTRON ACTIVATION ANALYSIS

Because of the conflicting evidence on the head wounds and movement, no definite conclusion can be reached about the number and direction of the fatal shot(s). There is, however, a scientific test by which objective and definitive conclusions about the head shots can be made.

Neutron activation analysis is a procedure whereby objects, such as bullet fragments, are bombarded with nuclear radiation. The irradiated objects will display different degrees of radiation according to their chemical composition. Each of the chemical elements composing the object will emit gamma rays, which can be measured in amounts as small as one-billionth of a gram. Each Mannlicher-Carcano bullet is composed of copper, lead, silver, antimony, bismuth, zinc, with traces of other elements. All bullets manufactured by the Western Cartridge Company, the firm which made the ammunition used in Oswald's rifle, were manufactured with the identical mixture of elements. Since each Carcano bullet contains the same volume and weight of each element, the results of neutron activation analysis totals will be the same for each element in all bullets or fragments from Oswald's rifle. If the totals do not match, then more than one type of ammunition was used.[42]

Neutron activation analysis was performed on Bullet 399, a bullet fragment removed from Governor Connally's wrist, one of the bullet fragments found in the front seat of the limousine, and two fragments removed from President Kennedy's head during the autopsy. Because of the precision of this test, it could have been an extremely useful aide in determining whether one or more different types of ammunition were used in the assassination. Unfortunately, many bullet fragments and other pieces of evidence were not tested. Of those fragments tested, only the silver and antimony were measured. No copper was measured, even though it composed a much higher proportion of the total weight of bullets than either silver or antimony. Despite these limitations, the results of the neutron activation analysis do provide very strong evidence of more than one assassin.[43]

The results for both silver and antimony demonstrate that Bullet 399 did not match the fragment removed from Governor Connally's wrist. This means that Bullet 399 could not have caused the Connally wrist wound. The Kennedy head fragments did not match the limousine fragment and therefore could not have been caused by it. The Kennedy head fragments did not even closely resemble the Connally wrist fragment or Bullet 399, nor did the limousine fragments.[44]

These results mean that at least two different types of ammunition were used in the assassination. Since the Kennedy head fragments contained 20 percent less silver and almost 40 percent less antimony than Bullet 399, the result is that there *must* have been different lots of ammunition. Since we know that Bullet 399 was a Mannlicher-Carcano round, the Kennedy head shot(s) may not have come from a Mannlicher-Carcano rifle.[45]

These comments are based on the assumption that the tests, which were conducted at the Atomic Energy Commission's nuclear testing facilities in Oak Ridge, Tennessee, were performed properly. Many vital pieces of evidence were not tested. For example, copper tracings around the bullet holes in President Kennedy's coat should have been compared with the copper jacketing in Bullet 399. *Both* fragments from the front seat of the limousine and the three fragments from the rear of the limousine should have been compared with each other in order to determine whether or not all came from the same bullet. The copper, silver, antimony, and other elements from the live bullet found inside the firing chamber of "Oswald's" rifle should have been compared with the elements in the other fragments to see if they matched.

Neutron activation analysis could be a positive, certain determination of the question of how many rifles were used in the assassination. It is the most precise and objective procedure available. Experts can and do disagree about the medical evidence, the Zapruder film, the ballistics test, and the like. The results of neutron activation analysis (or another new procedure, flameless atomic absorption spectrometry), however, are scientifically objective and beyond argument. Unfortunately, it was not done at the time, at least as completely and accurately as possible.

SUMMARY

The medical evidence about President Kennedy's head wounds is inconclusive. Assuming that the autopsy photographs and X-rays of the head are authentic, there is indisputable evidence of one shot, fired from above and behind, which entered the rear of the head. The photographs and X-rays clearly demonstrate this. These photographs do not, however, reveal whether this bullet exited or where. The large gaping hole on the right side of the president's head could be either a wound of exit or one of entrance. Because of its massive size, it could even be *both* an exit and an entrance wound.

The very severe damage to the skull and brain, the large degree of bullet fragmentation, the fact, conceded even by defenders of the *Warren Report,* that a very high-powered rifle must have been used, are not characteristic of the rifle and ammunition allegedly used by Lee Harvey Oswald. Wounds ballistics tests performed for the Warren Commission and by others fail either to confirm or refute the lone-assassin thesis. The double movement of the president's head suggests the possibility of a double impact. The neutron activation analysis strongly indicates more than one rifle.

The medical and ballistics evidence, therefore, does not prove beyond a reasonable doubt that all shots were fired from the rear. Neither does it prove beyond a reasonable doubt that any shots were fired from in front. Until the missing brain can be located and pathologically dissected, until complete and accurate neutron activation analysis can be performed, we shall not know with certainty how many shots were fired nor where they were fired from. The Warren Commission's contention that all the shots were fired from the sixth-floor southeast corner window of the Texas School Book Depository building is thus not proven by the available evidence.

CHAPTER 6

LEE HARVEY OSWALD: GUILTY OR INNOCENT?

HAVING DETERMINED that the shots were fired from the sixth-floor southeast corner window of the Texas School Book Depository building, the Warren Commission then concluded that "the shots which killed President Kennedy and wounded Governor Connally were fired by Lee Harvey Oswald." To substantiate its thesis that Oswald was the assassin, the commission supplied seven hypotheses, each backed up by some evidence.[1]

Its first contention was that "the Mannlicher-Carcano 6.5 mm. Italian rifle from which the shots were fired was owned by and in the possession of Oswald." This statement by the commission presupposes that all the shots were fired from the rifle found on the sixth floor of the building. As we have seen, the evidence does not even support the hypothesis that all shots were fired from the sixth-floor window, much less from that particular rifle. The Zapruder film, the bullet fragments, the medical evidence, and the neutron activation analysis all argue persuasively that at least one shot was fired from in front of the president and that at least two different types of weapons and ammunition were employed in the assassination.[2]

Even though the assumption that the rifle was used in the shooting is not proven by the evidence, the question of whether Oswald ever owned or possessed that rifle is worth analyzing. About an hour after the assassination, a Mannlicher-Carcano 6.5 mm. Italian rifle bearing the serial number C2766 was found hidden under a stack of boxes on the sixth floor of the Book Depository building. The FBI learned that the rifle had been shipped by Klein's Sporting Goods Company of Chicago to A. Hidell of Dallas on 20 March 1963. "A. Hiddell" and "Alex Hidell" were two of the many aliases used by Lee Harvey Oswald. Documents experts of the FBI and Treasury Department matched the printing on the purchase order for the rifle and the handwriting on the money order used to pay for it with Oswald's printing and handwriting. The Dallas Post Office box number (2915) to which the rifle was shipped had been leased to Oswald. This evidence proves beyond a reasonable doubt that Lee Harvey Oswald did indeed purchase a rifle.[3]

Other evidence connecting Oswald with the rifle is hardly as conclusive. A right palmprint, positively identified as Oswald's, was lifted from the underside of the rifle barrel by the Dallas Police. The print was lifted off the rifle with a piece of scotch tape. While the print on the tape was Oswald's, there is no objective evidence linking it to the rifle. Lieutenant Day of the Dallas Police told the Warren Commission that he dusted the barrel for prints and then lifted the print with the tape. This information was not made public until 27 November, five days after the assassination. The FBI laboratory found absolutely no traces of the print, the tape, or the dusting powder on the rifle. Customary procedure is to photograph prints on the objects where they are found. No photographs were made of the print on the rifle.[4]

Several fibers, similar to those in the shirt Oswald was wearing, were found on the rifle. The FBI expert testified that these fibers "most probably" came from Oswald's shirt, although he could not state positively that they did. The Dallas police, however, shipped the shirt and the rifle together to Washington. Neither objected was wrapped; both touched each other in the shipping carton. Therefore, since the shirt came into contact with the rifle before they were examined by the FBI, there is no way of telling how these fibers came to be on the rifle. They could have resulted from Oswald's touching the rifle, or from careless handling of the evidence by the Dallas police.[5]

Another piece of evidence trumpeted by the commission is a photograph of Oswald with a rifle in his hand. The authenticity of the photograph has been questioned by many commission critics. Regardless of whether the photograph is genuine, it is, in fact, totally irrelevant to the question of his ownership of the weapon. FBI photographic experts testified that they could not determine whether the rifle Oswald is holding is the sixth-floor Mannlicher-Carcano. Furthermore, the photograph was taken on 31 March 1963. Even if it were genuine, it hardly proves that Oswald possessed the rifle the following November.[6]

Marina Oswald told the Warren Commission that the rifle found on the sixth floor was "the fateful rifle of Lee Oswald." This statement is meaningless, since Marina Oswald's expertise in firearms identification included her inability even to distinguish between a rifle and a shotgun. She also testified that she heard Oswald practice operating the bolt action of his rifle. The commission produced no evidence to verify that Marina Oswald was able to distinguish the sound of this particular rifle, to the exclusion of all other weapons.[7]

She also told the commission that the rifle was wrapped up inside a blanket in the garage of the home in Irving, Texas, where she lived between 24 September and 22 November 1963. The owners of the Irving home, Ruth and Michael Paine, both testified they had actually picked up the blanket and moved it around in the garage and were completely unaware that it contained a rifle. In a memorandum that the Warren Commission suppressed from its *Report* and from its twenty-six volumes of published evidence, J. Wesley Liebler, the commission counsel responsible for this section of the *Warren Report*, stated that "the fact is that not one person alive today [including Marina] ever saw that rifle in the Paine garage in such a way it could be identified as being that [Oswald's] rifle."[8]

There is a very serious question of whether Oswald purchased the rifle found on the sixth floor. According to the Warren Commission, "this particular rifle was the only rifle of its type bearing serial number C2766," and "the number C2766 is the serial number of the rifle, and the rifle in question is the only one of its type bearing that serial number." The commission, however, failed to include in its published *Report* a report by J. Edgar Hoover that states, "since many concerns [Italian arms factories] were manufacturing the same weapon, the same serial number appears on weapons manufactured by more than one concern." At least ten factories manufactured Mannlicher-Carcano rifles in Italy in 1940. Each of the ten made Carcanos with the C2766 serial number, several of which are in the United States today. One of these rifles is even owned by Dr. John Lattimer, one of the Warren Commission's staunchest defenders. In a published article, Dr. Lattimer claims ownership of a Mannlicher-Carcano 6.5 mm. 91/38 rifle with serial number C2766. Since more than one rifle had the same serial number, it is impossible to demonstrate which of these is the one purchased by Lee Harvey Oswald.[9]

A fact first uncovered by commission critic Sylvia Meagher suggests that the Depository rifle may not have been the one ordered from Klein's Sporting Goods. The commission believed that Oswald ordered the rifle from a Klein's advertisement in the February 1963 issue of the *American Rifleman* magazine. The advertisement promotes a 36-inch Mannlicher-Carcano rifle weighing 5½ pounds. The Depository Carcano was 40.2 inches long and weighed 8 pounds. The commission did not publish the original Klein's advertisement.[10]

The evidence on Oswald's ownership of the rifle is thus inconclusive. The mail order, post office box number, handwriting analysis, and part of Marina Oswald's testimony indicate that he did purchase a weapon. The serial numbers and Klein's advertisement indicate that he may not have purchased the rifle found in the Depository building. In any event, except for the palmprint, the Warren Commission was unable to produce any evidence that the Mannlicher-Carcano was ever in the possession of Lee Harvey Oswald. If, as the commission alleged, the rifle was stored in the Paines' garage between 24 September and 22 November, it could not have been in Oswald's possession, for he did not live at the Paine home. Estranged from his wife, Lee Oswald lived in various rooming houses in Dallas during those two months. Even the commission itself admitted that Oswald did not actually come into contact with the rifle until the night before the assassination.[11]

The second statement of the commission implicating Oswald in the assassination is that "Oswald carried this rifle into the Depository Building on the morning of November 22, 1963." The commission believed that Oswald made an unusual trip to the Paine home on Thursday, 21 November, in order to pick up some curtain rods for his room in Dallas. The commission determined that the curtain rod story was a fabrication, for his landlady testified that his room already had curtains.[12]

In the commission's version, Oswald spent the night at the

Paine home. He woke up early on the morning of 22 November and left before Marina had awakened. He went to the garage, retrieved the rifle from the blanket, and put it in a paper bag that he had specifically manufactured for the purpose. Oswald walked down to the home of Mrs. Lillie Mae Randle, whose brother, Buell Wesley Frazier, drove Oswald to work that morning. Both Frazier and Mrs. Randle noticed that Lee Harvey Oswald carried a "long and bulky package" with him. After the assassination a bag containing a fingerprint and palmprint of Oswald's was allegedly found near the sixth-floor window. The bag also contained fibers that "could have come from the blanket in which the rifle was stored."[13]

Few sections of the *Warren Report* contain as many distortions of fact and evidence as this one. The physical and documentary evidence, as well as the testimony of eyewitnesses, clearly establish the fact that the Warren Commission had presumed Lee Harvey Oswald guilty and attempted to fabricate a case against him. An objective analysis of the facts reveals that few of the commission's assertions summarized above can be substantiated.

The commission decided that Oswald had lied when he told Frazier that he was going to Irving "to get some curtain rods." The landlady of the rooming house in which Oswald lived testified that Oswald's room had curtains and rods. Oswald did not mention the curtain rod story to either his wife or Ruth Paine. A search of the Depository building failed to uncover curtain rods. The commission, however, neglected to uncover evidence which strongly supports Oswald's story. First, a Dallas police photograph of the rooming house shows venetian blinds, but no curtains. Second, a news photographer witnessed the landlady and her husband hanging curtains and curtain rods in Oswald's room the day after the assassination. Third, two eyewitnesses who were in Oswald's room on 22 November state that it had no curtains or rods. Fourth, the commission conducted its investigation of whether curtain rods had been discovered in the Depository building in September 1964, over eight months later. That investigation began with a letter from Commission general counsel J. Lee Rankin to J. Edgar Hoover instructing the FBI to interview Roy Truly, the superintendent of the building. The purpose of the interview was "to establish that no curtain rods were found in the building." The letter is indicative of the way in which the commission conducted much of its investigating. Instead of trying to find out if *any* curtain rods had been found, it directed the FBI to establish that *none* had been found. This, however, is meaningless, since it is unlikely that a Depository employee would report such a discovery.[14]

Mrs. Randle saw Oswald carrying a package and then place it in Frazier's car. According to the *Warren Report,* she called it a "heavy brown bag." Frazier got in the car and drove Oswald to the company parking lot. Frazier remained in the vehicle while Oswald picked up the bag and left. "It was," the *Report* asserts, "the first time that Oswald had not walked with Frazier from the parking lot to the building entrance." To the commission, the bag contained not curtain rods, but the disassembled Mannlicher-Carcano rifle. The bag found on the sixth floor had been made from wrapping paper and tape from the Depository shipping and packaging department. The bag was custom-made by Oswald, the commission declared, because the rifle was too long and bulky to fit into an ordinary paper bag.[15]

There is, in fact, absolutely no evidence of any kind to prove whether or not Oswald manufactured this bag. The only evidence about the bag is that it was made from Depository paper and tape. This, of course, in no way even remotely suggests that Oswald made it. Both Frazier and Mrs. Randle swore that the bag found on the sixth floor was much longer than the package Oswald was carrying. Buell Wesley Frazier had previously worked in a department store and had handled curtain rods as part of his duties. When Oswald told him that his package contained curtain rods, Frazier saw nothing unusual about it.[16]

The bag found on the sixth floor was 38 inches long, and the disassembled rifle was 34.8 inches long. Both Frazier and Mrs. Randle swore that the bag Oswald carried was 27 or 28 inches long. Their accuracy in estimating lengths was tested by both the FBI and by the commission. Both times they accurately estimated a measured length of 27 to 27.5 inches. Mrs. Randle testified that when Oswald gripped the package at the top, with his arm extended fully downward, "the bottom [of the package] almost touched the ground." Frazier testified that Oswald held one end of the package cupped in his hand, in the same way a soldier would hold a rifle during military drill. The other end of the package, according to Frazier, was tucked under Oswald's armpit. Clearly, they were not describing a 36-inch-long package. The reader can demonstrate this by taking a yardstick, which is the same length as the package which the Warren Commission claimed Oswald held, and hold one end of the yardstick cupped in the hand. He will see that the other end will project beyond his shoulder. Yet Frazier swore that it came only to Oswald's armpit. The only way that Oswald could have carried the disassembled rifle and bag in the manner described by Frazier and Randle would have been if his arms hung down to his ankles.[17]

When they were shown the bag found on the sixth floor, Frazier and Randle swore that it was "too long" to be the bag Oswald carried. The commission distorted Mrs. Randle's testimony by quoting her as saying that Oswald carried a "heavy brown bag." The complete context of Mrs. Randle's testimony clearly demonstrates that she was referring to the texture of the paper rather than the weight of the package: "He was carrying a package in a sort of heavy brown bag, heavier than a grocery bag it looked like to me." The commission contended that this was the first time Oswald had ever walked ahead of Frazier into the Depository building. This carried the sinister implication that Oswald was trying to sneak into the building so Frazier could not see him hide the rifle. Frazier's actual testimony proved entirely different. He told the commission that he parked the car and then left the engine running in order to charge up his battery. Far from trying to sneak away, Oswald, package in hand, volunteered to wait with him. Frazier, however, told Oswald to go on alone.[18]

Since the eyewitness testimony hardly supported its claim that Oswald carried the gun in the bag, the commission stated that it "weighed the visual recollection of Frazier and Mrs. Randle against the evidence here presented that the bag Oswald carried contained the assassination weapon and has concluded that Frazier and Randle are mistaken as to the length of the bag." What was this evidence? The *Warren Report* has a section entitled "Scientific Evidence Linking Rifle and Oswald to Paper Bag."[19]

A paper bag was supposedly found near the sixth-floor window. The word "supposedly" is used because there is no contemporary evidence to verify this. No photographs of the bag on the floor near the window were taken. Dallas Deputy Sheriff Roger Craig, one of the first law enforcement officers to discover the "assassin's nest," stated that no bag was in the vicinity of the window at that time (approximately one hour after the assassination). Even if a bag had been there, there is no evidence that it contained the rifle. The Warren Commission nevertheless asserted, "The presence of the bag in this corner is cogent evidence that it was used as the container for the rifle." This inference from the mere location of the bag is indicative of the commission's predisposition to blame Lee Harvey Oswald for the crime. The fact that a bag was found near the window is obviously meaningless in itself. Over a dozen cardboard cartons were also found in that corner. It is a wonder that the commission did not state that the presence of the cartons in this corner is cogent evidence that they were used to carry the rifle.[20]

Oswald's right palmprint was found on the bottom of the bag and his left index fingerprint on one of its sides. To the commission, the location of the palmprint on the bottom of the bag "was consistent with the bag having contained a heavy or bulky object when he handled it since a light object is usually held by the fingers." It is true that heavy or bulky packages are usually held in the palm of the hand, but the fingers are also usually clutching the package on the other end. The reader is again invited to experiment. Carry a 35-inch, 8-pound object in a 38-inch-long bag. Rest the bag in your right palm and touch the bag *only* with your left index finger. You will see for yourself how absurd and ludicrous the position is. The existence of the palmprint and fingerprint mean only that Oswald touched the bag.[21]

The other "scientific evidence" linking the rifle and Oswald to the bag was the fact that the bag contained several fibers that "could have come" from the blanket in the Paine garage. Obviously, this evidence does not even connect the blanket to the bag, much less the rifle. The commission conjectured that the "rifle could have picked up fibers from the blanket and transferred them to the paper bag." While this is a possibility, another more plausible explanation exists. The Dallas police placed the bag, the blanket, the rifle, and other physical evidence in a box. None of these objects was wrapped; all bounced against each other. An official Dallas police photograph of the box, published by the commission, shows the bag, the blanket, and the rifle all resting against and touching each other. The photograph was taken *before* the fibers were discovered in the bag.[22]

In order to link Oswald to the blanket, the Warren Commission relied on one of its most incredible pieces of evidence. Limb and pubic hairs removed from Oswald matched limb and pubic hairs found on the blanket. Fortunately, the commission spared the public the graphic details of how Oswald's pubic hairs came into contact with the blanket. It did not spare it the tasteless and totally unnecessary publication of microphotographs of the pubic hairs of Lee Harvey Oswald. There was, of course, no need in the first place to link Oswald to the blanket, since it belonged to him.[23]

The most convincing evidence that the paper bag never contained the Mannlicher-Carcano rifle is the testimony of FBI documents expert James Cadigan: "I was requested to examine the bag to determine if there were *any* significant markings or scratches or abrasions or *anything* by which it [the bag] could be associated with the rifle, Commission Exhibit 139, that is, could I find any markings [on the bag] that I could tie to that rifle. . . . And I couldn't find any such markings." Despite this very convincing evidence, the commission concluded that Oswald "carried the rifle into the Depository Building, concealed in the bag."[24]

This section of the Warren Commission's case against Lee Harvey Oswald thus failed to prove any of the accusations made against him. There is not one scintilla of evidence that the blanket in the Paine garage *ever* contained the rifle. There is no evidence that Oswald ever manufactured the paper bag, only that he touched it. There is absolutely no evidence of any kind that the bag ever contained the rifle. The only two witnesses who saw Oswald carrying a package on 22 November testified that it could not have been the bag found on the sixth floor of the Depository building.

The third part of the Warren Commission's case against Oswald was that "Oswald, at the time of the assassination, was present at the window from which the shots were fired." This statement presupposes that there is irrefutable evidence that the window was the one "from which the shots were fired." As we have seen, there is indeed indisputable evidence that at least two shots were fired from a site behind the presidential limousine. There is, however, no reliable evidence proving that this site was the sixth-floor southeast corner window of the Texas School Book Depository building.[25]

To demonstrate that Oswald was present at the sixth-floor window at the time of the shooting, the commission analyzed the fact that several of Oswald's fingerprints were found on cartons of books located near the window. Of the three cartons located immediately adjacent to the window, only one contained Oswald's prints. They were a left palmprint and a right index fingerprint. Of sixteen other boxes located within five feet of the window, only one contained a print of Oswald's—a right palmprint.[26]

Of the three prints, only the right palmprint found on a box behind and to the left of the window boxes could be positively identified as less than three days old. The palm on this box was facing at an oblique angle toward the window. The commission stated that "someone sitting on the box facing the window would have his palm in this position if he placed his hand alongside his right hip." This is sheer speculation by the commission. It did not note that this print could also have been made under many different circumstances.[27]

The fact that handling the sixth-floor cartons was part of Oswald's normal duties at the Depository was considered by the Warren Commission. It did not reach the obvious conclusion that because Oswald worked on the sixth floor, the presence of his prints there is meaningless. The commission instead was led "to attach some probative value to the fingerprint and palmprint identifications in reaching the conclusion that Oswald was at the window . . . although the prints do not establish the exact time he was there."[28]

One "identifiable print," belonging neither to Oswald nor to any other Depository employee, nor to any law enforcement officials who touched the boxes, established beyond dispute that at least one unknown person touched at least one carton. This fact, coupled with the mysterious circumstances of the cartridge cases and the Hughes film showing two people at the sixth-floor window during the shooting, raises serious questions about the possibility of an accomplice. The commission failed to investigate this matter.[29]

The print evidence was obviously far too flimsy to place Oswald at the window at the time of the assassination. The commission therefore attempted to bolster its case by emphasizing the testimony of Charles Givens. One of Oswald's coworkers at the Depository, Givens told the commission that he saw Oswald on the sixth floor at 11:55 A.M., thirty-five minutes before the assassination. Obviously, this hardly places Oswald at the window at 12:30, when the shooting occurred. In thirty-five minutes Oswald had sufficient time to vacate not only the entire building, but the city of Dallas. Yet to the commission, the fact that he was seen on the sixth floor at 11:55 is strong evidence that he was there at 12:30.[30]

In the section treating Givens's testimony, the *Warren Report* asserts that "none of the Depository employees is known to have seen Oswald again [after 11:55 A.M.] until after the shooting." This statement is blatantly false. Depository janitor Eddie Piper swore in an affadavit that he saw and spoke with Oswald on the first floor at noon. Attempting to discredit Piper, the commission called him a "confused witness." The commission failed to mention that on 22 November 1963, Givens told the FBI that he saw Oswald on the fifth floor at 11:45. Four months later, he changed his mind and told the Warren Commission a different story. Piper told a consistent story both times he was questioned.[31]

The *Warren Report* also omits mention of the deposition of another Depository employee, Carolyn Arnold. She told the FBI that "as she was standing in front of the building, she stated that she thought she caught a fleeting glimpse of LEE HARVEY OSWALD standing . . . on the first floor. She could not be sure this was OSWALD, but said she felt it was and believed the time to be a few minutes before 12:15 P.M." In addition to Arnold and Piper, three other Depository employees saw Oswald on the fifth floor at 11:45, and assistant building superintendent William Shelly saw Oswald on the first floor at noon.[32]

Another vital aspect of this part of the case was ignored by the

Warren Commission in its section on Oswald's presence on the sixth floor at the time of the assassination. Bonnie Ray Williams, a Depository employee, ate his lunch on the sixth floor between 12:00 and 12:18 P.M. The precise location where Williams ate his lunch is not known. But it was near the sixth-floor southeast corner because plastic food wrap, an empty soda pop bottle, and bones from Williams's fried chicken lunch were found lying on the floor and on the cartons adjacent to the sixth-floor window. Williams testified that while he ate his lunch, he saw and heard "no one around." Williams's testimony, which the commission accepted as accurate and reliable, proves that Oswald could not have been in the vicinity of the "assassin's nest" between noon and 12:18. Thus, Oswald had less than twelve minutes to assemble his rifle, load it with ammunition, arrange the boxes as a "gun rest," and prepare himself for the shooting before the motorcade turned onto Elm Street. If the motorcade had been just five minutes early, Oswald would not have had time to assemble and load his weapon, since that operation takes at least ten minutes.[33]

The *Warren Report* emphasized the importance of Givens's testimony while omitting that of the other witnesses. It failed to cite the inconsistencies in Givens's story while distorting or ignoring the other witnesses who contradicted Givens. Despite the fact that six eyewitnesses saw Oswald elsewhere in the building and despite Williams's testimony that he saw "no one" on the sixth floor only ten minutes before the assassination, the commission nevertheless concluded that Oswald was present at the window.

In order to bolster its case that Oswald was at the window at the time of the shooting, the Warren Commission included a section entitled "Eyewitness Identification of Assassin" in its *Report*. This section begins with Howard Brennan's testimony (see Chapter One). The reader is reminded that Brennan actually viewed Oswald in a police lineup on 22 November and could not identify him. He stated the man he saw was standing up and shooting. Even the commission acknowledges Brennan's error. Since the window was open only fifteen inches from the floor, the assassin must have been lying, kneeling, or sitting as he shot. Brennan estimated the assassin's height and weight even though he had a view only of the upper half of the man from 120 feet away. Brennan had seen Oswald's picture on television on 22 November and "could not say" if this affected his identification of Oswald.[34]

Only one other witness, Amos Lee Euins, saw a man fire a rifle from the sixth-floor window. Euins believed the man was either a Negro or a "white man with a bald spot on top of his head." Neither of these descriptions fits Lee Harvey Oswald. Even Euins does not believe the man he saw was Oswald. Two witnesses, Ronald Fisher and Robert Edwards, saw a man *without* a rifle in the window. The man, who did *not* resemble Oswald, wore a "lightcolored, open neck shirt." According to the commission, Oswald wore a dark, rust-colored shirt. No other witnesses saw anyone in the sixth-floor window. The Hughes film of the assassination clearly shows *two* men only three feet from each other in adjoining windows on the sixth floor. Neither man resembles Oswald; neither is wearing a dark shirt; neither appears to be holding a rifle.[35]

There is no credible eyewitness identification of Lee Harvey Oswald as the assassin in the window. Several witnesses did see a gunman in the window, or a gun protruding out of the window. This does suggest that at least one shot was fired from there. However, none of the eyewitness testimony proves that the gunman was Oswald.

The commission determined that "Oswald's movements in the building immediately after the assassination are consistent with his having been at the window at 12:30 P.M." The first person to see Oswald after the shooting was Dallas Police Officer Marrion L. Baker. Riding his motorcycle in the press section of the motorcade, Patrolman Baker heard the shots. Believing that they may have come from the roof of the Book Depository building, Baker raced his vehicle to the corner of Elm and Houston streets. He jumped off, ran into the building, and was joined by Roy Truly, superintendent of the Depository building. After unsuccessfully trying to get an elevator, Baker, following Truly, ascended the stairs at the rear of the building. When he reached the second-floor stair landing, Baker noticed a man walking toward a Coke machine in a lunchroom. Baker drew his revolver and ordered the man to approach him. As the man did, Truly entered and identified the man as Lee Harvey Oswald, one of the Depository employees. Baker and Truly left the lunchroom and continued their stairway journey toward the roof. The time was 12:31:30 P.M., ninety seconds after the president had been shot.[36]

These events have given rise to a most perplexing aspect of the problem. If two eyewitnesses saw Oswald on the second floor only a minute and a half after the assassination, how could he have been on the sixth floor firing the shots? In order to resolve this problem, it is necessary, insofar as it is possible, to reconstruct the movements of Oswald, Baker, and Truly.

The Warren Commission naturally was aware of the problem and had Officer Baker and building superintendent Truly reconstruct their actions. Secret Service Agent John Howlett reconstructed Oswald's movements. The reconstruction times for Baker and Truly were 1 minute, 30 seconds at a "slow trot," and 1 minute, 15 seconds at a "fast trot." The times for "Oswald" were 1 minute, 14 seconds and 1 minute, 18 seconds. Since "Oswald's" time to reach the second floor was less than that required by Baker to reach the same place, the commission concluded that Oswald did have time to arrive in the lunchroom before Baker.[37]

The commission, however, failed to conduct a reconstruction that was faithful to the actual sequence of events on 22 November. In the reconstruction, the Warren Commission counsel timed Baker's movements from the first shot. Baker, however, testified that he began after the *last* shot. Since there was a minimum interval of four to seven seconds between the first and last shots, that much time must be added to Baker's reconstructed time in order to reach an accurate estimate. The adjusted times for Baker are 1 minute, 34 seconds, and 1 minute, 19 seconds.[38]

Secret Service Agent Howlett described his reconstruction of Oswald's movements. "I carried a rifle from the southeast corner of the sixth floor northernly along the east aisle to the northern corner, then westernly along the north wall past the elevators to the northwest corner. There I placed the rifle on the floor. I then entered the stairwell, walked down the stairway to the second floor landing, and then into the lunchroom." According to the commission, Howlett's reconstruction was a faithful rendering of Oswald's actions.[39]

Howlett's reconstruction, in fact, omitted several actions that Oswald must have engaged in, if the Warren Commission's version of the assassination is to be accepted. First, Howlett neglected to operate the bolt action of the rifle. Since a live cartridge case was in the firing chamber when the rifle was discovered, Oswald must have operated the bolt of the weapon after he fired the last shot. Second, Howlett did not have to clear any obstacles during his reconstruction. Yet, according to the commission, the sixth-floor window was surrounded by a shield of cartons. These boxes were stacked so tightly together that a man carrying a heavy, bulky weapon must have slowed down his movements in order to clear the area. The man who discovered the sixth-floor "assassin's nest," Deputy Sheriff Luke Mooney, testified that in order to reach the window, "I had to squeeze between these two stacks of boxes, I had to turn myself sideways to get in there." Roger Craig was there with Mooney. He has confirmed the physical impossibility of reaching the window without twisting through or climbing over the stacks of boxes.[40]

Third, Howlett testified that in his reconstruction of Oswald's actions, he "placed the rifle on the floor." The rifle was not merely placed on the floor. When discovered, it was very carefully hidden under a high stack of boxes. The man who discovered the weapon, Deputy Sheriff Eugene Boone, stated that he "caught a glimpse of the rifle, stuffed down between two rows of boxes with another box or so pulled over the top of it." According to Deputy Craig, the rifle was so well concealed under the boxes that it was necessary to lift and remove four 55-pound cartons before it could be retrieved.[41]

The commission allowed no time for Oswald either to escape from the shield of cartons or to conceal the rifle. It is not unreasonable to add 10 seconds to Oswald's reconstructed time. The more accurate times for Baker and Oswald are 1 minute, 26 seconds each. This would have the two men arriving in the lunchroom simultaneously. It is, of course, possible that Baker and Truly did not reconstruct their movements accurately. The hectic first couple of minutes after the shooting included large crowds of people converging in front of the Book Depository building. The crowds could have slowed Baker down. Oswald thus could have had sufficient time to reach the lunchroom before Baker. However, this does not mean that Oswald actually did. According to the commission, Oswald's actions were consistent with his having been on the sixth floor at the time of the assassination. This is inaccurate. Oswald's presence in the lunchroom a minute and a half after the shooting is consistent with his having been almost anywhere in the building. Officer Baker was over 150 feet away from the building during the shooting, yet he managed to reach the lunchroom within ninety seconds. Oswald's presence in the room, therefore, is consistent with his having been any place between the first and sixth floors of the building, as well as half a block away from it.[42]

There is only very disputable evidence that Oswald was present at the window at the time of the assassination. The fact that the rifle, the paper bag, and the cartons contained prints of Oswald's do suggest the possibility that he was there. On the other hand, none of the physical or eyewitness evidence provides proof that he was there *at the time of the assassination.* The only objective inference to be drawn from that evidence is that it is inconclusive.

The fifth part of the commission's case against Oswald is that a "rifleman of Lee Harvey Oswald's capabilities could have fired the shots from the rifle used in the assassination within the elapsed time of the shooting." It is true that the Mannlicher-Carcano rifle could be fired fast enough. Films of the assassination reveal that the minimum time between the first and last shots was five to eight seconds, more than sufficient time for even an amateur to fire the weapon three times.[43]

The commission determined that "Oswald possessed the capability with a rifle which enabled him to commit the assassination." Elaborate marksmanship tests were conducted for the commission by the FBI and by the United States Army. Three FBI experts and three master riflemen fired six shots each from Oswald's rifle at *stationary* targets. None of the shots hit the head or neck of the targets. Nevertheless, the commission concluded that Oswald could have fired the assassination shots. In 1967, CBS News conducted its own marksmanship tests. Its riflemen also failed to strike the targets with any consistent accuracy.

Commission critics have criticized the tests and the unsubstantiated conclusions drawn from them. They claim that Oswald's rating as a "poor shot" in the Marines and the failure of the commission's and CBS's experts to duplicate his alleged feat of marksmanship mean that he could not have been the sole assassin.[44]

Both the Warren Commission and its critics are mistaken. No one knows what the firing capabilities of Lee Harvey Oswald were. There is simply no evidence that Oswald ever fired a Mannlicher-Carcano rifle. The only substantial evidence about his marksmanship abilities comes from 1957 and 1959 Marine Corps tests of his firing an M-1 rifle. There is no dispute that the assassin(s) of President Kennedy exhibited a high degree of marksmanship. Whether Oswald was capable of such a feat is unanswerable. Lee Harvey Oswald is dead. He, and only he, could have resolved this problem.

To further bolster its case against Oswald, the commission stated that "Oswald lied to the police after his arrest concerning important substantive matters." This is an assumption that is not supported by evidence. Incredible as it may seem, the Dallas police made no tapes, notes, or transcripts of the twelve hours of interrogation sessions with Oswald. The only information available about what Oswald said during these sessions is the often confused and contradictory accounts, based solely upon memory, by various members of the Dallas police. There is no objective evidence to verify or refute these accounts. In any event, even if Oswald had lied to the police, this neither implicates nor exonerates him of guilt in the assassination.[45]

Finally, the *Warren Report* states that "Oswald had attempted to kill Maj. Gen. Edwin A. Walker (Resigned, U.S. Army) on April 10, 1963, thereby demonstrating his disposition to take human life." The story of the attempt on General Walker's life is beyond the scope of this book. Obviously, it has little bearing on the question of whether or not Oswald shot President Kennedy over seven months later.[46]

The Warren Commission brought out some evidence against Oswald. The facts that Oswald did purchase a rifle, that his palmprint was allegedly found on the rifle barrel, that fibers from the rifle could have come from his shirt, and that Oswald was in the physical vicinity of the sixth floor constitute the main concrete evidence against him. On the other hand, evidence in his favor includes the facts that there is no evidence that the rifle was in Oswald's possession after April 1963, that there is no evidence of any kind that Oswald brought a rifle into the building, that there were no prints of his on any part of the assembled rifle or the clip or the cartridge cases, that there is no evidence whatsoever that the bag ever contained the rifle, and that Oswald was seen on the second floor only ninety seconds after the shooting. An objective evaluation of the Warren Commission's case against Lee Harvey Oswald is that reasonable doubts about his guilt still remain.

CHAPTER 7

THE MURDER OF OFFICER TIPPIT

AT ABOUT 1:15 P.M. on 22 November 1963, forty-five minutes after the assassination, Dallas Police Officer J.D. Tippit was shot to death. The Warren Commission decided that Lee Harvey Oswald also killed Officer Tippit. The reason, according to the commission, was that Tippit stopped Oswald and questioned him because he suspected that Oswald may have been the man wanted for the slaying of President Kennedy. The commission's determination was made on the basis of eyewitness identification of Oswald, ballistics evidence linking Oswald's revolver with the bullets removed from Tippit's body, and assorted other evidence.

The Tippit murder occurred near the intersection of Tenth and Patton streets in a residential area of Dallas, approximately three and a half miles from Dealey Plaza. The Warren Commission first had to trace Oswald's movements from the scene of the assassination to the scene of the Tippit shooting. As we saw in Chapter Three, the commission arbitrarily assumed that Oswald departed through the front door of the Book Depository building at 12:33 P.M.

THE BUS RIDE

According to the commission, Oswald left the Depository building and walked east on Elm Street for seven blocks. He then caught a bus headed back toward the Depository en route to its regularly scheduled run in the Oak Cliff section of Dallas (the general area where Oswald lived and where Tippit was shot). The bus driver, Cecil McWatters, identified Oswald in a police lineup as the man who boarded his bus and who received a transfer when he left. The following day, a young man named Milton Jones entered McWatters's bus. McWatters immediately recognized Jones as the man who had boarded his bus on 22 November. He told the Warren Commission that he was wrong in selecting Oswald out of the lineup.[1]

The Dallas Police allegedly found a bus transfer in Oswald's possession when he was arrested. The transfer, according to the commission, was marked with the distinctive punchmarks of McWatters. The *Warren Report* claims that "on the basis of the date and time on the transfer, McWatters was able to testify that the transfer had been issued by him on a trip which passed a checkpoint at St. Paul and Elm Streets at 12:36 P.M., November 22, 1963." The transfer is indeed marked November 22, 1963, but the time is simply punched "P.M." How McWatters was able to determine the precise time from this general information is not known. Furthermore, since McWatters stated that he had mistaken Oswald for Milton Jones, Jones rather than Oswald must have received the transfer.[2]

Both McWatters and Jones remember a male passenger on the bus, a man who the commission claimed was Oswald. Both men remember the man as wearing a jacket. The commission, however, rejected this contention and stated that Oswald was not wearing a jacket. This is because the only witness who could positively identify Oswald on the bus was Mrs. Mary Bledsoe, a former landlady of Oswald's. Mrs. Bledsoe said that Oswald looked "like a maniac. His sleeve was out here . . . his shirt was undone . . . and his face was so distorted." Every other witness who saw Oswald after the assassination testified that he was calm, well-mannered, and neat. Mrs. Bledsoe swore that Oswald's shirt had a hole in the right sleeve at the elbow. How did she know this? A Secret Service man brought the shirt to her home and showed it to her shortly before her testimony to the commission. The Secret Service man also gave Mrs. Bledsoe prepared notes for her testimony before the commission because, as she observed, "*I forget what I have to say.*"[3]

The evidence of Oswald's bus ride is unconvincing. The bus transfer that he supposedly had in his pocket would be a certain identification. However, Deputy Sheriff Roger Craig and a former Dallas police officer have stated that no transfer was in his possession when he was arrested. This would imply that the police deliberately planted the transfer in order to implicate Oswald. In any event, Mrs. Bledsoe's testimony is the only other source of information that Oswald may have been on the bus. Her testimony that Oswald was wearing a shirt and no jacket conflicts with McWatters's and Jones's observations (if they did see Oswald on the bus). It should be noted that Patrolman Marrion Baker, who saw Oswald in the second-floor lunchroom, also testified that Oswald was wearing a jacket, as did William Whaley, the cab driver whom we shall discuss next. Despite the fact that Mrs. Bledsoe's descriptions of Oswald's clothing, appearance, and demeanor conflicted with every other description, the commission accepted her testimony as accurate.[4]

THE TAXI RIDE

After traveling a couple of blocks, McWatters's bus became caught in an immense traffic jam resulting from the frantic happenings at nearby Dealey Plaza. According to the commission, Oswald departed the bus at 12:44 and walked several blocks to a Greyhound bus station. There he entered a cab driven by William Whaley and rode to the 500 or 700 block of North Beckley Avenue, near his rooming house. After paying his taxi fare, Oswald then walked the remaining distance to the rooming house at 1026 North Beckley.[5]

The only evidence about the cab ride is the testimony of William Whaley. A few hours after Oswald was arrested, Whaley viewed a police lineup in which Oswald was one of the people. According to Whaley, "You could have picked him out without identifying him by just listening to him because he was bawling out the policeman, telling him it wasn't right to put him in line with these teenagers." The Warren Commission stated that it was "satisfied that the lineup was conducted fairly." Yet Whaley went on to note that Oswald "was the only one that had the bruise on his head . . . the only one who acted surly . . . you wouldn't have had to have known who it was to have picked him out by the way he acted." The other three men in the lineup looked like "young teenagers" to Whaley. He said they were all dressed differently from Oswald. Yet he *still* chose the wrong man, eighteen-year-old David Knapp, who did not even resemble Oswald.[6]

Whaley told the Warren Commission that the Dallas police made him sign an affadavit attesting to what he saw in the lineup *before* he saw the lineup. "I signed that statement before they carried me down to see the lineup. I signed this statement, and then they carried me down to the lineup." He was also not permitted to read what he had signed.[7]

The time Oswald entered Whaley's taxicab made the Warren Commission aware of the tight timetable which the events of 22 November created. The commission believed that Oswald killed Tippit at 1:15 P.M. and that he walked from his rooming house to the scene of the Tippit murder in twelve minutes. This had him leaving the house at 1:03 P.M. after staying there for about three minutes. Since he entered Whaley's cab at 12:48, and since it took six minutes to walk from where Whaley let him out to the rooming house, the cab ride could not have taken more than six minutes.[8]

The distance from the Greyhound bus terminal where Whaley picked Oswald up to the place where Oswald left the cab is 2.5 miles. If the trip took six minutes, as the commission claimed, then Whaley averaged 25 miles per hour, part of the journey being through the congested traffic conditions around Dealey Plaza. The reader is reminded that the commission refused to believe the two eyewitnesses who saw Jack Ruby at Parkland Hospital because it stated that the traffic was so congested that Ruby could not possibly have driven the three miles to the hospital in fifteen minutes. Yet, miraculously, Whaley managed to drive straight through the same traffic at the same time as Ruby. The commission obviously was going to get Oswald to his rooming house by 1 P.M. regardless of extenuating circumstances because it had a rigid timetable to meet. Ruby's presence at Parkland Hospital would have been an embarrassment to the commission's no-conspiracy thesis. Therefore, in spite of the strong eyewitness evidence, it refused to acknowledge that it was possible.[9]

In order to determine the time for the cab ride, the commission had Whaley reconstruct it. After driving his cab twice over the route, Whaley noted the time for the trip, without having to stop for a red light: nine minutes. Since this was too long to fit the commission's timetable, Whaley was driven over the route by a Secret Service agent, who made the trip in six minutes. The Secret Service driver drove to the 700 block of North Beckley, even though Whaley originally believed that he had let Oswald out in the 500 block. The extra two blocks made no difference to the Warren Commission. In discussing this matter, the *Report* makes one of its most astounding statements. "If he was discharged at Neely and Beckley (the 700 block) and walked directly to his roominghouse, he would have arrived there about 12:59 to 1 P.M. From the 500 block of North Beckley, the walk would be a few minutes longer, but in either event he would have been in the roominghouse at about 1 P.M." To the commission, Oswald could have walked the extra two blocks in no time![10]

THE TESTIMONY OF ROGER B. CRAIG

The *Warren Report* mentions that Dallas Deputy Sheriff Roger Craig claimed that about fifteen minutes after the assassination, he saw Oswald run from the rear of the Depository building, scamper down an incline to Elm Street, and enter a Rambler station wagon driven by a dark complected man. According to the commission, "Craig may have seen a person enter a white [*sic*] Rambler station wagon 15 or 20 minutes after the shooting . . . but the Commission has concluded that this man was not Lee Harvey Oswald, because of the overwhelming evidence that Oswald was far away from the building by that time."[11]

What was that "overwhelming evidence?" It should be mentioned first that even if the commission's version is accepted, Oswald was *not* "far away from the building by that time." According to the commission, at 12:44 Oswald was getting off McWatters's bus only five blocks east of the Depository building. He then walked for four minutes to the Greyhound bus station only four blocks away. The "overwhelming evidence" is the testimony of William Whaley. Remember that Whaley failed to select Oswald out of a police lineup as his taxicab passenger. He also testified that Oswald was wearing *two* jackets, while the commission claimed that he wore none. In his taxi logbook,

Whaley recorded the time of his pickup at the bus station as 12:30, yet the commission said that the real time was 12:48.[12]

Let us now examine Roger Craig's testimony in order to determine if it is consistent and accurate and supported by other evidence. Deputy Craig watched the motorcade in front of the Criminal Courts building on Houston Street. After hearing the shots, he raced to the Grassy Knoll area. Photographs of the scene show Craig in the large crowd of people converging on the knoll after the shooting. Craig then returned to the south side of Elm Street. As he was standing there with a group of law enforcement officials, he noticed a man run down the grassy embankment to the right front of the Texas School Book Depository building. A light green Rambler station wagon, driven by a heavy-set, dark-complected man, was traveling west on Elm Street. As the running man reached the curb, the station wagon stopped and the man entered.[13]

Later that afternoon Craig went to police headquarters. He entered the interrogation room where Oswald was being questioned. Craig identified Oswald as the man who entered the station wagon. The Warren Commission chose not to believe Deputy Sheriff Craig. The man who interrogated Oswald, Captain J. Will Fritz of the Dallas police, told the commission that Craig never entered his office. The commission, therefore, "could not accept important elements of Craig's testimony."[14]

There is, in fact, substantial evidence that provides far more corroboration for Craig's testimony than for the totally unsubstantiated statements of Whaley. Carolyn Walther was watching the motorcade from Houston Street. She saw a man standing on the fourth or fifth floor in the southeast corner window of the Depository building. He was holding a gun. Next to him was a man dressed in a brown sport coat. Shortly after the assassination, James Worrell saw a man run out of the back of the Depository. The man was five feet eight inches to five feet ten inches tall, average weight, had dark hair, and was wearing a dark sports jacket. The man was moving south on Houston Street.[15]

Richard Randolph Carr watched the motorcade from Houston and Commerce streets. Shortly before the shooting, he saw a man wearing a brown sport coat in an upper floor of the Book Depository building. A couple of minutes after the shooting, Carr saw this same man walking very fast heading south on Houston Street. After going around the block, the man entered a grey or green Rambler station wagon. Marvin Robinson was driving his car west on Elm Street about fifteen minutes after the shooting. He saw a man come down the grassy incline and enter a Rambler station wagon, which then drove away.[16]

Mrs. James Forrest was standing in a group of people who had gathered on the incline near the Grassy Knoll. As she was standing, she saw a man suddenly run from the rear of the Depository building, down the incline, and then enter a Rambler station wagon. The man she saw running down and entering the station wagon strongly resembled Lee Harvey Oswald. "If it wasn't Oswald," Mrs. Forrest has declared, "it was his identical twin." The testimony of Walther, Worrel, Carr, Robinson, and Forrest all provide strong substantiation for Roger Craig's story.[17]

Craig's story is also supported by photographic evidence. One photograph shows Deputy Craig running toward the Grassy Knoll. Another shows him standing near the Grassy Knoll. Another shows him standing on the south side of Elm Street looking toward the Book Depository building. In the same photograph, a light colored Rambler station wagon can be seen heading west on Elm Street. In another photograph, Craig is seen looking toward Elm Street in the general direction of the station wagon. Oswald is not visible in the picture. However, a large bus immediately in front of the station wagon blocks the view of anyone approaching it. Two photographs show Captain Fritz, Lee Harvey Oswald, and Deputy Sheriff Roger Craig all together in Fritz's interrogation room.[18]

Despite this impressive corroboration for Craig's testimony, the Warren Commission chose to reject it. Instead, it accepted the unsubstantiated and contradictory testimony of taxi driver William Whaley. There is no corroboration for Whaley's story. Whaley did tell the commission that when Oswald entered his cab, an elderly lady tried to enter it from the opposite side. Oswald volunteered to let her have the cab, but the lady refused because another taxi was waiting just behind Whaley's. There is no indication that the commission attempted to locate the other cab. Both the driver and the lady could have supported Whaley's observations. By studying the logbook of the other cab, it would be possible to attempt to trace the lady. Neither the police nor the commission did so.[19]

Whaley testified that Oswald "had on two jackets." The commission decided he wore none. At the police lineup, Whaley picked out eighteen-year-old David Knapp instead of twenty-four-year-old Lee Harvey Oswald (Knapp did not even resemble Oswald). Whaley registered 12:30 P.M. in his logbook as the time when his passenger entered the cab. This, of course, eliminated Oswald, since Oswald was in the Depository building at that time. The commission attempted to explain this by noting that Whaley recorded all trips at fifteen-minute intervals, regardless of how long the actual trip took. Since the commission decided that Oswald entered the cab at 12:47 or 12:48, it did not explain why Whaley entered 12:30 instead of 12:45 in his book. Nor did it explain why other trips were entered as 6:20, 7:50, 8:10, 9:40, 10:50, and 3:10, rather than regular quarter-hour intervals. In his original log, Whaley entered 500 North Beckley as the spot where he let Oswald out. The commission decided that Whaley was wrong here, also.[20]

It should be obvious to the disinterested observer that the Warren Commission was trying to fabricate a case against Oswald as a lone assassin and murderer. There is not one iota of evidence to substantiate Whaley's testimony about the cab ride. Deputy Sheriff Craig's story is supported by the testimony of five other witnesses as well as five photographs. Yet the commission believed Whaley's story and did not accept Craig's. The reason, no doubt, is that Craig's story would have built a very strong case for conspiracy.[21]

At 1 P.M. Oswald entered his rooming house at 1026 North Beckley Avenue. He went to his room and left, wearing a jacket, about three or four minutes later. The source of this information is the testimony of the housekeeper, Mrs. Earlene Roberts. Her testimony included several observations that cast doubt on the commission's story.

First, Mrs. Roberts told the commission that just after Oswald went to his room, a police car (Dallas squad car number 107 or 207), with two officers inside, parked in front of the rooming house. The driver sounded his horn twice, a "beep-beep" tone. The commission decided that Mrs. Roberts was mistaken about the police car because "investigation has not produced any evidence that there was a police vehicle in the area of 1026 N. Beckley at about 1 P.M. on November 22." This is not quite accurate. The last known location of Officer Tippit was Lancaster and Eighth, only a few blocks away from 1026 North Beckley. The number 207 squad car was, according to the commission, parked at the Depository Building at 1 P.M. But the driver of car 207 testified that he parked his car there and then went into the building. His car remained outside. It is possible that another police officer may have driven it away.[22]

Mrs. Roberts's testimony about Oswald's jacket also conflicts with the commission's. She stated that Oswald's jacket was dark, but the jacket allegedly discarded by the Tippit killer was very light gray. The commission claimed that Mrs. Roberts was unsure about the color of Oswald's jacket. Her actual testimony, however, was, "I recall the jacket was a dark color." Somehow Oswald managed either to change jackets or to lighten the color of the one he wore between the time he left the rooming house and the time he shot Tippit.[23]

Mrs. Roberts also stated that when Oswald left the rooming house, he stood by the bus stop. The bus stop is for the *north-bound* Beckley Avenue bus. The scene of the Tippit slaying was *south* of the rooming house. If Oswald was hurrying toward the Tippit rendezvous, then his actions were strange. Why he would have waited for a bus headed in the opposite direction was one question the commission failed to answer.[24]

It is nearly one mile, by the shortest route, from 1026 North Beckley to Tenth and Patton streets, where the Tippit slaying occurred. Although there is absolutely no evidence of any kind to indicate the route Oswald traveled to get to the scene of the Tippit murder, the Warren Commission arbitrarily decided that he took the shortest possible route. Commission Counsel David Belin walked the route, and it took 12 minutes. Several commission critics have falsely claimed that Belin took 17 minutes and 45 seconds. This longer time was, in actuality, when Belin took the long route to Tenth and Patton.[25]

Oswald left the rooming house at 1:03 P.M. It took him a minimum of 12 minutes to walk to Tenth and Patton. Therefore, he could not have arrived there before 1:15 P.M. The evidence is inconclusive about the exact time of the Tippit murder. But several bits of information strongly suggest that Tippit was killed *before* 1:15. The only two eyewitnesses who noted the time of the slaying, T.F. Bowley and Helen Markham, swore that it took place at 1:10 and 1:06, respectively. Bowley was never called as a witness before the commission. Mrs. Markham, the commission's star eyewitness, steadfastly contended that the time of the shooting was 1:06. If Bowley and Markham were correct, Oswald could not have shot Tippit. He simply did not have enough time to walk the mile in six to nine minutes (even the commission conceded that he did not run).[26]

At 1:16 P.M. the Dallas police received an emergency call from Tippit's car radio that an officer had been shot. The call came several minutes *after* the shooting. T.F. Bowley stated that as he turned his car onto Tenth Street, he saw a police officer lying on the street next to his squad car. Bowley got out of his car and walked to the scene. He looked at his watch and it said 1:10 P.M. "When I got there," Bowley stated in an affadavit, "the first thing I did was to try to help the officer." After concluding that Tippit was "beyond help," Bowley noticed a man trying to use Tippit's police radio. The man did not know how to operate it, so Bowley took the radio from him and called the police dispatcher and informed him that an officer had been shot.[27]

The man who tried to use the radio was Domingo Benavides, who had witnessed the actual shooting of Officer Tippit. Benavides was stopped in a truck about twenty-five feet from the scene. He stated to the commission that after the killer shot Tippit, he fled around the corner of a house. Benavides then "set there for just a few minutes . . . I thought he went in back of the house or something. At the time I thought maybe he might have lived in there and I didn't want to get out and rush right up. He might start shooting again." Then, after waiting a few minutes, Benavides went to the radio. At this time, Bowley appeared on the scene.[28]

The testimony of both Bowley and Benavides makes it clear that the actual murder of J.D. Tippit took place several minutes *before* the radio call to the Dallas police at 1:16. How long before

1:16 is not known, but the commission's estimate of 1:15 as the time of the shooting is obviously not in accordance with the testimony. The commission apparently was attempting to set the time of the shooting as late as possible in order to give Oswald more time to reach the scene of the crime.[29]

THE EYEWITNESSES

The Warren Commission based its conclusion that Oswald killed Tippit upon the testimony of eyewitnesses and upon certain physical evidence. Six eyewitnesses identified Oswald at a police lineup and three others identified him from a photograph. Of these nine witnesses, only one actually saw the shooting. The others identified Oswald as the man they saw fleeing the scene.

The only eyewitness to the shooting who identified Oswald was Helen Louise Markham. Mrs. Markham was standing on the corner of Tenth and Patton streets, approximately seventy feet from the shooting. In her testimony before the commission, Mrs. Markham was questioned by Commission Counsel Joseph Ball about her identification of Oswald at the police lineup.

Ball: "Now when you went into the room you looked these people over, these four men?"
Markham: "Yes, sir."
Ball: "Did you recognize anyone in the line-up?"
Markham: "No, sir."
Ball: "You did not? Did you see anybody—I have asked you that question before [Before the testimony began, Ball had told Mrs. Markham what he was going to ask]—did you recognize anybody from their face?"
Markham: "From their face, no." [In courts of law, identification by the *face* is the only admissible type].
Ball: "No one of the four?"
Markham: "No one of them."
Ball: "No one of all four."
Markham: "No, sir."
Ball: "Did you identify anybody in these four people?"
Markham: "I didn't know nobody [*sic*]. I had never seen none of them, none of these men."

By now the reader is undoubtedly wondering how the commission can label Mrs. Markham as a witness *against* Oswald. Her testimony to this point clearly establishes that she did *not* recognize Oswald in the lineup. The commission counsel was not to be deterred. Having asked five times whether Mrs. Markham could identify anyone in the lineup, he received an unequivocal "No" response each time. Ball then asked a question that can only be termed as a blatantly leading one. "Was there a number two man in there?" Mrs. Markham finally took this "hint" and replied, "Number two is the one I picked. . . . Number two was the man I saw shoot the policeman. . . . I looked at him. When I saw this man *I wasn't sure,* but I had cold chills just run all over me."[30]

Thus, it was "cold chills" rather than a recognition of Oswald's face which prompted Helen Markham to identify Oswald as Tippit's killer. Mrs. Markham, who cited the time of the slaying as 1:06 P.M., who did not recognize Oswald by his face, who "wasn't sure" when she looked at him, and whose "cold chills" convinced her, is nevertheless cited by the Warren Commission as a positive eyewitness identification of Oswald.

Helen Markham stated Oswald approached Tippit from the west, while another witness and the commission claimed he came from the east. She said she saw Oswald lean into an open window of the car; two witnesses and a photograph confirm that all windows were closed. She stated that Tippit tried to speak to her; all other witnesses, the commission, and the coroner found that he died instantly. She stated that she was alone with Tippit for twenty minutes; all other witnesses state that a large crowd gathered immediately. It is quite obvious that had Oswald been represented by a good defense attorney, Mrs. Markham would have had a few discrepancies to account for.[31]

In the commission's account, J.D. Tippit, who was a "fine, dedicated officer," was driving his patrol car when he saw a man who fit the general description of the suspect wanted in the murder of President Kennedy. This "fine, dedicated officer," who had the chance to make the arrest of a lifetime, did not try to arrest this dangerous suspect, nor did he draw his gun (according to the wanted description broadcast over the police radio, the suspect was carrying a 30.06 [*sic*] rifle). Instead, he called the man over to his car and began having a casual conversation with him.[32]

The closest eyewitness to the Tippit murder was Domingo Benavides, who was driving a truck on Tenth Street and was only about twenty-five feet away from the scene of the shooting. Benavides's description of the killer was of a man so unlike Oswald that he was not even taken to the lineup. Having viewed numerous pictures of Oswald on television and in magazines, Benavides steadfastly refused to identify him as the killer. When he appeared before a commission counsel in April 1964, Benavides again stated that he could not identify Oswald as the killer. Three years later, however, Benavides did tell CBS News that now he was sure that Lee Harvey Oswald had shot Officer Tippit. For some reason, Benavides had suffered an immediate loss of memory, and it took three years for it to be refreshed.[33]

One eyewitness was not even questioned by the Warren Commission or by the FBI. Mrs. Acquilla Clemons saw two men standing near the Tippit automobile. One of the men, "short and heavy," shot Tippit. The other man was tall and thin. After the shooting, they ran away in different directions. Mrs. Clemons stated that the Dallas police warned her not to reveal what she saw because she might get killed.[34]

Other witnesses not heard by the commission included Mr. and Mrs. Frank Wright, who also saw two men at the scene of the crime. Newly released FBI documents on the assassination reveal that a fourteen-year-old boy, also never questioned by the commission, witnessed the Tippit slaying. He stated that the man who shot Tippit was wearing dark pants and a very light-colored shirt. It is noteworthy that the first wanted description of the Tippit slaying suspect described him as "wearing white shirt and black slacks." The FBI was aware of both Mrs. Clemons and the Wrights. Yet, incredibly, J. Edgar Hoover ordered Gordon Shanklin, special agent in charge of the Dallas FBI office, *not* to interview these witnesses.[35]

Eight other witnesses identified Oswald as the man they saw fleeing the scene of the crime. Five of the witnesses identified Oswald in a lineup; three identified him from a photograph. The most persuasive of these witnesses was a cab driver, William Scoggins. Scoggins was sitting in his cab, heard the shooting, and saw Oswald fleeing the scene. Critics of the Warren Commission have either ignored or attempted to discredit the testimony of these witnesses. The evidence, however, strongly indicates that Oswald was in the vicinity of the Tippit murder scene. Whether he actually pulled the trigger is neither proven nor disproven by the eyewitness testimony.[36]

THE PHYSICAL EVIDENCE

The .38 caliber revolver was in Oswald's possession when he was arrested at the Texas theater approximately forty-five minutes after the Tippit slaying. Unlike the evidence concerning the rifle, which aroused controversy, there is overwhelming evidence that Oswald did own the revolver. The four cartridge cases were found lying on the ground near the scene of the murder. Apparently, the killer opened the chamber of his gun and manually ejected the cases. This is an unusual procedure, since revolvers usually contain automatic ejection mechanisms whereby all six shells are ejected at once. It is also unusual that the murderer did not attempt at once to flee the scene of the crime. Instead, he deliberately stopped and discarded four vital pieces of evidence that could have been used against him. The Warren Commission made no comment about these peculiar occurrences. Two of the commission's witnesses against Oswald, Ted Callaway and Sam Guinyard, both testified that they saw the killer fleeing the scene, but neither saw him drop the cartridge cases. In any event, the four cartridge cases were traced to Oswald's revolver, although they were never matched to the bullets.[37]

The Warren Commission claimed that four bullets were recovered from Officer Tippit's body, although it presented no evidence to substantiate this claim. It also failed to mention in its *Report* that only one of the four bullets was turned over to the FBI at the time of the slaying. The Dallas police turned it over to the FBI, stating that it was "the only bullet that was recovered." The other three bullets were located in a file drawer at Dallas police headquarters in March 1964, almost four months after the murder. The commission did not attempt to investigate these unusual circumstances in which the three extra bullets were discovered.[38]

FBI ballistics expert Cortlandt Cunningham examined the bullets and concluded that "it was not possible from an examination and comparison of these bullets to determine whether or not they had been fired—these bullets themselves—had been fired from one weapon, or whether or not they had been fired from Oswald's revolver." The reason was that Oswald's revolver had an oversized barrel. Bullets fired through the barrel were marked differently each time. In ballistics identification, several test bullets are fired from a weapon. If it is suspected that the test bullets have markings identical to the bullets in question, they can all be inspected through a comparison microscope to obtain confirmation. The bullet in question, for example, a bullet removed from a dead body, must match the test bullet in all observable markings, scratches, grooves, and the like. If the test bullet and the bullet removed from the body match, it is firm evidence that that bullet was fired from the same weapon that fired the test bullets.[39]

In the case of Oswald's revolver, however, the test bullets themselves did not match because of the oversized barrel. That is why Cunningham concluded that it was "not possible" to state that the Tippit bullets came from Oswald's revolver. Since the FBI could not verify the assumption that Oswald killed Tippit, the Warren Commission called on an obscure Illinois State Police expert, Joseph Nicol, to examine the bullets. Nicol concluded that one of the four bullets contained sufficient markings to enable him to state that it was fired from the same revolver that had fired the test bullets.[40]

Thus, the commission chose to ignore the best evidence and to accept that which was clearly of little value. The FBI expert, Cunningham, concluded that there was simply no way to determine if any of the bullets were fired from Oswald's revolver because the test bullets themselves bore different markings. Nicol, however, concluded that some of the lands and grooves on one of the bullets matched those on one of the test bullets, a feat of ballistics identification characterized by the FBI as "not possible."[41]

To add to the evidence against Oswald, the Warren Commission asserted that a jacket found several blocks from the scene of the Tippit killing had been discarded by Oswald during his flight away from the area. There is only very scanty evidence to support the commission's claim. Marina Oswald testified that her husband owned a similar jacket, and several witnesses believed that the jacket resembled one Oswald was wearing when they saw him. Most of the witnesses who saw Oswald, however, swore that he was wearing either no jacket or one of a darker color than the one found near the murder site. These witnesses included Mrs. Earlene Roberts and Mrs. Helen Markham, both of whom were extensively quoted by the commission as part of its case. No external physical evidence, such as fingerprints or shirt fibers, linking Oswald to the jacket was discovered. No evidence that Oswald ever purchased a jacket was discovered by the commission.[42]

Approximately forty minutes after Tippit was shot, Lee Harvey Oswald was arrested in the Texas theater, five blocks away from the scene of the crime. The commission had already described Oswald as a block-a-minute walker during his various escapades subsequent to the assassination. Yet somehow it took him, in the commission's own version, thirty minutes to *run* five blocks.[43]

SUMMARY

As is the case with the assassination of President Kennedy, the evidence about the murder of J.D. Tippit is inconclusive. On the one hand, the evidence of the bus transfer and Mrs. Bledsoe's testimony support the Warren Commission's contention that Oswald caught a bus several minutes after the assassination. The testimony of Mrs. Markham and the other witnesses establish Oswald's presence near the scene of the shooting of Officer Tippit. The fact that the four cartridge cases found near the scene were fired from Oswald's revolver indicate the possibility that he may have shot Tippit.

On the other hand, the testimony of Deputy Sheriff Roger Craig, strongly supported by eyewitness and photographic evidence, indicates that Oswald may have had accomplices in

Dealey Plaza, and that they transported him away from the area. The facts that three of the four eyewitnesses to the Tippit killing did not believe Oswald was the murderer and that three witnesses saw two men fleeing the scene of the crime contradict the commission's thesis. In any event, none of the four bullets could be linked to Oswald's revolver.

The Warren Commission clearly strained the evidence in order to find Oswald guilty of the murder of J.D. Tippit. That evidence simply does not establish Oswald's guilt, although, of course, neither does it establish his innocence.

CHAPTER 8

A PRESUMPTION OF GUILT

THE WARREN COMMISSION tried Lee Harvey Oswald for the murders of John F. Kennedy and J.D. Tippit and for the wounding of John B. Connally. It found him guilty on all three counts. Unfortunately, the commission chose not to conduct its investigation or hearings under the adversary process, which is the basis of the American system of justice. Nor did it tender Oswald the basic presumption of innocence until proven guilty, a presumption that forms another integral feature of our system of justice.

In the *Warren Report,* the commission stated that it did not operate as a court of law. Rather, it was a fact-finding body, assigned by President Lyndon Johnson the task of determining the truth about the assassination. It is true that the commission fell under no obligation to conduct its business under the prescribed processes of law. Nevertheless, considering the seriousness of the crime, it would have been far more in the interest of justice if the commission had so operated. This is particularly true since the chief justice of the United States was himself chairman of the commission, which bears his name.

Even though Lee Harvey Oswald was dead by the time the Warren Commission was established, he was widely publicized as the assassin. Less than two weeks after the commission was created, the FBI released its five-hundred-page report on the assassination. That report stated without reservation that Oswald was the sole assassin and that there was no evidence of a conspiracy. The commission accepted the conclusions of the FBI report from the beginning. Rather than conduct its own independent investigation, the commission relied entirely on the FBI report. The *Warren Report* is, in fact, little more than an expanded version of the FBI document. Indeed, the commission employed the FBI to do virtually all of its investigative work.[1]

The result is that from the beginning, the Warren Commission operated on the presumptions that Oswald was guilty and that there was no conspiracy. This is confirmed by a recently declassified memorandum from Deputy Attorney General Nicholas Katzenbach to Presidential Assistant Bill Moyers. Written only three days after the assassination, the memorandum explains why the president should appoint a commission to investigate the assassination. The purpose of such a commission, Katzenbach wrote, was not to investigate the facts of the case. Rather, "*the public must be satisfied that Oswald was the assassin;* that he did not have confederates who are still at large; and that the evidence is such that he would have been convicted at trial."[2]

In its investigation of the assassination, the commission demonstrated its presumption of Oswald's guilt. Only witnesses against Oswald, with but few exceptions, were permitted to testify. No cross-examination of witnesses was allowed. Numerous vital witnesses were never even questioned. For example, only seven of the over two dozen witnesses to the autopsy of President Kennedy were questioned. Such significant evidence as the Kennedy and Tippit autopsy photographs and X-rays, the original Zapruder film, and over three hundred photographs and films of the assassination were never examined by the commission. Such witnesses favorable to the commission's thesis as Howard Brennan and Mary Bledsoe were handled with kid gloves by commission counsels. Such witnesses unfavorable to the thesis as Arnold Rowland and Roger Craig were treated with disbelief and contempt. In some cases, evidence was deliberately distorted in order to make it conform to the official version. We have already seen numerous examples of the commission's mishandling of evidence. In this chapter we shall explore this matter in further detail.

THE AUTOPSY

The *Warren Report* leaves the public with the impression that there was never any controversy about the wounds inflicted on President Kennedy. It cites the autopsy report as the definitive statement about the wounds and clearly conveys the false impression that the autopsy surgeons concluded, during the autopsy, that only two bullets struck the president, both fired from above and behind him.[3]

The evidence indicates otherwise. First, the *Report* fails to mention that Dr. Humes, the chief autopsy surgeon, burned his notes made during the postmortem examination of the president's body. This deliberate destruction of important evidence by Dr. Hume was not questioned by the commission. Second, the *Report* did not mention the fact that none of the three doctors who performed the autopsy were competent forensic pathologists. Speaking of one of the autopsy doctors, Dr. J. Thorton Boswell, world-renowned forensic pathologist Milton Helpern stated that the *Warren Report* did not mention Dr. Boswell's qualifications "because he had absolutely none worthy of mention."[4]

The official autopsy report on President Kennedy is not dated. The exact date when it was prepared is unknown. New evidence recently made available indicates that the autopsy protocol published in the *Warren Report* was written *months after* the assassination. For over ten years, the transcripts of the secret Executive Sessions of the Warren Commission of 22 January 1964 and 27 January 1964 were classified Top Secret. The public release of the transcripts proves beyond question that the original autopsy was destroyed and replaced by one more favorable to the commission's lone-assassin theory.

The transcript of the 27 January 1964 meeting quotes J. Lee Rankin, chief counsel to the commission.

Rankin: then there is a great range of material in regard to the wounds, the autopsy and *this point of exit or entrance of the bullet in the front of the neck, and all that has to be developed much more than we have at the present time.*

We have an explanation there in the autopsy that probably a fragment came out of the front of the neck. . . .

Rep. Hale Boggs: I thought I read that bullet just went in a finger's length.

Rankin: That's what they first said. They reached in and they could feel where it came, *it didn't go any further than that,* about part of the finger or something. . . .

So the basic problem, what kind of a wound it is in the front of the neck is of great importance to the investigation.

We believe it must be related in some way to the three sheets [*sic*] from the rear.[5]

Thus, on 27 January 1964, over two months after the assassination and the autopsy, the Warren Commission was unable to determine whether or not President Kennedy was shot in the front of the neck. Obviously, if the wound in the front of the neck was an entrance wound, it could only have been inflicted by an assassin firing from the front of the limousine. Clearly, the autopsy report which the commission had at the time of the meeting was not nearly as definite about the wound as the autopsy published in the *Report.*

Other commission documents suggest the inaccuracy of information from the original autopsy. For example, in a 23 January 1964 memorandum, J. Lee Rankin noted that there was "a considerable amount of confusion as to the actual path of the bullets which hit President Kennedy, particularly the one which entered the right side of his back." A 12 March 1964 memorandum from Arlen Specter, commission counsel in charge of the medical evidence, to Rankin notes that "the autopsy surgeons made substantial efforts to determine if there was a missile in President Kennedy's body to explain what happened to the bullet which *apparently* entered the back of the body." Another 12 March 1964 memorandum by Specter states that "the bullet traveled in a consistent downward path, *on the assumption that it emerged in the opening on the President's throat.*"[6]

The most revealing document is another memorandum by Specter to Rankin. It is dated 30 April 1964, over five months after the "official autopsy report" and over six weeks after the three autopsy surgeons testified before the commission. "1. *The Commission should determine with certainty whether the shots came from the rear* . . . With all the outstanding controversy about the direction of the shots, there must be independent viewings of the films (X-rays and photographs) to verify testimony which has come only from Government doctors. 2. *The Commission should determine with certainty whether the shots came from above.*" This document was suppressed from the commission's files at the National Archives for over three years.[7]

The preponderance of evidence compels the conclusion that

the original autopsy report of President Kennedy was so vague and ambiguous about such essential matters as the source and direction of the shots that a new and greatly altered version of the autopsy was substituted for it. Over five months after the assassination, the Warren Commission was still uncertain whether the shots came from above and from the rear. It should be noted that the "independent viewings" of the autopsy materials called for by Specter were never forthcoming. On the contrary, the commission made no attempt to obtain expert medical advice besides that of the "Government doctors."

The autopsy surgeons apparently believed that a bullet entered the president's back, penetrated less than a finger's length, and then worked its way out of the body during external cardiac massage performed at Parkland Hospital. The official FBI report of the autopsy confirms this. If the bullet did not exit from the body, then the tiny hole in the president's throat must have been an entrance wound. The Warren Commission falsely reported that "further exploration during the autopsy disproved that theory."[8]

Two documents from the National Archives disclose the fact that a bullet was removed from the body during the autopsy. One is an FBI "receipt of a missile recovered by Commander James Humes." The other is an official receipt by the Protective Research Section (Secret Service) of the Treasury Department for various items including "one receipt from FBI for a missile removed during the examination of the body." Could this have been the bullet which struck him in the throat and, according to Dallas Dr. Kemp Clark, "ranged downward in his chest and did not exit"?[9]

THE REJECTION OF EVIDENCE

On 25 November 1963, three days after the assassination, two journalists were traveling to the Irving, Texas, home of Ruth Paine for an interview. As they entered the small community, they noticed a "gun repair" sign in a furniture store. They stopped at the store in order to see if Lee Harvey Oswald had ever been there. Two elderly ladies, Mrs. Edith Whitworth and Mrs. Gertrude Hunter, were sitting in the store. The reporters asked them if they had ever seen Oswald there. The ladies' response injected a new area of investigation in the Oswald saga.[10]

The ladies told the journalists that Oswald had come into the furniture store approximately two or three weeks before the assassination. He asked them where the gun repair shop referred to in the sign was. Mrs. Whitworth and Mrs. Hunter informed Oswald that there was no longer a gun shop in the furniture store and referred him to a gun repair shop several blocks away. Oswald remained in the store looking at furniture. He informed the ladies that he was looking for an apartment and wanted to buy some furniture.[11]

Later the same day Oswald returned to the store. This time he was accompanied by his wife and daughter. The Oswalds looked at furniture for about forty-five minutes and left. One feature of the story that deserves attention is that Oswald drove an automobile. Both times he entered the furniture store, Oswald had driven up in a 1957 blue Ford. Mrs. Hunter recalled the car because her son had one very similar.[12]

Corroboration for the ladies' story came when the journalists visited the Irving Sports Shop. There, gunsmith Dial Ryder told them that Oswald had indeed been to his shop on the same day that the ladies saw him in the furniture store. Oswald had Ryder bore holes in the rifle and mount a telescopic sight on it. The rifle was not the C2766 Mannlicher-Carcano. Ryder recalled it as a Mauser, a much more reliable and accurate weapon than the Mannlicher. He showed the journalists a repair tag with Oswald's name on it. The journalists cross-examined the ladies and Ryder three times. The three consistently picked Oswald's picture out of a group of photographs. The ladies picked Marina's picture from a group of photographs.[13]

The Warren Commission refused to accept the stories of Mrs. Whitworth, Mrs. Hunter, and Ryder. According to the *Warren Report,* Ryder does not remember that Oswald had ever been a customer. Ryder also failed to call the attention of his employer, Charles W. Greener, to the repair tag. "Marina Oswald," according to the *Report,* "testified that she had never been on the premises before," in referring to the furniture store. The commission determined that Oswald "apparently was not able to drive an automobile himself and does not appear to have had access to a car." The incident occurred on a weekday, and Oswald's worksheets showed that he was at work then. A friend of Mrs. Hunter's stated that she "has a strange obsession for attempting to inject herself into any big event."[14]

The commission concluded that Oswald had never been in the furniture store and that he did not leave another rifle at Ryder's repair shop. The journalists, however, both saw the repair tag with Oswald's name on it, and both interviewed the ladies and Ryder, who they decided were consistent and reliable witnesses. In its *Report* the commission did not mention the fact that Ryder's employer vouched for his veracity. Nor did it note that the ladies saw Marina in person and both swore that she was the woman who accompanied Oswald to the furniture store. By quoting a friend of Mrs. Hunter's, the commission attempted to cast her testimony in dubious light. Yet the commission refused to state that Helen Markham's own son believed that she was prone to fantasy and exaggeration.[15]

Indirect corroboration for the ladies' and for Ryder's stories can be found in the fact that substantial evidence exists that Oswald did possess a second rifle and that he did drive an automobile. This evidence was gathered by the reporters, by the FBI, and by the author.

The journalists visited several shooting ranges in Dallas and found one that Lee Harvey Oswald had practiced in. The manager of the rifle range stated that Oswald had come to the range in order to practice firing his rifle. The weapon was not a Mannlicher-Carcano, but an odd European weapon, possibly an altered Mauser. According to the range manager, Oswald caused a ruckus when he began shooting at other people's targets. After repeated complaints by the patrons, the manager asked Oswald to leave. Not only the range manager, but three other witnesses recall Oswald at the firing range. All four, experienced with and knowledgeable about different types of firearms, believe that Oswald had a different type of rifle from a Mannlicher-Carcano.[16]

One of the reporters rented a room at 1026 North Beckley Avenue, the house where Oswald lived at the time of the assassination. One of the tenants there recounted how Oswald had used his automobile, a 1957 Ford, which matched the description of the vehicle Mrs. Whitworth and Mrs. Hunter saw Oswald driving. Mrs. Earlene Roberts, the housekeeper at the rooming house, also observed Oswald driving a car. A Dallas used-car salesman remembered that Lee Harvey Oswald had test-driven an automobile only a couple of weeks before the assassination. Two service station owners, two service station employees, and three employees of cafes remember seeing Oswald driving a car during his trip from Mexico City to Dallas in October 1963. Newly declassified FBI documents disclose other examples of Oswald's driving. Six acquaintances of Oswald's during his stay in New Orleans in the summer of 1963 also verify the fact that Lee Harvey Oswald did drive a car. The only evidence to the contrary offered by the Warren Commission was that Oswald did not have a driver's license and that his wife testified that he did not drive.[17]

THE ODIO AFFAIR

The commission's handling of the Sylvia Odio affair is another example of its abuse of evidence. On 22 July 1964, Mrs. Odio told a Warren Commission lawyer that Lee Harvey Oswald, introduced to her as Leon Oswald, visited her in late September 1963. Leon was accompanied by two men who appeared to be Cuban or Mexican. One of the two Latins later told Mrs. Odio that Oswald was an ex-Marine and an expert rifleman, and that he planned to assassinate President Kennedy. The two Latins informed Mrs. Odio that they knew that she was engaged in clandestine anti-Castro activity and that they knew "incredible details" about her father, who was a political prisoner in Cuba.[18]

Mrs. Odio's testimony raised serious difficulties for the commission, for it presented the obvious possibility of a conspiracy. The commission's response was to request that the FBI conduct an investigation "to determine Mrs. Odio's veracity," a technique that it employed only against unfavorable witnesses. The FBI informed the commission that William Seymour, Lawrence Howard, and Loren Eugene Hall were the three men who visited Mrs. Odio. Seymour, Howard, and Hall were all associated with anti-Castro activities. None resembled Lee Harvey

Oswald, although J. Edgar Hoover speculated that Mrs. Odio mistook Hall for Oswald because the name Loren Hall sounds like Lee Oswald.[19]

The *Warren Report* was published before the FBI had completed its investigation of the Odio affair. Nevertheless, the *Report* concluded that Oswald could not have visited Mrs. Odio on 25 September 1963 because he was on a bus bound for Mexico City at the time and because the FBI said that Mrs. Odio mistook Hall for Oswald. The facts do not support the commission. Mrs. Odio did not remember the exact date when Oswald visited her. Mrs. Odio's sister also swore that Oswald was there. Hall admitted that he had lied, and that he, Howard, and Seymour had never visited Mrs. Odio. Mrs. Odio's description of Oswald as accompanied by Latins matched perfectly with the descriptions given by numerous witnesses from the New Orleans area. Finally, there is no indisputable evidence that Oswald was on a Mexico City bound bus on 25 September.[20]

THE DALLAS POLICE

The commission's treatment of the Dallas police is yet another example of its handling of evidence. We have already seen how the Dallas authorities conducted its lineups—placing Oswald in a lineup with men who looked much younger than he and who were dressed differently, having witnesses sign identification affadavits before they viewed the lineup, and listing witnesses as giving "positive identification" of Oswald, even though these witnesses were not certain. We have also seen how the commission dismissed these gross violations of justice with the simple remark that it was "satisfied that the lineups were conducted fairly."[21]

The commission also made no attempt to investigate the manner in which certain items of evidence incriminating Oswald mysteriously came into possession of the Dallas police. According to the *Warren Report,* Lieutenant J.C. Day, the Dallas police fingerprint expert, had lifted a palmprint of Oswald's from the underside of the rifle barrel. The "lifting" was accomplished with a strip of cellophane tape applied to the print, which had been dusted with powder. Day testified to the Warren Commission that after he had lifted the palmprint, "the print on the gun still remained. . . . there were traces of ridges still on the gun barrel." Yet, when the rifle was examined a few hours later by FBI fingerprint expert Sebastian Latona, no traces whatsoever of this print were found. Nor did Latona discover any evidence to indicate that Day had lifted a print off the barrel.[22]

This palmprint was the only print of Oswald's on the rifle and thus was an important link in the chain of evidence connecting Lee Harvey Oswald with the assassination. Nevertheless, the Dallas police did not divulge the existence of this print until it was sent to the FBI on 29 November, a week after the shooting. The commission was satisfied that the print was genuine because certain markings on the cellophane tape matched scratches and grooves on the rifle barrel. The commission, however, made no attempt to explain why the palmprint on the tape was flat, while one on a rifle barrel would necessarily have had to be curved in order to conform to the curvature of the barrel. Nor did it ascertain why Day thought traces of the print remained on the barrel, while Latona could find no evidence whatsoever of a print, dusting powder, or tape. Furthermore, usual police procedure is to photograph fingerprints in place, before they are lifted from their original locations. Although Day did photograph other prints on the rifle (none of which were complete enough to identify), he did not photograph the palmprint.[23]

The paper bag allegedly used by Oswald to carry the rifle into the Book Depository building is another piece of evidence magically produced by the Dallas police. There is absolutely no evidence of any kind that the bag was found near the sixth-floor southeast corner window of the building. Not even one of the first six Dallas police officers to enter the "assassin's nest" area remembers seeing a bag there. Numerous photographs were taken of the sixth floor, but not one reveals a bag. Dozens of photographs and newsreel films reveal Lieutenant Day removing the rifle from the building, but there are none of him with the bag. The Warren Commission nevertheless accepted without question Day's claim that the bag was found there. The commission even went so far as to publish a photograph of the sixth-floor area showing an empty space enclosed by a drawn-in dotted line as the location of the bag when discovered.[24]

The extraordinary circumstances surrounding the detention and death of Lee Harvey Oswald were also glossed over by the commission. It made no attempt to ascertain the reasons why the Dallas police made no tapes nor took any transcripts of the thirteen hours of interrogation of Oswald. Nor did the commission satisfactorily deal with the question of how Jack Ruby managed to evade seventy armed police officers and gun down Oswald on national television.[25]

The Dallas police arrested six individuals in Dealey Plaza within one hour of the Kennedy assassination. Photographic evidence of the arrests is ample. In a series of photographs, two Dallas policemen are shown leading three individuals from the railroad yards to the police command post at the corner of Elm and Houston streets and then toward the county jail on Houston Street. These three men have never been identified. Irresponsible critics of the Warren Commission have falsely claimed that two of the three men were E. Howard Hunt and Frank Sturgis, both of Watergate fame. The allegations about Hunt and Sturgis have been disproven. The real identities of the three men, however, have never been disclosed.[26]

The *Dallas Times-Herald* noted two other arrests in Dealey Plaza. A young man wearing horn-rimmed eyeglasses, a plaid coat, and a raincoat was apprehended near the Book Depository building. On 10 December 1963, the newspaper reported that a thirty-one-year-old man was arrested minutes after the assassination in the railroad yards, where a man was reported carrying a rifle. The suspect was arrested on charges of "investigation of conspiracy to commit murder." The charges were not dropped until three weeks after the assassination. Jim Braden, a man with a long FBI arrest record and with known ties to organized crime, was also arrested in Dealey Plaza. Finally, a Latin man was also arrested there shortly after the shooting and quickly released.[27]

The Warren Commission failed to investigate any of these curious events. In each arrest case, there are photographs of the suspects in police custody, testimony by law enforcement officials of the arrests, and, in the Jim Braden arrest, a documentary verification. The Dallas police failed to keep records of these arrests. Yet the commission neglected to uncover the reasons.[28]

That the Warren Commission presumed Lee Harvey Oswald guilty of the murder of John Kennedy is beyond dispute. The working papers of the commission, suppressed from public scrutiny for many years, clearly demonstrate the commission's bias against Oswald. For example, in a memorandum for members of the commission, Chairman Earl Warren referred to an outline of the investigation. The outline, prepared by Chief Counsel J. Lee Rankin, was drawn up in early January 1964, *before* the commission had done any investigating. The longest part of the outline was entitled "Lee Harvey Oswald as the Assassin of President Kennedy." The commission thus began its investigation with the *a priori* conjecture that Oswald was the assassin. Nowhere, in any of the transcripts of commission sessions nor in the documentary evidence of commission procedure, can the simple question "Who killed President Kennedy?" be found.[29]

The evidence also explicitly proves that the commission relied almost entirely on the 9 December 1963 FBI report of the assassination. That report clearly concludes that Oswald was guilty and that no conspiracy was involved. In the 27 January 1964 executive session of the commission, Rankin refers to the FBI report: "They have decided that it is Oswald who committed the assassination." Commission member Senator Richard Russell agreed: "They [the FBI] have tried the case and reached a verdict on every aspect." Even though the commission was aware of the FBI findings, it made no attempt to conduct an inquiry independent of the bureau. On the contrary, it relied on the FBI for almost all of its investigative work and for analysis of most of the material evidence.[30]

On 14 March 1964, *before* the commission had heard most witnesses and *before* it had examined such crucial aspects of the case as the medical and ballistics evidence, a "Proposed Outline of Report of the Commission" was prepared by Commission Counsel Norman Redlich. Section IV of the outline was labeled "Lee H. Oswald as the Assassin." Article I of Section IV reads "Appraisal of Oswald's Actions of November 21 and 22 in Light of Assassination." Under Article I, Redlich remarked, "This will be a difficult section, but I feel we must face up the various paradoxical aspects of Oswald's behavior *in light of his being the assassin.*" Redlich's proposed outline was approved by Rankin and became the basis for the *Warren Report.* How Rankin and his staff could know what the *Report* would state before most of the evidence had been analyzed is not explained.[31]

In a 27 January 1964 memorandum to Rankin, staff lawyer W. David Slawson wrote, "This tends to shorten the time slightly during which Oswald would have had to pull the trigger three times on his rifle." Before any testimony or evidence had been studied, Slawson was already certain that Oswald fired the rifle three times. In another memorandum to Rankin, Norman Redlich noted, "our intention . . . is to substantiate the *hypothesis* which underlies the conclusion that Oswald was the sole assassin." Three days later Rankin told the commission that it is "reasonable to *assume* that he did what the Commission concludes that he [Oswald] did do."[32]

The Warren Commission's work was handled mainly by staff lawyers, who did the greater portion of interviewing witnesses and supervising the various tests on ballistics and other physical evidence. Of the 552 witnesses interviewed by the commission staff, only 94 actually testified before the commission itself. Many important witnesses were never questioned by any commission members. Of the seven commission members, only Earl Warren was present during the questioning of the 94 witnesses. The total time devoted by the commission to the assassination itself occupied less than one-third of its hearings. Forty-three percent of the hearings were devoted to Oswald's background; 12 percent consisted of testimony about the internal operations of such federal agencies as the FBI and the Secret Service; and 26 percent entailed testimony about Jack Ruby, the Dallas police, Castro, and other subjects not directly related to the assassination.[33]

Of the twenty-six volumes of hearings and exhibits published by the commission, the first fifteen were transcripts of hearings before the commission. Volumes sixteen through twenty-six were photographic and other exhibits. A very large proportion of the exhibits are matters unrelated to the assassination. For example, there are such irrelevant and unnecessary materials as microphotographs of Oswald's limb and pubic hairs, a dental chart revealing the condition of Jack Ruby's mother's teeth in 1938, a detailed analysis of Marina Oswald's pregnancy, cheesecake photographs of strippers from Jack Ruby's nightclub, traffic tickets incurred by Ruby in the 1950s, Oswald's vaccination certificates, and personal letters from Marina to her girl friends.[34]

It should be obvious that the *Warren Report* did not result from an objective and independent investigation of the assassination of President Kennedy. It is more of a brief for the prosecution than an unbiased analysis of all the evidence. Although one of the original goals of members of the Warren Commission was to "reassure" the public that there was no conspiracy, the heavily prejudiced and distorted version of the assassination that the commission published only served to provoke controversy and disbelief. The publication of the *Warren Report* in September 1964 touched off a debate that continues to this day—a debate about the validity of the *Report*'s contentions that Oswald was the sole assassin and that there was no conspiracy.

CHAPTER 9

CONGRESS INVESTIGATES

WHEN the *Warren Report* was published in September 1964, its initial reception proved overwhelmingly favorable. The national television and radio networks gave the *Report* extensive and sympathetic coverage. The leading newspapers and magazines also lauded the commission's work. For over a year, it appeared that the Warren Commission had provided the definitive answers to the identity of President Kennedy's assassin and to his motivation.[1]

In 1966, however, the first of many works critical of the *Warren Report* was published. Written by attorney Mark Lane, that work, *Rush to Judgment,* attacked virtually all of the commission's central conclusions. Lane raised the serious possibility of a conspiracy in the assassination. He disputed the commission's single-bullet theory, its contention that all the shots were fired from the rear, its account of the murder of Officer Tippit, and its version of Ruby's slaying of Oswald. An instant bestseller, *Rush to Judgment* raised doubts in the public mind and provoked an enormous amount of controversy. Generally denounced as irresponsible and mercenary by the national press, Mark Lane nevertheless began the public disbelief in the lone-assassin thesis of the Warren Commission.[2]

Many other authors critical of the *Warren Report* published works, some careful, documented critiques, others reckless speculation. All added to the public distrust that *Rush to Judgment* had generated. Strong defenses of the Warren Commission by such well-known authors as William Manchester and Jim Bishop failed to silence the growing criticism of the commission. More fuel was added to the critics' fire in February 1967, when New Orleans District Attorney Jim Garrison launched his infamous investigation of the assassination. Garrison's sensational investigation received an enormous amount of national publicity, ranging from *Playboy* magazine to the "Tonight Show." Garrison's public denunciations of the Warren Commission prompted CBS to telecast an unprecedented four-hour-long special news program on the assassination. Despite the network's spirited defense of the *Warren Report,* a 1967 Gallup Poll revealed that over two-thirds of the American people doubted the commission's conclusions.[3]

The March 1969 trial of Clay Shaw, whose acquittal discredited Garrison's reputation, the growing controversy over the Vietnam war, and the Watergate scandals all reduced public interest in the assassination. But in March 1975, the Zapruder film was shown on national television. For the first time, Americans saw the graphic, full-color footage and experienced the shock of seeing John Kennedy's brains blown apart. This episode, repeated several weeks later, convinced many that the Warren Commission had erred. Optics expert Robert Groden's specially enhanced version of the Zapruder film appeared to depict a crossfire, since Kennedy's violent backward and leftward movement indicated that the fatal head shot came from in front, from the Grassy Knoll.[4]

Even before the television programs, movements to reopen the assassination controversy developed. From 31 January to 2 February 1975, a "Politics of Conspiracy" conference, sponsored by the Assassination Information Bureau, was held at Boston University. The large crowds in attendance heard numerous critics attack the Warren Commission's conclusion. On 19 February 1975, Representative Henry Gonzalez, a rider in the Dallas motorcade, introduced a resolution calling for a congressional investigation into the murders of John and Robert Kennedy and Martin Luther King and into the wounding of George Wallace. In March, Mark Lane organized a Citizens Commission of Inquiry, whose purpose was to persuade Congress to reopen the investigation. On 18 April, *New Times* magazine published "JFK: The Truth Is Still At Large," an article that generated a storm of public controversy. The *New Times* article preceded a series of articles in such journals as the *Saturday Evening Post, Penthouse, Rolling Stone,* and the *New York Review of Books.* The national television networks joined this spate of new publicity by telecasting many programs about the assassination. In November 1975, for example, CBS produced a two-hour documentary and NBC and ABC one hour each on the JFK killing.[5]

The federal response to this renewed interest in the assassination included a reexamination of the Kennedy autopsy materials by a medical panel appointed by the Rockefeller Commission (a commission headed by Vice-President Nelson Rockefeller, whose main purpose was to investigate domestic activities by the CIA). The Rockefeller Commission's vigorous defense of the *Warren Report* failed to stifle public belief in an assassination conspiracy. In September 1975, a United States Senate Select Committee to study the relationship of federal intelligence agencies with the government appointed a subcommittee under Senator Richard Schweiker. Its purpose was to investigate the performance of intelligence agencies in the investigation of the Kennedy assassination. Released in May 1976, the Schweiker subcommittee report detailed the failure of the federal intelligence agencies to examine possible assassination conspiracies.[6]

The Schweiker subcommittee's sensational disclosures enhanced the growing distrust in United States agencies. The full committee, chaired by Senator Frank Church, had uncovered evidence of CIA-Mafia assassination plots against Fidel Castro and other secretive activities calling the CIA's integrity into question. Convinced that vital evidence was deliberately withheld from the Warren Commission, members of the House of Representatives sponsored a resolution calling for a congressional investigation of Kennedy's death. To obtain additional support, especially from the House's Black Caucus, the resolution also called for an investigation of the assassination of Martin Luther King. On 17 September 1976, the resolution passed the House by a vote of 280 to 65. It established a Select Committee on Assassinations, consisting of twelve congressmen. Chaired by Representative Henry Gonzalez, the committee appointed famed criminal prosecutor Richard A. Sprague as its chief counsel. Internal dissension among the committee staff and open hostility between Gonzalez and Sprague resulted in the resignations of both men. A new House Select Committee on Assassinations was created, and its tenure authorized from

30 March 1977 to 3 January 1979. Congressman Louis Stokes of Ohio was named chairman, and G. Robert Blakey, a lawyer with congressional committee staff experience, was named chief counsel and staff director.[7]

The House Select Committee on Assassinations comprised twelve representatives, eight Democrats and four Republicans. The full committee was divided up into two subcommittees, one on the Kennedy assassination, the other on the King assassination. The Subcommittee on the Assassination of John F. Kennedy was chaired by Congressman Richardson Preyer of North Carolina and included Congressmen Yvonne Brathwaite Burke, Christopher J. Dodd, Charles Thone, and Harold S. Sawyer. Committee Chairman Louis Stokes and Congressman Samuel L. Devine, the ranking Republican on the committee, served as *ex officio* members of the subcommittee.[8]

Just as the men who served on the Warren Commission held a variety of demanding jobs that prevented them from devoting full time to the commission's daily activities, so, too, did the members of the House Select Committee. Busy with the manifold duties of congressmen, including service on other congressional committees, engaged in such other activities as campaigning for reelection, the committee members spent only part of their time with the assassination case. The day-to-day tasks of research, evaluating evidence, selecting expert consultants, interviewing witnesses, and arranging the format of the entire investigation were left to the committee's John F. Kennedy Task Force. Under the overall direction of Chief Counsel Blakey, the task force was composed of young lawyers, none of whom had any expertise in studying the Kennedy assassination.[9]

The House of Representatives gave its Select Committee on Assassinations four mandates: (1) Who assassinated President Kennedy? (2) Did the assassin(s) receive any assistance? (3) Did United States government agencies adequately collect and share information prior to the assassination, protect President Kennedy properly, and conduct a thorough investigation into the assassination? (4) Should new legislation on these matters be enacted by Congress? To fulfill these mandates, the committee spent the last six months of 1977 assembling a staff, reviewing the critical literature about the assassination, and organizing its gathering of evidence, the conduct of its public hearings, and the preparation of its final report. The actual investigation lasted from January to July 1978. The public hearings were held in September and December of that year, and the *Report* was issued on 29 March 1979.[10]

The House Select Committee based its investigation on three categories of factual information: scientific evidence, government files, and the testimony of witnesses. The committee relied mainly on scientific evidence, the findings of its expert consultants in the fields of forensic pathology, ballistics and firearms, handwriting analysis, photographic interpretation, acoustics, fingerprinting, and the like. It used the government files, assassination materials of the FBI, CIA, Secret Service, and other agencies with considerably more caution. It placed the least credence on witness testimony because of the fifteen-year lapse between the assassination and its investigation, the faulty memory of many witnesses, and the tendency of some witnesses to bias or falsehood.[11]

The results of the committee's work were published in a 686-page *Report,* supported by twelve volumes of hearings and appendices. The committee's central conclusion that John Kennedy's assassination was probably due to a conspiracy represented a sharp contradiction of the Warren Commission's conclusion that no conspiracy existed. Because of the obvious significance of this finding, it is necessary for us to take a detailed look at the method the committee used to arrive at it.

The committee's first conclusion strongly reinforced the *Warren Report.* It found that President Kennedy was struck by two rifle shots fired from behind him. The most obvious evidence for this was the autopsy photographs and X-rays of Kennedy's body. A team of expert photographic analysts, forensic anthropologists, and radiologists scrutinized the materials and determined that all were genuine. This determination was significant, for many Warren Commission critics had questioned the authenticity of the autopsy photographs and X-rays. The committee's experts laid to rest any serious question about this issue.[12]

The House Select Committee contracted a distinguished panel of forensic pathologists to examine the autopsy materials and other medical evidence. Headed by Dr. Michael Baden, chief medical examiner of New York City, the panel included three pathologists who had previously reviewed the autopsy evidence and six who had not. In order to provide its members with the most complete information available, the panel had specially prepared computer-assisted image enhancement techniques applied to the photographs and X-rays. It also enlisted the aid of several experienced radiologists in interpreting the X-rays. In addition to the photographs and X-rays, the panel studied bullets, clothing, films, medical and autopsy reports from Parkland and Bethesda hospitals, and numerous articles in professional journals. Finally, the panel members interviewed many of the Dallas doctors and autopsy pathologists who worked on President Kennedy and Governor Connally. The result of their deliberations is contained in the report that forms the most detailed and extensive analysis of the medical evidence in the Kennedy assassination available.[13]

The medical panel concluded first that a bullet struck Kennedy high in the upper back on the right side. While the precise location of the entrance hole could not be determined, the existence of bullet holes in the president's coat and shirt permitted the estimation that it was situated about two to three inches below the junction of the shoulder and the neck. The color photographs clearly revealed the wound to be a bullet entrance wound. It was very small, less than a half inch at its widest part. The oval shape of the hole indicated that the bullet entered at an angle. The bruising around the hole, especially prominent in the lower left and upper right margins, suggested that the missile entered from below the president. The bruising also proved that the wound was indeed one of entrance.[14]

The panel's second conclusion was that John Kennedy had a bullet exit wound in his throat. The autopsy photographs of the front of the neck showed the large two-inch wide tracheotomy incision made by Dr. Perry during the emergency resuscitation procedures taken at Parkland Hospital. At the bottom center of the incision is a small semicircular hole, which the panel concluded represented a bullet exit hole. Even though exit wounds typically range from two to five times larger than entrance wounds, the panel believed that Kennedy's buttoned shirt collar and tie knot caused his skin to be stretched tight, thus resulting in a small hole of exit. The slitlike tears in the president's shirt collar confirmed the contention that the bullet exited at that location.[15]

Since the president had an entrance hole in his upper back and an exit hole in the lower throat, the panel surmised that one bullet had caused both wounds. The X-rays and autopsy information disclosed bruising of the tip of the right lung, damage to the windpipe, and blood and air in the chest. Those clinical signs were consistent with a bullet's passing through the president's upper chest in its passage from the entrance hole in the back to the exit hole in the throat.[16]

The Forensic Pathology Panel then examined the head wounds. Several photographs of the back of Kennedy's head show a vertical, oval hole located high on the head, almost near the top. This wound, in the "cowlick," measured over three-quarters of an inch long and two-fifths of an inch wide. The X-rays of the skull showed sharp fracture lines and a large bullet fragment at the point where the hole was located. Based on this evidence, the panel concluded that a bullet entered John Kennedy's skull high on the back of his head, about four inches above the bone that protrudes from the back of the skull.[17]

The panel's location of the entrance wound contrasted sharply with that of the autopsy, which located it much lower down in the head. In interviews with members of the panel, the three autopsy pathologists insisted that the entrance hole was located near the base of the skull, just above the hairline. However, the objective evidence of the photographs and X-rays, including sophisticated computer-enhanced analyses of these materials, supported the panel's contention that the bullet entered near the top of the head. And in public testimony, Dr. Humes admitted that the entrance hole was indeed high on the back of the head.[18]

Finding the place where this bullet exited John Kennedy's head proved a difficult task for the pathologists. The skull lost so much bone that only a very large cavity remained in the right front portion of the head. However, from the available autopsy material, the panel concluded that the bullet exited the right side of the head approximately midway between the forehead and the ear and about three inches below the top of the skull.[19]

The panel also examined the evidence about Governor Connally's wounds. It found that a bullet entered the right side of his upper back, entered his chest, bouncing along his fifth rib and causing it to shatter. The same bullet exited the chest and entered the right wrist, breaking the radius, the large bone on the thumb side. After exiting the wrist, the bullet penetrated a very short distance into the governor's thigh.[20]

The Forensic Pathology Panel concluded that two bullets, both fired from the rear, struck President Kennedy, and that one bullet, fired from the rear, struck Governor Connally. It also declared that the weight of the evidence supported the single-bullet theory—that the same bullet that went through Kennedy's chest also caused Connally's injuries. Thus, in all significant respects, the panel fully supported the Warren Commission's contention that all shots came from the rear.

One of the panel's members, Allegheny County, Pennsylvania, Coroner Dr. Cyril Wecht, vigorously dissented. Dr. Wecht asserted that the single-bullet theory was medically impossible and that the evidence did not rule out the possibility of a shot's being fired from the right front and striking the president in the head. The eight other panel members, however, disagreed, and the House Select Committee properly accepted their findings as representing the consensus of medical expertise.[21]

Strongly reinforcing the pathologists' conclusions was the testimony of wounds ballistics expert Larry Sturdivan. In testimony before the committee, Sturdivan stated that, in his opinion, the Zapruder film, the autopsy material, and the ballistics evidence all substantiated the Warren Commission's finding that all shots were fired from Oswald's rifle. Sturdivan also showed the committee a film of goats being shot to explain the apparent discrepancy between Kennedy's backward head movement and a shot's entering the rear of his head. Sturdivan asserted that the reason for Kennedy's backward head movement was a neuromuscular reaction to the massive destruction of neurological tissue that the bullet caused.[22]

While Sturdivan provided only conjecture to support his arguments, another committee witness, Dr. Vincent P. Guinn, a chemistry professor at the University of California at Irvine, presented hard scientific evidence to substantiate his. Dr. Guinn subjected various bullet fragments to neutron activation analysis, a process whereby objects are irradiated with nuclear radiation and the different levels of radiation according to their weight is measured; the precise chemical composition of a substance can be measured in units as tiny as parts per billion. In the field of ballistics, neutron activation analysis has proven a valuable instrument for identifying bullets and bullet fragments.[23]

In the Kennedy assassination case, neutron activation analysis could be used to determine whether Bullet 399, bullet fragments removed from the president's brain and from the governor's wrist, and the limousine fragments came from the same ammunition and if that ammunition matched Oswald's rifle. In September 1977, Dr. Guinn tested these materials and surmised that the fragments from the governor's wrist came from Bullet 399, a powerful and convincing scientific substantiation of the single-bullet theory. Guinn also found that the fragments removed from President Kennedy's brain matched the fragments found in the limousine, proof that only one bullet, fired from Oswald's rifle, struck the president in the head. Dr. Guinn reported that neutron activation analysis revealed evidence of only two bullets, both Mannlicher-Carcanos of the exact type used in Oswald's rifle. Dr. Guinn's analysis, therefore, fully supported the medical evidence and the Warren Commission's findings that all bullets striking the president and the governor were fired from Oswald's rifle.[24]

The committee's second conclusion was that "the shots that struck President Kennedy from behind were fired from the sixth floor window of the southeast corner of the Texas School Book Depository Building." This conclusion relied on medical, ballistics, photographic, and other experts, and, of course, fully substantiated the Warren Commission's identification of the source of the shots.[25]

The Forensic Pathology Panel had already determined that the fatal head shot came from above and behind the president, but it was unable to determine, from the available medical evidence, whether the bullet that entered Kennedy's back had been fired from above, below, or on a level plane. The House Select Committee, therefore, decided to have an expert conduct a trajectory analysis to pinpoint the origin of the shots. The expert, Thomas Canning, a NASA engineer, used the medical panel's location of the wounds, the photographic experts' analysis of the timing of the shots, and the locations of the limousine and its occupants. Very careful measurements enabled Canning to conclude that the shots all could have been fired from the sixth-floor window the Book Depository building.[26]

The weight of the other evidence also confirmed the Depository as the source of the shots. The discovery of the rifle and the cartridge cases on the sixth floor, the ballistics match between the limousine fragments and the rifle, and the eyewitness testimony all gave the committee ample reason for its assertion that the Depository window was the place whence shots were fired. The ownership of the rifle by Oswald was proved beyond question through the analysis of mail orders, money orders, and other documents. Handwriting experts concluded that all of the writing and signatures on the documents were Oswald's. The committee's photographic panel also proved beyond question that, contrary to the claims of many Warren Commission critics, all photographs of Oswald holding the rifle reveal the rifle in the photographs was the same rifle discovered on the sixth floor of the Depository building.[27]

The committee concluded that Lee Harvey Oswald was on the sixth floor shortly before the assassination and that "Oswald's other actions tend to support the conclusion that he assassinated President Kennedy." Oswald's access to the sixth floor, his prints on cartons near the window, and eyewitness identification of him in the building shortly before the shooting confirm the probability that he was at the window at the time of the shots. Oswald's murder of Officer Tippit, his attempt to murder Major General Edwin A. Walker on 10 April 1963, his capacity for violence, and his "twisted ideological view of himself and the world around him" all promote the likelihood that he shot Kennedy.[28]

Thus far, the House Select Committee on Assassinations agreed in every respect with the conclusions of the Warren Commission. But an additional item of evidence forced the committee to alter its original presumption that a sole assassin fired all the shots from the rear. That evidence was a Dallas police tape of the gunshots. Expert acoustical analysis of the tape determined that of the four shots fired, three came from the rear and one from the front. This forced the committee to draw its second main conclusion: "Scientific acoustical evidence establishes a high probability that two gunmen fired at President John F. Kennedy."[29]

As the presidential motorcade proceeded into Dealey Plaza, one of the motorcycle police officers used his police radio microphone to call the central dispatcher. The policeman depressed the button on the microphone. After finishing his conversation, the officer released the button, but the button remained depressed. The microphones are voiced activated, i.e., they transmit the sounds of voices of persons speaking directly into them. Extraneous noises, such as the cheering of crowds, cannot be picked up by the microphone. Very loud noises, however, such as gunshots, sirens, and engine noises, are transmitted. Thus, the microphone, in a stuck open position, transmitted the sounds of the gunfire in Dealey Plaza during the assassination. A dictabelt at Dallas police headquarters recorded the transmission from the microphone. Shortly after the assassination, the recordings were transferred to a reel-to-reel tape, thus providing a permanent record of the sounds. (The dictabelt, commonly used by secretaries to transcribe messages, is easily erased).[30]

To the naked ear, the Dallas police tape contains nothing resembling gunshots. The only audible sounds that can be distinguished from static interference are the voices of various police officers, motorcycle engines, sirens, and a bell. Several years ago, Gary Mack, a Dallas radio executive, filtered some of the background noise and static and discovered seven noises that he believed were gunshots. But without expertise in acoustics, Mack was unable to test his theory.[31]

The House Select Committee obtained copies of the tape and subjected them to acoustical analysis, but the results proved inconclusive. In March 1978, however, the committee discovered the original dictabelt and tape recording. Stored in a cabinet until 1969, the materials then were turned over to Paul McCaghren, director of the Dallas Police Intelligence Division. McCaghren retained them until he released them to the committee nine years later. The committee hired Bolt, Beranek, and Newman (BBN), a firm specializing in scientific acoustical analysis. BBN had pioneered the analysis of sound recordings to determine the timing and direction of gunfire through its study of a tape recording of the 1970 Kent State shootings.[32]

Dr. James E. Barger, BBN's chief scientist, conducted a series of tests. First, he determined that the reel-to-reel tape was an exact duplicate of the original dictabelt. Then he converted the tape recording to digitized waveforms, similar to the peaks and valleys of an electrocardiogram. Then, Barger filtered out such noise as the repeated firings of a motorcycle engine. Then, he selected six sequences of impulses that might possibly represent gunshots. Finally, Barger established that all six impulse sequences occurred during the time of the assassination (the central dispatcher's office recorded the precise time that every message received came in).[33]

Barger's initial analysis established a distinct possibility that the tape contained the sounds of gunshots. Now it was necessary to record the sounds of gunfire in Dealey Plaza in order to compare them with the impulses on the tape. In August 1978, BBN recorded the sounds of shots fired from the sixth-floor window of the Texas School Book Depository building and from the Grassy Knoll. Barger discovered that four of the impulses on the Dallas police tape matched the recorded sounds of gunfire in the reconstruction. Because the matches were not exact, Barger concluded that there was a 95 percent probability that two shots were fired from the building, a 75 percent likelihood that three shots came from the building, but only a 50 percent chance that a shot was fired from the Grassy Knoll.[34]

One can easily imagine the Committee's astonishment when it heard Dr. Barger's testimony. The medical, ballistics, and other scientific evidence clearly pointed to a lone assassin firing from the rear. Now, Barger raised the distinct possibility of shots fired from the front and rear. If that turned out to be the case, then at least two assassins must have shot at the president. To refine Barger's analysis, the committee hired acoustics expert Mark Weiss of Queens College of the City University of New York and his research associate, Ernest Aschkenasy. The committee charged Weiss and Aschkenasy with determining whether or not a shot was indeed fired from the Grassy Knoll.[35]

Using a precise scale plot map of Dealey Plaza, Weiss and Aschkenasy computed the type of impulses that a Grassy Knoll shot would have caused. Then they carefully examined the Dallas police tape to search for such impulses. They found an impulse sequence on the tape that matched their calculations to within 1/1,000 of a second. The precision of the match was so great that they concluded that there was a 95 percent probability of a shot's being fired from the Grassy Knoll, a probability so strong that it ruled out random tape noise and other possible causes for the impulses on the tape. Weiss and Aschkenasy testified that their acoustical analysis proved beyond any reasonable doubt that a supersonic bullet was fired at the presidential limousine from the Grassy Knoll.[36]

The acoustical studies by Weiss and Aschkenasy, reviewed and supported by Barger, convinced a majority of the committee members that the assassination of John Kennedy resulted from a conspiracy. Having established the high probability of a conspiracy, the committee sought to identify its nature and the individuals involved in it. First, it eliminated the Soviet and Cuban governments. Neither country, the committee argued, would dare risk war against the United States, which surely would have resulted if agents of either had committed the assassination. The committee also absolved the Secret Service, FBI, and CIA from complicity in the assassination. Although all three agencies proved deficient in their gathering of information, and although all three failed to provide the Warren Commission with complete information relevant to the assassination, the committee could find no evidence implicating any in the event itself.[37]

The House Select Committee on Assassinations uncovered evidence of a possible conspiracy involving individuals associated with anti-Castro organizations in the United States. Within a few months after his accession to power in May 1959, Fidel Castro began consolidating his dictatorship in Cuba. He confiscated large amounts of private property, jailed thousands of opponents of his regime, and suppressed civil liberties. By the beginning of 1960, tens of thousands of Cuban opponents of the Castro regime emigrated to the United States and concentrated in such places as Miami, New Orleans, and Dallas.[38]

Most of the Cuban exiles resigned themselves to permanent life in the United States. Many exiles, however, refused to acquiesce in Castro's domination of their homeland and began organizing numerous groups whose purpose was to overthrow Castro. Under Presidents Eisenhower and Kennedy, the United States government furnished these anti-Castro organizations with arms, supplies, training, and logistical support. These activities were carried out by the CIA. On 17 April 1961, a brigade of Cuban exiles, trained and equipped by the United States, invaded Cuba at the Bay of Pigs. The failure of the United States to support the invasion with air power resulted in the annihilation of the brigade. President Kennedy's public acceptance of full responsibility for the Bay of Pigs fiasco intensified the Cuban exiles' animosity toward Kennedy.[39]

The Cuban Missile Crisis of October 1962 also heightened the exiles' bitterness against Kennedy. In return for the removal of Soviet missiles from Cuba, the United States pledged not to invade it. Shortly thereafter, the government began closing down Cuban refugee training camps and confiscating weapons and supplies from the refugees. By the fall of 1963, the anti-Castro Cubans felt betrayed by the Kennedy administration. In October 1963, a Cuban named Nestor Castellanos told a meeting of anti-Castro Cubans, "We're waiting for Kennedy the 22d, buddy. We're going to see him in one way or another. We're going to give him the works when he gets in Dallas." On 21 November 1963, a Cuban activist, Homer S. Echevarria, told a Secret Service informant that his organization had "plenty of money" and would take action against Castro "as soon as we take care of Kennedy." Finally, the House Committee learned that in the summer of 1963, Lee Harvey Oswald came into contact with David Ferrie and possibly Guy Bannister, both right-wing activists associated with anti-Castro organizations in the New Orleans area. Although it could not produce complete evidence verifying this, the committee concluded that individuals active in anti-Castro activities had the motive, means, and opportunity to assassinate President Kennedy, and may have done so.[40]

The committee also concluded that certain individuals associated with organized crime in the United States may have been involved in the assassination. A primary factor in the committee's opinion was the close ties between Jack Ruby and organized crime. In the month prior to the assassination, Ruby telephoned Irwin Weiner, a "frontman for organized crime"; Robert "Barney" Baker, an associate of Jimmy Hoffa's; Nofio J. Pecora, a lieutenant of the reputed Louisiana Mafia boss Carlos Marcello; Lewis McWillie, who had ties with organized crime figures Santos Trafficante and Meyer Lansky; and Murray "Dusty" Miller, another individual closely allied with Hoffa and the Mafia.[41]

President Kennedy and his brother, Attorney General Robert F. Kennedy, had spent more than a decade combating organized crime and labor racketeering. The Kennedy administration authorized the FBI to conduct electronic surveillance of the Mafia leaders. The tapes of certain conversations revealed deepseated resentment and, indeed, hatred of the Kennedy brothers. In February 1962, for example, Willie Weisburg told his boss, Angelo Bruno of Philadelphia, "Somebody should kill [President Kennedy]." In October 1963, Stefano Magaddino, the Mafia boss of Buffalo, remarked that Kennedy "should drop dead." An FBI informant reported that in September 1962, reputed Louisiana underworld leader Carlos Marcello stated that President Kennedy would be assassinated. And Jose Aleman, a prominent Cuban exile, told the committee that in September 1962, the Miami Mafia boss, Santos Trafficante, told him that President Kennedy was "going to be hit." In 1962, Edward Grady Partin, an associate of Teamster boss Jimmy Hoffa, told the FBI that Hoffa stated that President Kennedy would be shot while riding in an open convertible.[42]

The House Select Committee on Assassinations thus contradicted a central conclusion of the Warren Commission. The second official U.S. government investigation into the assassination of President Kennedy decided that the assassination probably resulted from a conspiracy. Because of the continuing controversy about the assassination, we shall now turn to an intensive, objective analysis of the evidence produced by the committee.

CHAPTER 10

THE HOUSE COMMITTEE REPORT: EVIDENCE AND ANALYSIS

IN THIS CHAPTER we shall examine the central conclusions of the House Select Committee on Assassinations in order to test their validity. Since some of those conclusions simply repeated those of the Warren Commission, only those portions of the House Committee's *Report* that present significantly new findings will be analyzed here.

THE MEDICAL EVIDENCE

Because of the outstanding controversy about the medical evidence, the House Select Committee hired a panel of forensic pathologists to examine the autopsy materials and other medical evidence relating to the assassination. As recounted in Chapter Nine, the Forensic Pathology Panel agreed with the autopsy pathologists and with the Warren Commission in all essential matters, e.g., the nature of the bullet wounds in President Kennedy and Governor Connally. However, the panel did offer interpretations of the medical evidence that differed sharply from the original autopsy and Warren Commission findings.

The panel first considered the wound in President Kennedy's back. It concluded that a bullet hole, 0.9 by 0.9 cm., was located in the upper portion of Kennedy's back, approximately two inches below the shoulder and slightly to the right of the middle of the back. In contrast, the Warren Commission concluded that the bullet struck the president in the lower neck. Furthermore, the autopsy pathologists measured the wound as 4 x 7 mm., significantly smaller than the 9 x 9 mm. measured by the panel. The panel made no mention of these discrepancies in its report to the committee.[1]

The panel also concluded that the bullet entered President Kennedy's back at an upward angle because the abrasion collar of bruising around the wound was larger at the bottom than at the top. When bullets enter the body, they leave abrasion collars around the wound of entrance. The angle at which a bullet enters can be estimated from the size of the collar. Thus, a bullet fired from above will leave more bruising around the top of the entrance hole. But in President Kennedy's case, the panel stated that the "abrasion collar is larger at the lower margin of the wound, evidence that the bullet's trajectory at the instant of penetration was slightly upward in relation to the body."[2]

Neither the Forensic Pathology Panel nor the Select Committee realized the significance of this finding, so significant that it completely refutes the single-bullet theory. If the bullet entered Kennedy's body at an upward angle, it could hardly have gone on to strike Governor Connally at a downward angle. Since Kennedy sat directly behind and approximately three inches above Connally, it is apparent that any bullet striking Connally at a downward angle could not have first gone through Kennedy at an upward angle. Despite this obvious fact, the panel concluded that "the medical evidence is consistent with this hypothesis" that the bullet which struck Governor Connally "had previously struck President Kennedy in the upper right back."[3]

The panel's conclusion that the bullet that struck the president in the back entered at an upward angle also refutes the Warren Commission's and the House Committee's claim that this bullet was fired by Lee Harvey Oswald from the sixth-floor window of the Book Depository building. That window stood 60 feet above Elm Street and 55 feet above President Kennedy. Any bullet fired from that window must have entered its victim at a downward angle. Since the bullet that hit Kennedy entered at an upward angle, it must have been fired from below him, because he sat erect when he was struck.[4]

Not only did the House Select Committee ignore this, it published drawings that distorted the panel's evidence. One drawing, for example, shows the bullet entering the president at a sharp downward angle of almost forty-five degrees. The reason for the committee's twisting of the evidence was undoubtedly to force it to conform to the presupposition that Oswald was the assassin.[5]

In direct testimony before the committee, Dr. Michael Baden, the head of the panel, stated that the bullet entering the president's back could have traveled "upward, approximately horizontally, or downward. Each of these trajectories could produce the autopsy findings. . . . We cannot . . . determine from whence [*sic*] the bullet came." The committee neglected to ask Dr. Baden how a bullet traveling downward could have struck Kennedy's back at an upward angle. The only possible explanation for a bullet fired from the sixth floor of the Depository building entering the back at an upward angle is if the president had been leaning forward parallel to the limousine floor at the instant of impact. All films and photographs of the assassination clearly depict President Kennedy sitting erect at that instant. The committee, however, ignored this objective evidence and assumed that the Depository window was the only conceivable source of the shot.[6]

The Forensic Pathology Panel next considered the alleged exit hole in the front of Kennedy's neck. As we have seen, Dr. Malcolm Perry cut a tracheotomy incision directly through that hole, and the autopsy photographs showed only that incision. Dr. Perry's incision was so large (50 x 40 mm.) that it totally obscured the original bullet hole. Because of the very large size of the tracheotomy incision, the autopsy pathologists failed to recognize any visible signs of the bullet hole. Despite this, the panel decided that the autopsy photographs did show a "semicircular missile defect near the center of the lower margin of the tracheotomy incision."[7]

This revelation by the panel defies the objective evidence. First, the panel admitted that none of the photographs were in sharp focus. Yet, magically, it discovered a bullet hole in the poorly focused photos, while the pathologists could not find the hole in the actual body. Second, the semicircular defect visible in the incision does not resemble a bullet exit wound. Exit wounds are typically large and jagged, exhibiting considerable damage to the skin and underlying tissues. The photographs show the defect to be small, round, with no serious skin damage, and with the skin inverted into the body rather than exuding outward, as exit wounds usually do. Third, Drs. Malcolm Perry and James Carrico of the emergency team at Parkland

Hospital were among the only physicians to see the actual bullet wound in the president's neck. Dr. Carrico told a committee staff interviewer that "there was some injury to the trachea behind it, so the thing must have been going front to back. . . ." Dr. Perry said that the wound was "roughly round [and] the edges were bruised." Bruising of the edges of a wound is one of the positive indicators of entrance wounds, as the panel itself noted in describing the entrance wound in Kennedy's back. Yet, it ignored the observations of the Dallas doctors and, without a scintilla of evidence, determined that the hole in the neck was one of exit.[8]

The panel noticed an entrance wound in the rear of the president's head. It located the wound high on the top of the head because of the autopsy photographs. The autopsy pathologists, however, located the entrance hole low down, near the base of the skull. The discrepancy of over four inches in descriptions of the bullet hole's location raises obvious questions about the validity of the panel's interpretation of the evidence. After viewing the photographs, all three autopsy pathologists reaffirmed their original location of the hole. As the panel noted, "Dr. Finck [an autopsy pathologist] believed strongly that the observations of the autopsy pathologists were more valid than those of individuals who might subsequently examine photographs." The panel dismissed Dr. Finck's reasonable remark and concluded that he and his colleagues had erred, even though they had Kennedy's body before them when they made their observations.[9]

The panel assumed that the large gaping wound in the right front of President Kennedy's head was an exit wound caused by the bullet that entered the back of his head. To substantiate this, the panel noted that some of the bones around the margin of the huge (130 mm.) hole were beveled outward. It neglected to observe that other bones in the margin area were beveled inward. It also observed that X-rays of the brain reveal bullet fragments extending "from the back to the front." It did not mention that the fragments simultaneously extend from front to back. In both instances, the panel distorted the evidence to make it weigh more heavily on the side of its hypothesis of a rear-entering bullet.[10]

The bias of the panel was clearly revealed in its remark that the "brain was not coronally sectioned. . . . The Panel stresses that coronal sectioning is the most acceptable and accurate method of determining precisely the effects of a missile on the brain, as well as the angle of a bullet track in the head." Since the brain was not sectioned, one would expect the panel to have concluded that the incomplete nature of the evidence does not permit a definitive conclusion about the precise nature of the head wounds on President Kennedy. The panel, however, concluded that one bullet struck him in the rear of the head and exploded out the right front.[11]

The panel also concluded that the oval, elongated entrance wound in Governor Connally's back was caused by a "tumbling bullet," i.e., a bullet that had previously struck something else. The obvious implication of this assertion was that the bullet had gone through Kennedy's neck before it struck Connally. The panel did not mention that the size and shape of Connally's back wound matched those of the rear wound in Kennedy's head. Despite the identical nature of the two wounds, Dr. Baden insisted that the Kennedy bullet had not "tumbled," while the Connally bullet had. The panel completely discounted the remarks of Dr. Robert Shaw, the surgeon who operated on the governor's back. Dr. Shaw stated explicitly that the bullet that struck the governor "had not struck any other objects." Dr. Shaw asserted that Bullet 399, the infamous "single bullet," could not have caused all of Connally's wounds. Another of the Connally surgeons, Dr. Thomas Shires, also informed committee interviewers that the governor's wounds were probably caused by more than one missile.[12]

These selected examples clearly illustrate the predisposition of the Forensic Pathology Panel toward the lone-assassin hypothesis. By carefully selecting only those parts of the medical evidence that tended to support the hypothesis, the panel succeeded only in adding more uncertainty to an already hopelessly complex issue. The panel either overlooked or ignored such relevant aspects of the medical evidence as the highly significant testimony of the Dallas physicians, the nature of the ammunition allegedly employed in the assassination, and the direct observations of the autopsy pathologists. Lacking expertise in pathology, the committee failed to subject the panel's conclusions to the rigorous cross-examination procedures used in the adversary process in court. Nor did the committee consult physicians experienced in treating gunshot wounds. As the author discovered after numerous interviews with many such physicians, a far more critical analysis of the evidence would have resulted.

To bolster the medical panel's conclusions, the committee heard wounds ballistics expert Larry Sturdivan testify about some elements of the ballistics evidence as they pertained to the Kennedy and Connally wounds. First, Sturdivan testified that the reason Bullet 399 broke the governor's rib and wrist bones without suffering deformity was that the missile had lost substantial velocity by first going through President Kennedy's neck. Since there is no evidence whatsoever that Bullet 399 wounded either man, Sturdivan's statement was meaningless. Also, tests conducted for the Warren Commission in 1964 revealed that bullets from Oswald's rifle fired into such diverse substances as a goat's ribs, a cadaver's wrist, a gelatin compound, and cotton invariably suffered damage and mutilation that sharply distinguished them from the virtually intact Bullet 399.[13]

Sturdivan also stated that Kennedy was not struck in the front of his head by an exploding bullet fired from the Grassy Knoll. The reason, Sturdivan declared, was that the computer-enhanced X-rays of Kennedy's skull do not depict "a cloud of metallic fragments very near the entrance wound." In cases where exploding bullets impact, he asserted that "you would definitely have seen" such a cloud of fragments in the X-ray. Sturdivan's remarks betrayed both his own ignorance of the medical evidence and the committee's careful manipulation of that evidence. Sturdivan saw only the computer-enhanced X-ray of the skull, not the original, unretouched X-rays. Had he seen the originals, he would have observed a cloud of metallic fragments clustered in the right front portion of the head. Furthermore, the closeup photograph of the margins of the large wound in the head shows numerous small fragments. The Forensic Pathology Panel itself noted the presence of "missile dust" near the wound in the front of the head. One of the expert radiologists who examined the X-rays noticed "a linear alignment of tiny metallic fragments" located in the "posterior aspect of the right frontal bone." The chief autopsy pathologist, Dr. James J. Humes, remarked about the numerous metallic fragments like grains of sand scattered near the front head wound. The medical evidence, then, definitely proves the existence of a cloud of fragments in the right front portion of Kennedy's head, convincing evidence, according to Sturdivan, that an exploding bullet actually did strike the president there.[14]

Sturdivan's final observation was that the backward movement of President Kennedy's head was not due to the impact of a bullet fired from the front, but from a neuromuscular reaction caused by massive destruction of his central nervous system. To substantiate this, Sturdivan told the committee that jackrabbits shot in the head automatically spring upward because they experience a similar neuromuscular reaction resulting in the release of tension in their leg muscles. Then Sturdivan showed the committee a film of a goat, its horns taped to a bar, shot between the eyes. Its response to the fatal shot was an arching of the back and a stiffening of the legs. According to Sturdivan, Kennedy's backward movement was identical to the animal's.[15]

That the committee should accept such material as Sturdivan's demonstration as "scientific evidence" furnishes an outstanding example of its lack of objectivity. To the disinterested observer, it is obvious that President Kennedy was neither a jackrabbit nor a goat, that he neither sprang upward nor arched his back and straightened his legs after being shot, and that he was not shot between the eyes. The utter irrelevance of the animal films to the Kennedy assassination requires no further demonstration. Yet the committee accepted them as proof that President Kennedy was not shot from the front. For example, committee member Harold Sawyer wrote that the film "of the goat shooting episodes convincingly explained the rearward reaction of the President's head as seen in the Zapruder film and very convincingly demonstrates that it could not have been caused by the frontal impact of a bullet."[16]

Had the committee exhibited interest in discovering the true explanation of the backward movement of Kennedy's head, it would have studied the evidence about human, rather than animal, response to bullet wounds. The committee, in fact, already possessed one instance provided in its investigation of the assassination of Dr. Martin Luther King, Jr. As Dr. King leaned forward on the balcony outside his motel room, a bullet fired from the front struck him in the jaw, tore through his mouth, and exploded into his neck. According to Sturdivan's analysis, this front-entering bullet should have propelled Dr. King forward off the balcony onto the ground below. Instead, the bullet knocked Dr. King violently backward, causing him to fall on his back on the balcony floor. Countless other examples, including war films of soldiers shot in the head, verify without exception the fact that bullets striking people in the head cause the head to move in the direction of the path of the bullet.[17]

Further divorcing the committee's investigation from reliability was its dependence upon the analysis of NASA expert Thomas Canning for determining the trajectory of the bullets that struck President Kennedy and Governor Connally. Canning used the location of the wounds on the two men, the position of the limousine, the alignment of the occupants of the vehicle, and other information to arrive at his calculations. Those calculations demonstrated that both the "single bullet" and the fatal head shot could have been fired from the sixth-floor southeast corner window of the Book Depository building.[18]

In permitting Canning to perform his trajectory analysis, the committee ignored the advice of the Pathology Panel. The panel cautioned that there is no reliable method of "determining the missile trajectory . . . particularly if precision within the range of a few degrees is required." This was illustrated by Canning's rejection of the objective medical evidence. Instead of using the true location of the entrance wound in Kennedy's back (approximately four inches below the shoulder), Canning arbitrarily raised it three inches in order to arrive at a trajectory consistent with the sixth-floor window. He also computed the angle of the wound as twenty-one degrees downward. This was nothing less than a blatant distortion of the medical evidence, which proved that the bullet entered the president's back at a "slightly upward" angle. Despite similar distortions of other parts of the objective medical data, Canning's trajectory analysis resulted in margins of error, by his own admission, that would have permitted the assassins to have fired from such diverse locations as the fourth, fifth, sixth, and seventh floors, and the roof of the Depository, as well as from the two upper floors of the neighboring Dal-Tex building. The total number of sniper locations that would fit Canning's analysis is seventy! Clearly, such lack of precision, as well as the manipulation of the objective medical data, belies any serious inferences to be drawn from the trajectory analysis.[19]

One of the House Select Committee's most important witnesses, Dr. Vincent P. Guinn of the Chemistry Department at the University of California at Irvine, performed neutron activation analysis on several of the items of physical evidence in the Kennedy assassination. Dr. Guinn compared the chemical composition of bullet fragments removed from Governor Connally's wrist with that of Bullet 399, and the composition of two Kennedy head fragments with the fragments found on the floor of the limousine. He concluded that the Connally wrist fragments and Bullet 399 were from the same bullet, while the Kennedy head fragments and the limousine fragments came from the same bullet. Dr. Guinn stated that only two bullets were used, and that both were Mannlicher-Carcanos.[20]

On the surface, the neutron activation analysis tests performed by Dr. Guinn provided strong support both for the single-bullet theory and for the contention that the fatal head shot was fired from Lee Harvey Oswald's rifle. Since the wrist fragments and Bullet 399 matched each other, the committee accepted Dr. Guinn's thesis that they came from the same bullet. Likewise, the committee endorsed the Guinn theory that the head and limousine fragments came from the same bullet.[21]

A more careful analysis of the neutron activation analysis tests, however, shows numerous deficiencies that contest all of Dr. Guinn's central conclusions. First, of the more than thirty bullet fragments in John Kennedy's head, only two were subjected to the test. The rest remained embedded in brain tissue and skull bone. That two head fragments matched each other does not mean that the others did so. Second, Dr. Guinn did not analyze the large copper fragment found in the limousine. The origin of that fragment, therefore, remains scientifically unproven. Third, Dr. Guinn had previously performed neutron activation analysis on Mannlicher-Carcano ammunition, one of the bullets being from the same manufacture and production lot (Western Cartridge Company, lot 6003) as bullets from Oswald's rifle. *None* of the bullets matched each other. Moreover, Guinn analyzed pieces of the same bullet, and they, too, failed to match. For example, the four pieces of the bullet from lot 6003 had figures ranging from 7.9 to 15.9 parts per million (ppm.) silver, from 80 to 732 ppm. antimony, and from 17 to 62 ppm. copper. Dr. Guinn himself admitted that "some Mannlicher-Carcano bullets cannot be distinguished from each other."[22]

The most serious shortcoming in Dr. Guinn's analysis is his failure properly to interpret that data from the assassination fragments. For example, the Connally wrist fragment contained 25 percent more silver and 850 percent more copper than Bullet 399. It also contained 2400 percent more sodium and 1100 percent more chlorine, and it contained 8.1 ppm. aluminum, while Bullet 399 contained none. Similarly, the Kennedy head fragments and limousine fragments contained wide disparities in their chemical composition. Guinn and the committee, therefore, were hardly justified in their conclusions about "matches." Since different parts of the same bullet show different chemical values, and since the actual assassination fragments tested differed sharply in their values, the neutron activation analysis hardly lent scientific weight to the single-bullet and lone-assassin theories.[23]

Having dealt with the "scientific" evidence supporting the theory that the shots were fired from the sixth-floor southeast corner window of the Texas School Book Depository building, the House Select Committee on Assassinations turned to proof that Lee Harvey Oswald fired those shots. First, through handwriting and photographic analysis, committee experts proved that Oswald purchased the rifle found on the sixth floor and had possession of it in March and April 1963. However, the committee failed to discover even the slightest evidence that Oswald possessed the rifle at the time of the assassination.[24]

The committee stated that shortly before the assassination, Lee Harvey Oswald "had access to and was present on the sixth floor" of the Book Depository building. In this brief section of its *Report,* the committee did nothing more than rehash some of the Warren Commission's previous investigation. For example, the committee concluded that Oswald's fingerprints and palmprints on the cartons and paper sack and the way the boxes were stacked "must be considered as evidence that he handled the boxes in the process of preparing the so-called sniper's nest and that he had used the paper sack to carry the rifle into the depository." The existence of Oswald's prints on the boxes and sack mean only that he touched them. No inference can be read into this, since there is not an iota of evidence to define the circumstances in which he touched these objects.[25]

The committee also stated that Oswald could easily have been present on the sixth floor at the time of the assassination. Several of his coworkers saw him there a half-hour previously. However, the committee, forgetting Howard Brennan's Warren Commission testimony, claimed that "there was no witness who said he saw Oswald anywhere at the time of the assassination." As we have seen, Depository employee Bonnie Ray Williams ate his lunch on the sixth floor less than ten feet from the "sniper's nest" and testified that he heard and saw no one there between 12:00 and 12:20. Carolyn Arnold, another Depository employee, asserted that she saw Oswald in the second-floor lunchroom at 12:15, only fifteen minutes before the assassination. Since two other eyewitnesses, Oswald's boss and a policeman, saw him in the same second-floor lunchroom less than two minutes after the shooting, the committee's conclusion that Oswald fired the shots from the sixth floor remains open to question.[26]

Oswald's actions immediately after the shooting appeared "significant" to the committee. Of all the Depository employees, only Lee Harvey Oswald neither returned to the building nor had an alibi. This finding by the committee contradicted the evidence. Other Depository employees also left the building right after the assassination. Without attempting to trace Oswald's journey from the Depository building, the committee concluded that he shot and killed Officer J.D. Tippit. It relied on eyewitness identification of Oswald and the fact that the four cartridge cases found at the scene of the Tippit slaying were fired from his revolver. The committee ignored the other evidence in the Tippit case: the statements by Acquila Clemmons and Frank Wright that two men were involved, the failure to match any of the bullets recovered from Tippit's body with Oswald's revolver, the possibility that Oswald did not have time to reach the murder scene, and the confused and contradictory accounts of many eyewitnesses.[27]

The committee's bias against Oswald is illustrated by its belief that the Tippit murder, "committed while fleeing the scene of the assassination, was consistent with a finding that Oswald assassinated the President." The committee failed to produce even an iota of evidence that the murder of Officer Tippit was committed as Oswald fled the scene of the Kennedy killing. Oswald's presence at the Tippit scene, in a residential neighborhood four miles from Dealey Plaza, had no direct connection with his alleged involvement in the assassination. Furthermore, even if Oswald actually murdered Tippit, there is no evidence whatsoever linking that crime with the assassination.[28]

Oswald's motive for the assassination was "his conception of political action, rooted in his twisted ideological view of himself and the world around him." It hardly seems necessary to remark that this statement by the House Select Committee embodies little more than speculation. Only Lee Harvey Oswald could possibly have known his own motives. Since Oswald denied shooting Kennedy, even to his dying breath, there is no objective means of determining his inner thoughts. Lee Oswald's well-documented obsession with Marxism, Socialism, and other radical theories no more implicated him than it did the thousands of other Americans who espouse unpopular causes. Lee Harvey Oswald's behavior is no more capable of complete explanation than is the behavior of George Lincoln Rockwell, Gus Hall, and Charles Manson.[29]

Of all the conclusions of the House Select Committee on Assassinations, none has aroused as much controversy as the contention that scientific acoustical analysis of a Dallas police tape recording of the gunshots establishes a "high probability that two gunmen fired at President John F. Kennedy." This, of course, led to the further conclusion that President Kennedy "was probably assassinated as a result of a conspiracy." The reason for these conclusions, so contrary to the Warren Commission's lone-assassin thesis, was that the acoustical analysis of the tape recording demonstrated that three shots came from the rear of President Kennedy and one from in front. Since two gunmen fired shots, they must have engaged in a conspiracy. Delighted with this scientific verification of their long-standing belief in the existence of a Grassy Knoll assassin, many Warren Commission critics accepted the acoustical analysis uncritically.[30]

A final, definitive interpretation of the acoustical analysis has not yet been produced. However, it is possible to present several tentative observations about it. First, the authenticity of the tapes has never been established. While Professors Weiss and Aschkenasy proved that the tape was recorded in Dealey Plaza, they did not prove that it was recorded at 12:30 P.M. on 22 November 1963. The implication that someone may have deliberately manufactured a doctored tape is serious, but in the light of the mysterious circumstances surrounding such other material evidence as Bullet 399 and the autopsy photographs, this possibility cannot be dismissed. Second, there is no evidence concerning the whereabouts of the tape between 1964 and 1969, when it was discovered in a file cabinet at Dallas police headquarters. The missing five years in the tape's history obviously warrant detailed investigation. Third, the tape may not have recorded all the sounds of gunfire. An assassin could have used a silencer, or a voice of a policeman could have drowned out the sound of shooting on the voice-activated microphones. Also, in the reconstruction of the shooting, done to provide the acoustics experts with an objective standard with which to compare the tape, shots were fired only from the sixth-floor window of the Depository building and from the Grassy Knoll. The tape may have recorded impulses from shots fired elsewhere in Dealey Plaza, but, inexplicably, the committee failed to authorize the proper tests for the other places.[31]

If the tape is authentic, it definitely disproves the lone-assassin thesis. Not only does the tape reveal the existence of a gunman on the knoll, it also establishes the time between the first and second shots as 1.66 seconds. Since Oswald's rifle could not be fired twice in less than 2.25 seconds, the tape proves that there must have been two gunmen firing from the rear. To avert this embarrassing possibility, the committee hired a team of expert marksmen from the District of Columbia Police Department to conduct firing tests. Oswald's rifle was too worn to be used, so a similar Mannlicher-Carcano was employed. Using a rifle different from Oswald's and firing at stationary targets, the police experts were unable to fire two shots in less than 2.0 seconds. Committee Chief Counsel G. Robert Blakey and Assistant Counsel Gary Cornwell then fired from the hip, i.e., without aiming, and were able to fire two shots in 1.6 seconds. With the exception of Congressman Christopher Dodd, all committee members agreed that Oswald aimed, fired, and missed his target on the first shot, then, *without aiming,* fired so accurately that the bullet went through both President Kennedy and Governor Connally. That this explanation defies logic is obvious. A far more reasonable interpretation of the data than the committee's illogical, remote possibility is that one assassin missed and another fired and struck his target.[32]

The committee decided that the first shot was fired from the Depository at Zapruder frames Z157–161 and missed. The second shot, also from the Depository, came at Z188–191 and struck both Kennedy and Connally. The third shot, from the Grassy Knoll, came at Z295–296 and missed. The fourth shot, again from the Depository, came at Z312, struck President Kennedy in the head, and killed him. While the committee's scenario cannot be ruled out, several factors militate against it. First, the evidence against the single-bullet theory is overwhelming. Second, it hardly seems credible that an assassin firing from the knoll, only 50 feet from the president, missed, while one in the Depository, 300 feet away, hit his target. Third, the medical and ballistics evidence already covered argue strongly in favor of a hit from the Grassy Knoll.[33]

A much more plausible scenario, one that fits the constraints both of the Zapruder film and tapes, as well as the medical and ballistics evidence, follows. The first shot, from the Depository, came at Zapruder frame Z177 and struck Kennedy in the back. The second shot, also from the Depository, struck Connally in the back. It came at Z208. The third shot, from the knoll, struck Kennedy in the head at Z313. The fourth and final shot, at frame Z327, came from the Depository and also hit Kennedy in the head. Even the committeee conceded the possibility of this sequence, although it did not place much credence in it.[34]

Having established the existence of a conspiracy in the Kennedy assassination, the House Select Committee then attempted to identify the conspirators. It eliminated the United States, Soviet, and Cuban governments from complicity but concluded that individuals associated with organized crime or with anti-Castro Cuban exile organizations "may have been involved." Despite certain scraps of evidence hinting of links between Lee Harvey Oswald with the two organizations, the committee produced no credible evidence to substantiate its remark.[35]

The committee's belief that the Soviet government would hardly have risked war with the United States appears reasonable. However, the committee's attempts to procure information from the Soviets and its interview of Fidel Castro proved utterly futile. Likewise, its suggestion that individuals associated with organized crime may have been involved in the Kennedy assassination is totally without corroboration. The alleged involvement of organized crime individuals in such infamous murders as the St. Valentine's Day Massacre, the executions of Albert Anastasia, Sam Giancana, and Johnny Rosselli, and the disappearance of Jimmy Hoffa—all perfectly executed with no traces of evidence left behind—provides little support for the theory that they may have been behind the Kennedy murder. Similarly, the anti-Castro organizations, however outraged they may have been with certain actions of the Kennedy administration, were riddled with dissension, seriously divided among themselves, and had no previous history of domestic violence.[36]

The *Report* of the House Select Committee on Assassinations, then, failed to resolve the main problems raised by the assassination of President Kennedy. Its investigation uncovered some new evidence, particularly the acoustical analysis, but, on the whole, it proved as limited and faulty as that of the Warren Commission. Lacking expertise in the manifold aspects of the assassination, the committee staff members under Chief Counsel Blakey spent the last six months of 1977 merely familiarizing themselves with the evidence that already existed. They had only eight months in 1978 to gather new evidence, interpret the available facts, study the analyses and recommendations of their expert consultants, and prepare for the public hearings in September.[37]

The committee staff functioned under Blakey's rigid rules of secrecy. Instead of opening its investigation to the public, the committee operated in secret, taking great pains not to share the information it gathered with the numerous individuals who could have shared their expertise with the committee staff and provided it with badly needed constructive criticism. Consequently, the staff wasted precious time investigating peripheral and irrelevant matters and neglected far more significant ones. For example, the committee hired the Forensic Pathology Panel to study the medical evidence, but it neglected to consult physicians with experience in treating gunshot wounds. The committee devoted much time to photographic analysis of the famous photographs depicting Lee Harvey Oswald standing in his backyard and holding a rifle, but it neglected to give serious attention to the extremely significant frames Z321–339 of the Zapruder film.[38]

Burdened with an enormous amount of evidence to study and limited by its rigid timetable (the law establishing the committee stipulated that it would cease to exist on 3 January 1979), the House Select Committee on Assassinations proved unable to examine the murder of John Kennedy in the proper manner. The committee's refusal to operate publicly, its lack of expert cross-examination of witnesses, its failure to attach the proper significance to numerous pieces of evidence resulted in an investigation of the assassination that raised more questions than it originally sought to answer.

CHAPTER 11

SOME QUESTIONS

WHEN A HISTORIAN investigates a past event, he usually begins by asking questions about that event. Innumerable questions about the Kennedy assassination have been raised. Some of them are worth considering, for they touch upon the most critical features of the assassination mysteries. The available evidence does not permit definitive answers to all those questions, but they do deserve attention.

1. Who killed President Kennedy?

This, of course, remains the central mystery in the entire assassination saga. Unfortunately, we do not know the answer. That more than one individual fired shots at the president cannot seriously be doubted. Their identities, however, are unknown.

2. Did Lee Harvey Oswald fire any of the shots?

The evidence against Oswald is impressive: the discovery of his rifle bearing his palmprint on the sixth floor of the Book Depository building; the testimony of eyewitness Howard Brennan; Oswald's prints on the cartons and paper sack at the window; the discovery of three cartridge cases from his rifle by the window; the discovery of two bullet fragments fired from his rifle in the limousine; his departure from the building soon after the shooting.

On the other side of the coin, the evidence in Oswald's favor is equally impressive: eyewitness identification of him on the second floor of the Depository building fifteen minutes before the assassination and two minutes after it; the lack of his prints on the outside of the rifle; the questions as to whether the cartridge cases had actually been fired from the rifle during the assassination; the extremely difficult feat of marksmanship an assassin firing from the window faced; the lack of corroboration for Brennan's contradictory and confused identification.

Thus, the evidence about Lee Harvey Oswald's involvement in the assassination is inconclusive. The fact that Oswald *may* have shot the president does not, of course, preclude the possibility that he *may not* have. Obviously, Oswald remains a prime suspect. But an objective evaluation of the evidence simply does not permit a definitive conclusion about his guilt or innocence.

3. How did Lee Harvey Oswald escape the scene of the assassination?

There is no evidence to support the claim of the Warren Commission that Oswald walked out through the front door of the Book Depository building at 12:33. With the exception of the bus transfer allegedly found in Oswald's pocket, neither is there any evidence to support the commission's claim that Oswald caught a bus and a taxi. Replete with contradictions, the testimony of Mary Bledsoe and William Whaley hardly prove that the bus and taxi ride took place.

In contrast, the eyewitness and photographic evidence strongly supports Deputy Sheriff Roger Craig's testimony that he saw Oswald run from the rear of the building about fifteen minutes after the assassination and enter a station wagon driven by a dark-skinned man. Eyewitness Helen Monaghan saw Oswald in an upper floor of the building five to ten minutes after the shots. Eyewitnesses Helen Forrest and James Pennington corroborated Craig's story, for they, too, saw Oswald flee the building and enter the station wagon. While not conclusive, this evidence very solidly supports the conspiracy theory.

4. Was Oswald's gun fired at President Kennedy and Governor Connally?

The fact that two large bullet fragments, ballistically proven traceable to Oswald's rifle, were found in the front seat of the presidential limousine supplies very strong evidence that the rifle was fired once, although the possibility that the fragments were planted in the car cannot be disproven.

No other evidence proves that the rifle was fired more than once. Even if they could be proven beyond question to have been fired from Oswald's rifle, the three empty cartridge cases found on the floor by the sixth-floor window of the Depository building provide no indication that they were fired from the weapon on 22 November 1963. Obviously, the possibility exists that they were fired previously and dropped there to implicate Oswald. Even if the rifle was one of the assassination weapons, there is no proof that Oswald fired it.

5. Are the backyard photographs of Oswald holding a rifle authentic?

Because of several apparent discrepancies between the man pictured in the photographs and known pictures of the real Oswald, many Warren Commission critics questioned the authenticity of the backyard photographs. The panel of photographic experts appointed by the House Select Committee did exhaustive tests on the photographs and negatives and concluded that they were authentic.

For all of the commotion about the photographs, their relevance to the assassination is obscure. They were taken in April 1963, seven months before the assassination. Photographs of Oswald holding a weapon at that time hardly prove or disprove that he discharged that weapon seven months later.

6. How many shots were fired?

The Warren Commission based its three-shot theory primarily on the three cartridge cases, and the House Committee based its four-shot theory primarily on the Dallas police tape. The earwitnesses provide little assistance, for their accounts of the number of shots range from none to seven. Nor do the wounds on Kennedy and Connally provide an answer. Connally's wounds could have been caused by as few as one and as many as three shots, while Kennedy's may have been caused by from two to four shots. The bulk of the evidence points to four shots, three from the rear and one from the front.

7. How many shots struck President Kennedy?

On the surface, the two bullet wounds in the rear of Kennedy's body and the two in front suggest four as the answer to the question. However, the possibility that the two front holes were exit wounds for the rear holes demands close analysis. The rear holes of entrance in the head and back are positive evidence of two shots. As we have seen, the huge, gaping wound in the right front of the president's head could not simply have been an exit hole from one of Oswald's bullets. Almost certainly, it was also an entrance wound caused by a "dum-dum" or exploding bullet fired from the Grassy Knoll. The front wound in Kennedy's throat was probably *not* caused by a separate bullet. The answer, therefore, is at least three.

8. What caused the tiny bullet hole in President Kennedy's throat?

The Warren Commission's and House Committee's claim that this hole was the exit hole for the bullet that entered Kennedy's back is not supported by the evidence. The wound in the president's throat was round, clean, and encircled by a ring of bruising. Moreover, it was extremely small, smaller than the diameter of most bullets. The Forensic Pathology Panel's assertion that the buttoned collar of Kennedy's shirt caused his skin to stretch taut, thus resulting in a small exit wound, appears erroneous. Ordinarily, bullets exiting through taut skin cause large exit wounds because the bullets push tissue and matter through the skin causing it to explode outward, much as a paper bag filled with air will expand and rupture in an uneven, jagged manner as the air rushes out.

If the throat wound were an entrance wound, as some critics have charged, there would have to be some evidence of its path through the body. Since there is none, this explanation can likewise be discounted.

The most plausible explanation for the wound is that it was caused by a fragment of bone or bullet from the head shot. No hole in the neck is visible in enlargements of individual frames of the Zapruder film and in other visual records. This virtually eliminates both the exit and entrance wound theories. The most reasonable explanation, then, is that a fragment was forced through the skull cavity by the tremendous cranial pressure of the head shot and exited through the president's neck.

9. Was Bullet 399 a genuine assassination bullet?

The overwhelming weight of the evidence indicates that Bullet 399 played no role in the Kennedy assassination. The bullet's almost intact condition precludes it as the cause of Governor Connally's wounds. The removal of bullet fragments from the governor's wrist, the extensive damage to his rib and wrist, and the wounds ballistics tests results all argue persuasively against Bullet 399 as having caused any of Connally's injuries.

A bullet was discovered on a hospital stretcher that had no connection with the assassination. Darrell Tomlinson and O.P. Wright, the only two witnesses who saw the bullet on the stretcher, refused to believe that Bullet 399 was the one they saw. Nor would the two Secret Service officials who handled the stretcher bullet agree that Bullet 399 was the one they handled.

Although Bullet 399 was fired from Oswald's rifle, there is no evidence whatsoever to suggest that it caused any of the wounds on Kennedy and Connally. The Warren Commission and the House Committee assumed that Bullet 399 was the infamous single bullet, primarily because it could be traced to Oswald's rifle. Both bodies, however, failed to investigate the possibility that the bullet was planted in order to implicate Oswald.

It is possible that Bullet 399 entered Kennedy's back, penetrated only a couple of inches into the body, and did not exit—later falling out during external cardiac massage. This, in fact, was the original impression of the autopsy pathologists. If this is the case, we do not know how it wound up on a hospital stretcher that had no connection with the assassination.

Because of the incomplete information available, we still do not know when Bullet 399 was fired or how it came into the possession of the FBI as an item of ballistics evidence.

10. Did an assassin fire shots from the Grassy Knoll?

Yes. The huge, gaping hole in the right front of President Kennedy's head was almost certainly caused by an exploding bullet fired from the knoll. The rapid backward and leftward movement of Kennedy's head, as well as the backward and leftward spray of brain tissue, skull bone, and blood are very strong indicators of a shot from the right front. Assuming that it is authentic, the acoustical tape actually recorded the sound of a knoll shot.

Eye and earwitness testimony furnishes further evidence of a shot from the knoll. Almost three-quarters of the witnesses who testified heard shots from the knoll during the shooting, and three people saw a flash of light there. Five witnesses smelled gunpowder in the knoll area. A witness saw a man fleeing the knoll immediately after the shooting, and two law enforcement officials encountered phony "Secret Service" men in the parking lot behind the knoll within minutes after the gunfire.

11. If a shot came from the Grassy Knoll, why was no physical evidence of it discovered?

The answer to this question, so frequently asked by defenders of the *Warren Report,* is as simple as it is obvious. Common sense should be sufficient to explain that anyone taking the risk of killing the President of the United States would also have taken the precautions necessary to avoid leaving physical evidence of his guilt. The peculiar part of this aspect of the assassination case is not the lack of physical evidence on the knoll, but the plethora of evidence scattered all over the sixth floor of the Book Depository building. The two government investigations insist that Lee Harvey Oswald did not even bother to pick up the three cartridge cases and paper bag near the sixth-floor window but, in the process of descending the building stairs, paused for the refreshment of a Coke before departing the building.

An assassin with even the slightest concern with making a successful escape would hardly have selected the sixth floor of the Depository Building for his firing site. He would have been trapped on an upper floor of the building. His only means of escape would have been to descend six flights of stairs and then weave his way through the crowd of spectators and police to freedom.

The Grassy Knoll, on the other hand, provided a natural and ideal sniper's position. The six-foot-high wooden fence and the abundance of shrubbery concealed him from the crowd, yet gave him an undisturbed line of fire at the president. The parking lot right behind the knoll gave him quick access to a getaway vehicle.

12. Who were the "Secret Service" men encountered on the knoll right after the shots?

We know that they were not genuine Secret Service agents since all agents remained with the motorcade during its dash to Parkland Hospital. The men who flashed "Secret Service" credentials to Officer Smith and Constable Weizman, therefore, were imposters, and their identities have never been discovered. It need hardly be mentioned that the Warren Commission made no attempt to investigate this obviously serious matter.

13. Who were the three "tramps" arrested in the railroad yards behind the Grassy Knoll?

The theory that two of the three men were E. Howard Hunt and Frank Sturgis may be dismissed as unwarranted speculation. However, their true identities have never been determined. The Dallas police must have had some reason for arresting them but destroyed the records of the arrest. It is unlikely that the police would have suspended their search for the president's assassin to look for vagrants. However, as with so many other aspects of this case, the incomplete evidence does not permit an answer to the question.

14. Were two men seen together on an upper floor of the Texas School Book Depository building?

Yes. Witnesses Carolyn Walther, Richard Carr, Ruby Henderson, Arnold Rowland, and Johnny L. Powell saw two men, one of them dark-complected, together on the sixth floor. The Hughes and Bronson films of the assassination apparently show two men near the sixth-floor window.

15. Why did the Secret Service fail to respond to the initial gunshots and attempt to protect President Kennedy?

The Zapruder and other films and photographs of the assassination clearly reveal the utter lack of response by Secret Service agents Roy Kellerman and James Greer, who were in the front seat of the presidential limousine. After the first two shots, Greer actually slowed the vehicle to less than five miles an hour. Kellerman merely sat in the front seat, seemingly oblivious to the shooting. In contrast, Secret Service Agent Rufus Youngblood responded instantly to the first shot, and before the head shots were fired, had covered Vice-President Lyndon Johnson with his body.

Trained to react instantaneously, as in the attempted assassinations of President Gerald Ford by Lynette Fromme and Sara Jane Moore and of President Ronald Reagan by John Warnock Hinckley, the Secret Service agents assigned to protect President Kennedy simply neglected their duty. The reason for their neglect remains one of the more intriguing mysteries of the assassination.

16. Why have so many important witnesses in the assassination case met strange deaths?

It is true that certain key individuals in the Kennedy assassination case have met with sudden death under rather unusual circumstances. Among these are Lee Harvey Oswald, David Ferrie, and Jimmy Hoffa. Oswald was gunned down by Jack Ruby in the presence of seventy armed policemen. Ferrie died of natural causes after typing two suicide notes. Hoffa mysteriously disappeared.

The deaths of these and other persons connected with the case have prompted some assassination researchers to speculate that certain sinister forces responsible for Kennedy's murder are responsible for these deaths. However, there is no concrete evidence linking any of the deaths with the assassination itself. Unless such evidence is produced, all attempts to establish such a connection must remain in the realm of conjecture.

17. Was a paper bag found on the floor by the sixth-floor window?

The *Warren Report* claims that it was. However, the bag was not photographed in place, and Dallas law enforcement officers Luke Mooney, Roger Craig, and Gerald Hill, the first three policemen to reach the "sniper's nest," testified that they did *not* see the 38-inch-long sack, which, according to the *Report,* lay only two feet from the window. Three officers who arrived later remember seeing a bag there.

Once again, we are faced with conflicting evidence, and the reader has to decide for himself which appears more reliable.

18. Were all the eyewitnesses to the assassination interviewed?

No. Incredibly, the Dallas police did not seal off Dealey Plaza right after the assassination. They permitted traffic to proceed on Elm Street, just as if nothing had happened there. Over half the eyewitnesses simply left and went home without ever being questioned. Many inmates in the Dallas County Jail watched the motorcade from their prison cells. Even though these men literally constituted a captive audience, none was ever interrogated.

19. Did the Dallas police mishandle the physical evidence?

Yes. The paper bag allegedly found near the sixth-floor window was not photographed in place. The three empty cartridge cases were placed in an envelope, with no indication of the precise location in which each case was found. The police mishandled the book cartons around the window so badly that while only three of Oswald's prints were found on the nineteen cartons, twenty-four prints of policemen were found. The police permitted the press to enter the Depository building shortly after the discovery of the rifle. Before a thorough search of the building had taken place, the press roamed all over it, conceivably destroying evidence. The Dallas police neglected to mark and seal each item of physical evidence, e.g., the rifle, the revolver, the cartridge cases, thus separating each from the others. Instead, they put all the evidence in a large box, an action that resulted in their needlessly touching each other. The police, moreover, gave the Warren Commission three separate and contradictory versions of the transcription of the police radio calls at the time of the assassination. The Dallas police also produced four different, contradictory versions of the way in which the boxes by the window were stacked.

20. Why did the authorities change the motorcade route?

The original route, published in the *Dallas Morning-News* on 22 November 1963, called for the motorcade to proceed directly on Main Street through the triple underpass, *without* making the cumbersome turns onto Houston and Elm streets. The motorcade, however, did make the turn onto Elm, so it could take the Elm Street ramp to Stemmons Freeway. This was not the most direct route to President Kennedy's destination, the Trade Mart building. It would have been quicker and safer for the caravan to go straight on Main Street to Industrial Boulevard, where the Trade Mart is located. We do not know why the change was made.

21. Why did Officer Tippit stop Oswald?

It is difficult to accept the Warren Commission's claim that Tippit stopped Oswald because Oswald fitted the description of the suspect in the Kennedy assassination. That description was so general that it could have described thousands of individuals. Since Tippit had a view only of Oswald's rear, one wonders how he could have matched him with the suspect. Furthermore, if Tippit really suspected Oswald, he almost surely would have drawn his revolver against such a dangerous suspect. Yet, according to the commission's star eyewitness, Helen Markham, Tippit not only made no attempt to make the arrest of a lifetime, he engaged him in friendly conversation.

Neither the Warren Commission nor the House Select Committee on Assassinations tried to explore the unusual circumstances surrounding Tippit's presence in the area. Almost every other police officer in Dallas was ordered to proceed to Dealey Plaza, Parkland Hospital, or Love Field Airport. Tippit alone received instructions to remain where he was, in the residential Oak Cliffs section, where no suspicion of criminal activity had been raised. The police dispatcher also ordered Tippit to "be at large for any emergency that comes in," most unusual instructions, since the primary duty of all policemen is to "be at large" for emergencies.

22. Did Oswald murder J.D. Tippit?

The evidence against Oswald is strong. Eyewitness Helen Markham identified Oswald as the murderer. The House Select Committee located another eyewitness, Jack Tatum, who also identified Oswald as the killer. Six other witnesses saw Oswald fleeing the murder scene, and four cartridge cases fired from Oswald's revolver were found at the scene.

On the other hand, eyewitnesses Aquila Clemmons and

Frank Wright saw two men kill Tippit. A witness, questioned by the FBI but never called before the Warren Commission, saw a man who did not resemble Oswald kill Tippit. The bullets removed from Tippit's body were too mutilated to permit identification of them with Oswald's revolver. Moreover, the cartridge cases and the bullets did not match, the cases coming from different manufacturers than the bullets.

Clearly, the proper channel for resolving this conflicting evidence was a court of law, but Oswald's death made this impossible. As noted, neither the commission nor the committee conducted its inquiry under the adversary process to help settle such issues. The question, therefore, must remain unanswered.

23. Why was Officer Tippit patrolling an area outside his assigned district when he was shot?

Only J.D. Tippit could answer that question, and he is dead. At 12:45 P.M., fifteen minutes after the assassination, the Dallas police dispatcher ordered Tippit to proceed to the "central Oak Cliffs area," which is outside his regularly assigned district. The original Dallas police version of the police tape contains no reference to Tippit. The second version, transcribed five months later, contains the order to Tippit. J.D. Tippit was the only policeman in Dallas who was given instructions to patrol a quiet residential area, where no crime had been committed. Every available police officer was ordered to proceed immediately to Dealey Plaza or to Parkland Hospital. The last known location of Officer Tippit was Lancaster and Eighth, about eight blocks from the murder scene. Tippit reported this location at 12:54, twenty-one minutes before he was shot. The Warren Commission would have us believe that Tippit was so careful and methodical in his duties that it took him twenty-one minutes to travel eight blocks. This is a speed of about two miles an hour, slower than a normal walking pace. Obviously, this is yet another matter requiring further investigation.

24. Why did it take Oswald thirty minutes to run from the scene of the Tippit murder to the Texas theater only five blocks away?

Officer Tippit was killed at 1:15 P.M. and Oswald ran into the

Texas Theater at 1:45. Clearly, it did not take him a half-hour to run five blocks. Neither the Warren Commission nor the House Select Committee produced any evidence to indicate what Oswald did during that time span.

25. How many shots were fired at Officer Tippit?

The official Tippit autopsy report states that four bullets were recovered from Tippit's body. Four bullets now form part of the physical evidence in the case. Yet, as with so many other parts of the Kennedy assassination, some of the circumstances underlying the discovery of this evidence appear strange and indeed mysterious.

The original Dallas police inventory of evidence turned over to the FBI lists "bullet [*sic*] recovered from body of Officer J.D. Tippit." The other three bullets did not turn up until four months after the murder, when they were discovered in a file cabinet at Dallas police headquarters (the same cabinet that contained the tape?).

On 11 December 1963, Secret Service agents Edward Moore and Forrest Sorrels reported their conversation with Dallas medical examiner Dr. Earl Rose: "only three of the four bullets penetrated into Tippit's body. The fourth apparently hit a button on the officer's coat. . . . When the examination [autopsy] was performed, three bullets were removed from the body and turned over to the Police Crime Lab." The police homicide report confirms this. According to that report, Tippit was shot "once in the right temple, once in the right side of the chest, and once in center of stomach." The actual autopsy, however, states that three bullets struck Tippit in the chest and one struck him in the head. A letter from J. Edgar Hoover to J. Lee Rankin notifies the commission that the FBI did not receive the "three" [*sic*] bullets until late March 1964, four months after the assassination. Yet Secret Service agents Moore and Sorrels reported on 11 December, only three weeks after the murder, that the bullets "are now in the possession of the FBI."[1]

The obvious contradictions in the evidence leave unanswered the questions of whether three or four shots struck Tippit and what happened to the bullets. Considering the fact that three of the bullets were Remingtons and one was a Winchester, while two of the cartridge cases found at the Tippit murder scene were Remingtons and two were Winchesters, it is not unreasonable to conclude that the Tippit murder requires clarification.

26. Why did Jack Ruby kill Lee Harvey Oswald?

The Warren Commission's claim that Ruby wanted to spare Mrs. Kennedy the personal ordeal of a trial seems flimsy. When Earl Warren interviewed Ruby in his Dallas jail, Ruby pleaded with the chief justice to let him testify in Washington, where he would tell the real story behind the whole assassination controversy. Inexplicably, Warren denied Ruby's request.[2]

While it is possible to imagine numerous motives for Ruby's act, there is no reliable, independent evidence to substantiate such speculation. Whatever Ruby's reasons, they remain unknown.

27. How did Ruby gain access to the heavily guarded basement of Dallas police headquarters?

The House Select Committee on Assassinations uncovered evidence that indicated the likelihood that a Dallas police officer assisted Ruby in entering the basement.

The fact that Ruby managed to walk past seventy armed law enforcement officials and gun down Oswald obviously raises suspicions of a conspiracy in this murder. The available evidence, however, does not permit a conclusive determination either of the nature or extent of that conspiracy.[3]

28. Did Jack Ruby and Lee Harvey Oswald know each other?

Over a dozen reliable witnesses claim to have seen the two men together during the four months prior to the assassination. Six separate eyewitnesses saw Ruby and Oswald in Ruby's Carousel Club in November 1963. Those witnesses included three employees and three patrons of the club. The author has interviewed a journalist who saw a photograph of Ruby and Oswald together.

The other witnesses included a lady who saw Ruby and Oswald together in New Orleans in the summer of 1963. While the FBI dismissed her account, Ruby, in fact, did visit New Orleans during that period.[4]

Again, the evidence is not conclusive, but it does strongly

14. *Oswald in New Orleans.* Lee Harvey Oswald passing out pro-Castro leaflets in New Orleans. Note the Latinos near him.

suggest that Ruby and Oswald may very well have known each other before the assassination.[5]

29. Did the Dallas police violate Lee Harvey Oswald's legal rights while they held him in custody?

Despite the Warren Commission's disclaimer, the answer is a decided affirmative. At his midnight press conference on 22 November, Oswald told newsmen that he was "not allowed legal representation" and requested "someone to come forward to give me legal assistance." The Dallas police chief, Jesse Curry, admitted that "we were violating every principle of interrogation." As we have seen, the police lineups appeared rigged to make identification of Oswald almost certain. He was the only suspect with a bruised and cut face and with disheveled clothing. He was dressed differently from the other men in the lineup. He was put in a lineup with three teenagers. At least one witness was persuaded by the police to sign an affidavit identifying Oswald *before* he viewed the lineup. The search warrant authorizing the search of Oswald's room did not specify the objects being sought by the police.

30. Did Oswald drive an automobile?

The Warren Commission claims that he did not, but there is substantial evidence to the contrary. Albert Bogard, a Dallas new car salesman, swore that he took Oswald for a test drive of a car less than two weeks before the assassination. Edith Whitworth and Gertrude Hunter saw Oswald driving a blue 1957 Ford about two weeks before the assassination. One of the lodgers in Oswald's rooming house at 1026 North Beckley Avenue let him drive his blue Ford sedan. Two service station operators recalled Oswald's driving a car and having it serviced. Journalists attempting to trace Oswald's route from Laredo, Mexico, to Dallas interviewed numerous service station operators, cafe owners, and other proprietors who recalled Oswald's stopping at their establishments.[6]

31. With whom did Oswald associate during his stay in New Orleans in the spring and summer of 1963?

Although the Warren Commission concluded that Oswald's Marxist, pro-Castro views led him to various activities promoting those views, it failed to demonstrate that Oswald contacted even one individual of similar views during his New Orleans stay. The evidence, in fact, demonstrated that *all* of Oswald's known associations were with individuals of right-wing persuasion. The author's extensive research into this topic has produced much new evidence of Lee Harvey Oswald's right-wing activities in New Orleans.[7]

On numerous occasions, Oswald associated with Guy Bannister, an ex-FBI official and a private investigator. Militantly anti-Castro and rabidly segregationist, Bannister was well known in the New Orleans area for his extremist views. Twice, Bannister and Oswald visited the campus of Louisiana State University in New Orleans and engaged students in heated discussions of federal racial policies. During these discussions, Oswald vehemently attacked the civil rights policies of the Kennedy administration.[8]

Another right-wing extremist with whom Oswald associated was David William Ferrie. A defrocked Eastern Orthodox priest, an expert pilot, a research chemist, and a sexual deviate, Ferrie also actively participated in anti-Castro organizations and smuggled supplies to anti-Castro rebels in Cuba. Once, Ferrie and Oswald attended a party, where they discussed the desirability of a *coup d'état* against the Kennedy administration. On another occasion, Oswald and Ferrie were seen at Ponchartrain Beach, a New Orleans amusement park. Oswald and Ferrie also frequented the Napoleon House bar, a popular hangout for college students. There they often debated Kennedy's foreign policy with the students. Accompanied by two "Latins," Ferrie and Oswald were observed in Baton Rouge, where they openly denounced Kennedy's foreign and domestic policies.[9]

One of the most significant eyewitness observations was of Ferrie, Oswald, and numerous Cubans, all dressed in military fatigues and carrying automatic rifles, conducting what appeared to be a "military training maneuver." This event took place near Bedico Creek, a swampy inland body of water near Lake Ponchartrain, about fifty miles north of New Orleans. This occurred in early September 1963, two months after the final government raid on anti-Castro guerrilla camps in the United States.[10]

The night of 22 November, David Ferrie drove 250 miles from New Orleans to Galveston, Texas, in a blinding thunderstorm. At Galveston, Ferrie received and made several long-distance telephone calls. The following day, he drove to Houston, then Alexandria, Louisiana, and then to Hammond, where he spent the night in the dormitory room of a friend who was a student at a local college. Then he returned to New Orleans, where he underwent questioning by the FBI. Shortly after the assassination, Ferrie deposited over seven thousand dollars in his bank account, even though he did not have a steady job.[11]

Obviously, these New Orleans activities of Oswald's warrant further investigation. The House Select Committee on Assassinations appreciated the significance of Oswald's New Orleans activities but failed to investigate them properly. Instead, it devoted much attention to such irrelevant matters as Ferrie's tenuous link to Carlos Marcello and the bookmaking activities of Oswald's uncle.[12]

What relationship these matters have to the assassination of President Kennedy is unclear. As we have seen, the evidence does not permit a definitive statement about Oswald's role in the Kennedy murder. As far as David Ferrie and Guy Bannister are concerned, there is no evidence at all to link them to the crime. The New Orleans evidence, however, does demonstrate that Oswald's public image as a pro-Castro Marxist was a facade masking the anti-Castro and anti-Communist agitator beneath.

32. How significant was the Garrison investigation?

In February 1967, New Orleans District Attorney Jim Garrison announced that his office was investigating the assassination. This sensational news aroused a storm of controversy and publicity. The Garrison investigation resulted in the arrest and trial of New Orleans businessman Clay Shaw for conspiracy to murder John F. Kennedy. The 1969 trial resulted in Shaw's acquittal.

During the two-year investigation, Garrison made many irresponsible statements about the FBI, CIA, and other government agencies and about assassins firing from manholes and escaping through underground sewers. However, he did reveal the large exent to which the federal government had suppressed evidence about the assassination, demonstrated the relationship between Oswald and Bannister and Ferrie, and brought out much new information about the Zapruder film, the Kennedy autopsy, and ballistics evidence.

33. Did Oswald work for an intelligence agency of the United States government?

No. The evidence clearly shows that Oswald had no direct relationship with United States intelligence. After his defection to the Soviet Union, both the FBI and CIA maintained dossiers on Oswald, but these files contain no information pertinent to the assassination. Those writers who have suggested that Oswald's sojourn in the U.S.S.R., his trip to Mexico City, or his contacts with FBI Agent James Hosty proved significant to the assassination have failed to substantiate their theories.

34. Was an imposter buried in Lee Harvey Oswald's grave?

Differences of up to three inches in reports of Oswald's height, plus minor variations in the reports of certain physical marks on Oswald's body (wrist scars, mastoidectomy scar, etc.) have led some critics, most notably Michael Eddowes, a British investigator, to call for a disinterrment of Oswald's coffin and an exhumation autopsy on the body in it.

Eddowes's theory that while he was in the Soviet Union, Oswald was eliminated by the KGB and his place taken by a trained imposter is far-fetched. Oswald lived with his wife for over a year after they left the U.S.S.R. Oswald's mother, brother, and other relatives all saw him and had close contact with him and did not notice anything unusual about him.

35. Is vital evidence in the Kennedy assassination missing from the National Archives collection of assassination materials?

Numerous items of critical significance are indeed missing: the president's brain, tissue slides of his wounds, several autopsy photographs and X-rays, some bullet fragments originally tested by the FBI, and miscellaneous documents and other materials. The lack of these materials obviously presents a formidable obstacle to any attempt to answer some of the key questions about the assassination. Why they are missing is not known.

36. Why did the FBI and CIA withhold information from the Warren Commission?

As far as the FBI is concerned, it seems that the main reason was J. Edgar Hoover's precipitous decision that there was no assassination conspiracy and his almost paranoid desire not to tarnish the bureau's public image. Hoover tried to dissuade Lyndon Johnson from appointing a presidential commission to investigate the assassination, but Johnson bowed to public pressure. One of Hoover's top assistants, William Sullivan, stated that Hoover regarded the Warren Commission as an adversary and even periodically leaked information to the press to force the commission to conduct its inquiry along the lines of the already completed FBI report. The acting attorney general, Nicholas deB. Katzenbach, testified that if the FBI had come across evidence of a conspiracy, "what would have happened to that information, God only knows." The 125,000 pages of FBI assassination files, many of them marked by Hoover himself, contain much information that the bureau never shared with the commission.[13]

The CIA, too, failed to share all of its information with the Warren Commission. But its refusal to do so stemmed from the nature of the agency itself. The purpose of the CIA is to gather intelligence, a function that requires secrecy. The agency investigated the assassination only as it related to foreign activities. It appointed Richard Helms as its liaison with the Warren Commission, and Helms gave the commission only information that did not compromise the CIA's extensive network of agents. It is true that the CIA did not inform the Warren Commission about various matters, but in almost all instances, the information withheld had only an indirect connection with the assassination.[14]

37. In his book *Best Evidence,* David Lifton asserted that the body of President Kennedy was altered to conceal evidence of shots from the front. How valid is Lifton's theory?

In his book, Lifton asserted that an unidentified group of conspirators planned, executed, and concealed the assassination of President Kennedy. Even though the Zapruder film and certain other evidence indicated gunfire from the Grassy Knoll, the "best evidence" in the case and the evidence that would be given the most credence in a court of law was the official autopsy. Therefore, the conspirators altered the body of President Kennedy to make it appear he had been shot from behind.

When the president was rushed into the emergency room at Parkland Hospital, the doctors noticed a tiny hole in the throat. They all believed that this hole was clearly a wound of entrance, as the remarks to the press by the Parkland physicians indicated. Furthermore, the Dallas doctors stated, both in their written medical reports and in their testimony before the Warren Commission, that there was a very large wound of exit in the rear of the president's head. These observations were substantiated by those of laboratory and X-ray technicians, photographers, and physicians at Bethesda Naval Hospital who saw the body before the autopsy began.

To assure the success of their scheme, the plotters had to change the nature of the wounds on the body in order to make it appear that it contained only evidence of rear-entry wounds. The conspirators, therefore, carried out an elaborate plot of what Lifton calls "deception and disguise," a fantastic plot that entailed altering the body of John Kennedy.

From interviews with witnesses at Bethesda and from other sources, Lifton concludes that the body was removed from its bronze coffin while the presidential party was aboard Air Force One on the trip from Dallas to Washington. As the television cameras focused on the removal of the bronze coffin from the plane, the conspirators put the body in a helicopter and flew it to Bethesda. There they arranged various means, including two ambulances, to deceive the official party awaiting the arrival of the bronze coffin.

As this deception took place, the body was altered to give it the appearance of having been struck from the rear. The conspirators removed the brain and "reconstructed" the skull, eradicating all signs of the massive exit hole in the back of the head. They also placed small entrance holes in the upper back and in the rear of the head. When the actual autopsy was performed, the pathologists inspected a body that gave the appearance of being hit twice from behind. Lifton quotes the Sibert-O'Neill FBI autopsy report that "surgery of the head area" had been performed prior to the start of the postmortem. This, Lifton believes, was the alteration done on the original head wounds.

David Lifton's theory is not only novel, but it presents a startling account of an assassination plot conceived, executed, and disguised by the executive branch of the federal government. David Lifton has a reputation as one of the most thorough assassination researchers. His work is well documented and displays a careful attention to detail. For these reasons, and because of the sensational nature of Lifton's theory, an analysis of his main points will now be presented.

The documentary record substantiates Lifton's contention that medical descriptions of the Kennedy head wounds vary widely. Most of the Dallas doctors did testify that they saw a large exit wound in the back of the head, whereas the autopsy describes a small entrance wound in the back of the head and a large exit wound to the front. Lifton, however, ignored the fact that not all the Dallas doctors saw a large wound in the rear of the head. Dr. Charles Baxter stated that he saw a wound in the "temporal parietal plate of bone" in the side of the head. Dr. Adolph Giesecke noted the absence of skull from the top of the head to the ear, and from the browline to the back of the head. Dr. Kenneth Salyer observed a wound of the right temporal region on the side of the head. And Dr. Marion Jenkins mentioned "a great laceration of the right side of the head." Lifton quoted only those Dallas physicians who saw the large hole in the rear of the head and thus presented a misleading impression to his readers.

More significantly, Lifton ignored a vital aspect of the evidence. Throughout the emergency room treatment, President Kennedy lay on his back, with the back of his head resting on the mattress of the emergency cart. As Dr. Malcolm Perry told the Warren Commission, "He was lying supine [on his back] on the emergency cart." At no time was he turned over. If there was one point on which all the Dallas doctors agreed, it was that they never saw the president's back, including the rear of his head.

During the twenty minutes in which they worked to save

President Kennedy's life, the Parkland physicians did not even attempt to treat the head wound. Their efforts at resuscitation centered on the tracheotomy and on closed chest massage. Busy with these emergency measures, the doctors did not examine the head wound closely. During the time in which they were in the emergency room, the Dallas doctors glanced at the head wound and saw blood and brain tissue oozing out and two large flaps of scalp covering much of the hair and exposing the cranial cavity. They did not see the head after it was cleaned, and they took no measurements to record the exact nature of the wounds. As one of the Dallas physicians remarked to the author, the reason he and his colleagues mentioned a large wound in the rear of the head is that from their brief glances at the head, it looked like a rear wound. However, after seeing the Zapruder film and the autopsy drawings, he was perfectly satisfied that the wound was indeed in the right front of the head.

Another omission in Lifton's theory is his belief that the conspirators inflicted wounds on the body over six hours after the assassination. Although he claims to have read widely in textbooks on forensic pathology, Lifton apparently did not notice one of the most elementary principles of autopsy procedure: damage inflicted on a body after death is easily distinguishable from that inflicted on a living body. If the conspirators had reconstructed Kennedy's skull and produced two entrance wounds on the body, the Bethesda pathologists would have recognized the postmortem changes. By the time of the autopsy, the body was in the beginning stages of rigor mortis and exhibited signs of livor mortis and algor mortis (three of the stages a corpse undergoes after death). Any damage inflicted on that body would have displayed definite pathological signs of alteration, and the entrance wounds in the back and the head would not have shown microscopic indications of "coagulation necrosis," since the blood had long since ceased circulating.

Lifton claims that John Kennedy was shot in the front of the head by gunfire from the Grassy Knoll, thus causing the large exit wound in the rear observed by the Dallas doctors. Yet he fails to account for the fact that no one at Dallas or Bethesda saw an entrance wound in the front of the head. If the Dallas doctors were so observant as to see an exit wound in the rear of the head while the president lay face-up on the cart, why did they not see the entrance wound also?

Instead of the contradictory recollections of the Dallas doctors, we possess the objective evidence of the Zapruder film. Frames Z314–335 clearly depict the very large wound on the right front side of John Kennedy's head. The film also shows that the rear of the head remains intact throughout the assassination. Lifton argues that the CIA must have "doctored" the film to produce a false image. In addition to producing no evidence whatsoever to support this speculation, Lifton ignored the fact that the film graphically shows the violent backward movement of the head, hardly evidence of a rear-entering shot.

The autopsy X-rays and photographs depict the entrance holes in the back and in the rear of the head and also the huge, gaping wound in the right front of the head. According to Lifton, the photographs and X-rays were taken after the reconstruction of the body, so they would corroborate the autopsy findings. As we have seen, the photographs and X-rays do not provide irrefutable evidence of wounds inflicted only from the rear. The very large wound on the right side of the head depicted in these visual records could have been made by the explosion of a "dumdum" bullet fired from the right front. In addition, through dental identification and precise comparisons of certain anatomical features, experts hired by the House Select Committee on Assassinations positively identified the X-rays and photographs as authentic and the body depicted in them as that of John F. Kennedy. If the skull were "reconstructed," as Lifton claims, the X-rays would not contain the anatomical features essential to proper authentication.

In his work, Lifton quotes extensively from the FBI agents present at the autopsy and from laboratory technicians. FBI Agents Sibert and O'Neill, for example, stated that "surgery of the head area" had been performed prior to the autopsy. To Lifton, this is proof that the conspirators had reconstructed the skull. In fact, the Sibert-O'Neill report was written by the agents the day after the autopsy. It is neither a verbatim record of the proceedings nor a detailed medical recounting of the events that took place. The laboratory technicians and other witnesses to the autopsy provided widely divergent accounts of the wounds. By quoting only those that supported his thesis, Lifton provided a very misleading account to his readers, as he did with the Dallas doctors.

Another of Lifton's arguments is that during the autopsy, Dr. Humes removed the brain from the cranial vault without recourse to the surgical procedures normally required. To Lifton, this was evidence that the brain had been removed prior to the autopsy by the conspirators in order to alter it. This argument has little basis. The autopsy protocol, as well as the testimony of the pathologists, attest to the enormous damage done to the head. The skull was shattered. Almost three-quarters of the right half of the brain had been blown out of the head. When Dr. Humes began his examination of the head, pieces of the skull came apart in his hands, vivid testimony to the explosive impact of the bullet. All of the damage to the head that Lifton details as unusual can be explained as the result of an exploding bullet literally blowing the head apart.

Lifton believes that the autopsy photographs showing the large, gaping wound in the right front of President Kennedy's head were deliberately altered to make the wound appear as an exit wound. That it was an exit wound is precisely what the autopsy pathologists believed and what all subsequent medical inspections of the photographs concluded. However, the wound is not necessarily one of exit. An exploding bullet fired from the right front could have caused that wound. In the first volume of the House Select Committee on Assassinations hearings on the murder of Martin Luther King, drawings made from autopsy photographs of Dr. King clearly show a huge hole almost four inches long and two inches wide on the lower right side of the face, just above the jaw. According to the committee's Forensic Pathology Panel, this huge wound in Dr. King's face was an *entrance* wound caused by the explosion of a soft-nosed 30.06 bullet. Dr. Michael Baden, the chairman of the panel, told the committee that "the injuries seen on Dr. King with the bursting explosive-like injury to the face" were "entirely consistent" with an entrance wound of an exploding bullet.

David Lifton's theory, as sensational as it may appear, simply does not stand verified by the objective evidence. As detailed here, the autopsy left much room for criticism, and the fact that certain items of the medical evidence are missing obviously raises suspicions of a possible cover-up. The questions surrounding the death of President Kennedy are numerous, many of them still unanswered. Those posed by David Lifton, however, do not fall into this category.

CHAPTER 12

SUMMARY

ALTHOUGH it has been the object of two intensive federal investigations and the subject of countless books, articles, and other works, the assassination of President Kennedy has not yet received the thorough, disinterested attention it deserves. Both the Warren Commission and the House Select Committee on Assassinations proved unable to free themselves of the political constraints that forced their investigations into certain narrow channels. With few exceptions, those who have written about the assassination have colored their works with political partisanship and obvious bias. As a result, the central questions about Kennedy's murder remain unanswered.

As we have seen, the Warren Commission originated more out of Lyndon Johnson's desire to avert other investigations into the assassination than from a genuine desire to find out what actually happened. Johnson's decision to staff the commission with seven distinguished political leaders was clearly a propaganda move, for none of the seven possessed expertise in medicine, ballistics, and related areas. The legal staff chosen by the commission to conduct its actual investigation also lacked expertise in precisely those areas they investigated. Consequently, they overlooked vital evidence, failed to follow numerous clues, and neglected to interview crucial witnesses.

The FBI provided the Warren Commission with a substantial portion of the facts it employed to arrive at its conclusions. Unaware of the FBI's real attitude toward it, the commission accepted the bureau's assistance without hesitation. The recent investigation of the House Select Committee on Assassinations disclosed the fact that J. Edgar Hoover viewed the Warren Commission as an adversary and that he periodically leaked information to the press in order to divert the commission from investigating too thoroughly areas that the FBI had not acted on. Acting Attorney General Nicholas Katzenbach told the House committee that Hoover may very well have destroyed or concealed information that challenged the FBI's original lone-assassin, no-conspiracy theory.

The voluminous 125,000-page collection of FBI papers on the Kennedy assassination contains many items indicating the bureau's efforts to reinforce the lone-assassin thesis. For example, many witnesses gave FBI agents information about a possible assassination conspiracy. In almost all cases, the bureau either ignored these witnesses or tried to disparage their credibility. A large number of the papers are either partially or entirely censored. Ostensibly, the reason for the censorship is national security or personal confidentiality. The titles of some of the censored documents, however, suggest that they may contain information concerning Lee Harvey Oswald's still puzzling foreign activities: "Lee Harvey Oswald—Internal Security—Russia," "Lee Harvey Oswald—Internal Security—Cuba," "Fair Play for Cuba Committee."

The CIA also failed to share all of its evidence with the Warren Commission. Richard Helms, the agency's contact with the commission, recently admitted that he did not provide the commission with information about certain CIA activities that would possibly compromise the agency's work. Several former Warren Commission staff members stated that had they known about such matters as CIA-sponsored assassination plots against Fidel Castro, they would have looked into the possibility of a conspiracy much more carefully. The CIA assassination papers also include many censored documents concerning such topics as Lee Harvey Oswald, David Ferrie, Cuba, and Russia.

Faced with a "definitive" five-hundred-page FBI assassination report, pressured to meet its deadline, and hampered by the lack of complete evidence, the Warren Commission failed to accomplish its prescribed duty of ascertaining all the facts about the assassination. The commission operated in secret and under procedural rules that virtually guaranteed a biased investigation. Presuming Lee Harvey Oswald guilty, the commission simply ignored evidence to the contrary. The internal commission staff memoranda and other working papers clearly reveal the extent of confusion and uncertainty about such matters as the nature of the wounds on President Kennedy and Governor Connally. In its *Report,* however, the commission presented a version of the assassination that is definitive and devoid of controversy over its main conclusions.

With its numerous deficiencies, the *Warren Report* proved fair game for criticism. That criticism was not long in coming. Within three years after its publication, the *Warren Report* provoked hundreds of works sharply criticizing its main conclusions. Vigorous defenses of the *Report* by William Manchester, Jim Bishop, and other writers failed to stifle the critics. These critical works may be divided into three categories. The first includes those irresponsible muckrakers who attributed the president's death to everything from a Lyndon Johnson–inspired conspiracy to a plot hatched by the same sinister elements responsible for the fall of China to the Communists. The second category includes critics like Mark Lane, Harold Weisberg, and Sylvia Meagher, who uncovered many of the Warren Commission's gross errors but who also proved incapable of distinguishing reliable evidence from speculation. The third category includes such critics as Josiah Thompson, Cyril Wecht, and Howard Roffman, who relied almost exclusively on scientific evidence to offer convincing critiques of such issues as the single-bullet theory.

The House Select Committee on Assassinations was created in an atmosphere of political partisanship, and the first few months of the committee's existence were so embroiled in the feud between Chairman Henry Gonzales and Chief Counsel Richard Sprague that the committee did not really function until it was reconstituted in June 1977. By the time a new staff had been chosen, the committee had just a half-year to investigate the assassination, far too little time to evaluate properly the enormous mass of assassination source materials.

Unlike the Warren Commission, the House Select Committee on Assassinations did hold public hearings, but only a fifth of the hearings covered the scientific, physical evidence in the case. The rest were devoted to peripheral issues that had only an indirect relationship to the assassination itself. Witnesses favorable to the single-bullet theory and similar controversial issues escaped rigorous cross-examination, while the few witnesses like Dr. Cyril Wecht, who dared to challenge some of the central conclusions of the Warren Commission, were subjected to grueling cross-examination.

The committee's scientific "experts" frequently distorted the evidence to prove their theses and often engaged in pseudoscientific speculation. For example, the committee's Photographic Panel decided by a vote of fifteen to one that President Kennedy and Governor Connally were aligned in accordance with the single-bullet theory. Clearly, photographic analysis is not an issue to be decided by a democratic vote, but by hard, objective evidence. That same panel devoted more space in its report to the irrelevant issue of the validity of the backyard photographs of Oswald holding a rifle than to analysis of the Zapruder film. Similarly, the committee's published volumes of evidence devote considerably more space to peripheral issues than to the fundamental ones dealing with the assassination itself. By far the largest of the committee's published volumes is entitled "Staff Reports on Organized Crime," a volume that barely treats the assassination.

An objective evaluation of the evidence compels the conclusion that John Kennedy was assassinated as a result of a conspiracy. The scientific, medical, and ballistic evidence proves that shots were fired from the front and from the rear of the president. It also proves that two assassins fired from the rear, and one from in front. Lee Harvey Oswald's precise role in the assassination cannot be determined. The evidence neither proves that he fired shots at President Kennedy, nor that he did not fire shots. The evidence also does not permit an identification either of the assassins or of those involved in the conspiracy. Perhaps that is why the assassination continues to fascinate the American people. It is an unsolved mystery. That this unsolved murder mystery should entail the assassination of a President of the United States justifies its description as the crime of the century.

CHAPTER 13

THE PLOTTERS AND THEIR DEED

FOREWORD TO CHAPTER THIRTEEN

In the first twelve chapters, an analysis of the evidence in the assassination of President Kennedy has been given. This analysis has been based on primary source materials from the National Archives, the papers of the FBI and CIA, and the published volumes of the Warren Commission and the House Select Committee on Assassinations. One inescapable conclusion gathered from a careful scrutiny of that evidence is that President Kennedy was assassinated because of a conspiracy.

Although the book could end here, the author believes that he would be remiss in not presenting his version of the assassination and of the conspiracy behind it. Chapter Thirteen presents that version. The reader should separate this chapter from the rest of the book because it necessarily entails some speculation by the author. This is because all the evidence in the assassination is not yet available for research. What follows is the author's interpretation of how the actual events in Dealey Plaza took place, as well as a synopsis of the main conspiracy theories. It is based on the author's thorough analysis of the available evidence and presents the most reasonable version of the assassination.

ON 9 NOVEMBER 1963, the head of the intelligence division of the Miami police listened to a tape recording of a conversation between a police informant and Joseph Milteer, a well-known right-wing extremist. The conversation contained ominous allusions to a possible assassination attempt against President Kennedy when he visited Miami on 18 November.

Informant: Well, how in the hell do you figure would be the best way to get him [Kennedy]?

Milteer: From an office building with a high-powered rifle.
Informant: They are really going to try to kill him?
Milteer: Oh, yeah, it is in the working. . . .[1]

The Miami police relayed this information to the Secret Service, which then made last-minute changes in President Kennedy's Miami appearance. Instead of a motorcade, the agency arranged to have Kennedy flown by helicopter from the airport to the hotel where a speech would be given and then back to the airport. Such precautions clearly reduced the possibility of an assassination attempt.[2]

During the middle of the night of 20 November 1963, Lieutenant Francis Fruge of the Louisiana state police drove a woman to a hospital near Eunice, Louisiana. Since the lady, Rose Cheramie, was a known narcotics addict, Fruge paid little attention to her rambling, half-incoherent tale. Cheramie claimed that she and two male companions were making a "drug run" from Louisiana to Houston, Texas. During the automobile ride, they discussed the imminence of an assassination attempt against President Kennedy in Dallas on Friday, 22 November. After Cheramie got high on drugs, the men threw her out of the car. Lieutenant Fruge thought nothing of Rose Cheramie's story, nor did the physician to whom she repeated it. After learning of the Dallas murder, however, Fruge called the Dallas police and informed them of Cheramie's tale, but the Texas authorities were uninterested.[3]

Two days before the assassination, two Dallas police officers were making their usual rounds on patrol. As they entered Dealey Plaza, they observed several men engaged in target practice with a rifle. The men were situated behind the wooden fence on the Grassy Knoll. By the time the policemen reached the area, the men had vanished, apparently leaving in a car parked nearby.[4]

These incidents obviously raise the distinct possibility of an assassination conspiracy. Several documents from the FBI and CIA assassination files also hint that foreknowledge of the president's murder was fairly widespread. On 21 November, a Cuban told Gregory Basila, a San Antonio pharmacist, that "Kennedy will be killed in Dallas tomorrow." An informant told the FBI's Miami office that $25,000 to $50,000 was being offered to assassinate the president. Early in the morning of 22 November, a CIA source in Madrid heard a former Cuban journalist say that "Kennedy would be killed that day."[5]

Even more suggestive were two incidents that occurred before the assassination. In late September 1963, Sylvia and Anne Odio were visited in their Dallas apartment by two Cubans and an American. A couple of days later one of the Cubans, Leopoldo, telephoned Sylvia and told her that the American was so "loco" that he might even shoot the president of the United States. On the day of the assassination, Sylvia Odio fainted when she saw Lee Harvey Oswald's picture on television and immediately recognized him as the American companion of her two Cuban visitors.[6]

Late in the night of 22 November 1963, Clare Boothe Luce, one of America's most distinguished women, received a telephone call from a Cuban exile friend. He told her that he and several friends had met Oswald when he tried to infiltrate their anti-Castro free Cuba organization in New Orleans in the summer of 1963. He also told her that Oswald had made several trips to Mexico City and had returned with a large sum of money. Mrs. Luce recalled her friend's remarking about Oswald's boast that he was a "crack marksman and could shoot anybody," even the president. The last thing the friend told Mrs. Luce was that there "is a Cuban Communist assassination team at large, and Oswald was their hired gun."[7]

These events strongly point to an assassination plot. One or two together may be dismissed as coincidences, but their sheer numbers eliminate that possibility. As we have already seen, the medical, ballistics, and other physical evidence provides overwhelming proof of a conspiracy in the assassination of President Kennedy. It is now appropriate to gather the evidence and to reconstruct the assassination, insofar as that evidence permits. The reconstruction that follows is based on the author's careful analysis of the most reliable evidence available. It contains gaps, for the evidence is incomplete. New evidence not yet uncovered may, of course, change it.

THE "PATSY"

Whatever their reasons, the conspirators had already decided that John Kennedy must die, and they had already selected Dealey Plaza in Dallas as the ideal site for their team of expert marksmen to cut Kennedy down in a crossfire. Now they needed a scapegoat, someone on whom they could draw suspicion during the critical hours when the real assassins made their escape. In Lee Harvey Oswald, they found an ideal candidate.

Oswald's background—his coming from a broken home, dropping out of high school, receiving a dishonorable discharge from the Marines, defecting to the Soviet Union, ardently advocating unpopular causes—was in itself sufficient to cast suspicion on him. In addition, Oswald had a big mouth, frequently boasting about his expertise with a rifle and engaging people in debates about foreign and domestic policy. Oswald's Marxism—he was even married to a Russian woman—made him just the right choice.

During the two months prior to the assassination, the conspirators used an individual who closely resembled Lee Harvey Oswald to engage in a series of suspicious actions designed to call attention to Oswald. First, there was the Odio incident in late September. Then in October, Mrs. Lovell Penn of Dallas noticed three men firing a rifle on her property. She asked them to leave and afterward found an empty cartridge case. It was a 6.5 mm. Mannlicher-Carcano case. On 13 October, "Oswald" was seen at a meeting of a radical anti-Castro group in Dallas.[8]

On 1 November, "Oswald" entered Morgan's Gunshop in Fort Worth and acted "rude and impertinent." A few days later, the night manager of the Dallas Western Union office saw "Oswald" pick up several money orders. On 9 November, "Oswald" test drove a car. The salesman, Albert Bogard, remembered "Oswald's" telling him that he would return in a couple of weeks when he would have "a lot of money." On 10 November, "Oswald" applied for a job as a parking attendant at Allright Parking Systems in Dallas. As he talked with Hubert Morrow, the manager, "Oswald" inquired about the Southland Hotel, where the parking lot was located, and whether the building provided a good view of downtown Dallas.[9]

On the afternoon of 22 November, Dr. Homer Wood saw Oswald's picture on television and recognized him as the man he saw at the Sports Drome Rifle Range in Dallas on 16 November. Dr. Wood, his account corroborated by his son, remembered "Oswald's" firing a 6.5 mm. Italian rifle with a four-power scope. Considering "Oswald's" purchase of ammunition a few days before, the repair work done on his rifle by Dial Ryder, as recounted in Chapter Eight, we see a pattern clearly emerging. "Oswald" bought ammunition, had his rifle repaired, inquired about the view from a Dallas building, remarked about coming into possession of a lot of money very soon, and called attention to himself at the firing range.[10]

All these incidents clearly cast suspicion on Oswald. Yet, the real Lee Harvey Oswald did not participate in any of them. The evidence demonstrates that he was elsewhere when each of these events took place. Yet the evidence also demonstrates that they did take place and that numerous reliable eyewitnesses saw a man who they believed was Lee Harvey Oswald participate in them. While no absolute evidence exists to explain this curiosity, it is not unreasonable to hypothesize that someone impersonating Oswald went to great lengths to focus attention on himself during the three weeks prior to the assassination.[11]

THE ASSASSINATION: A RECONSTRUCTION

They arrived early. The motorcade was not scheduled to reach Dealey Plaza until 12:25 P.M., but the assassins got there much sooner. About an hour before the shooting, Julia Ann Mercer saw a man get out of a panel truck, walk up an embankment, and disappear behind the bushes on the Grassy Knoll. She noticed that he carried "what appeared to be a gun case" in his hand. At the other end of Elm Street, Helen Forrest saw a man with a rifle on the second floor of the Book Depository building. The time was "around noon." About fifteen minutes later, Arnold Rowland saw a man with a rifle in the far southwest window on the sixth floor of the Depository building. About the same time, Carolyn Walther and Ruby Henderson observed two men in the far southeast corner window on the sixth floor of the building. Waiting for the motorcade, inmate

John Powell looked across from his cell on the sixth floor of the Dallas County jail. He, too, saw the two men in the window and watched one of them manipulating the telescopic sight of his rifle.[12]

As the motorcade wound onto Elm Street, the assassins got ready for their prearranged synchronized crossfire. When the limousine reached the agreed-on place, the equivalent of Zapruder frame Z177, the gunman on the lower floor of the Depository building fired. The shot struck the president high on his upper back, but it did not penetrate very far into him. The firecracker-like noise heard by some of the witnesses at this time suggested that the weapon had not fired at its full potential.[13]

Less than two seconds later, at Zapruder frame Z208, the gunman in the sixth-floor southwest corner window fired. As he depressed the trigger, President Kennedy jerked forward and downward, apparently in response to the shot that had hit him in the back. The president's sudden motion moved his body out of the line of fire, the bullet instead slamming into Governor Connally's back.[14]

At this point, the assassins had not achieved their goal of killing President Kennedy, but their insurance against failure had not yet been cashed. The marksman behind the Grassy Knoll's wooden fence moved the scope of his rifle and focused the crosshairs on John Kennedy's right temple. As the slow-moving limousine reached the right spot, Zapruder frame Z312, the knoll assassin squeezed the trigger, and the "dum-dum" bullet exploded against the right front side of Kennedy's head.[15]

The gunman in the sixth-floor southeast corner window of the Depository also focused on the president's head. Now, at Zapruder frame Z327, he fired the final shot in the carefully planned crossfire. Discharged less than a second after the Knoll shot hit the president, this shot entered the rear of the skull near the top of the head, and it exploded out of the huge hole in the front caused by the shot from the knoll.[16]

The escape was as meticulously planned as the assassination. The Grassy Knoll assassin ran from the area, got into a waiting car, and sped away. The gunman on the second floor of the Depository simply left through the unguarded rear door of the building. The sixth-floor assassins waited until they were cer-

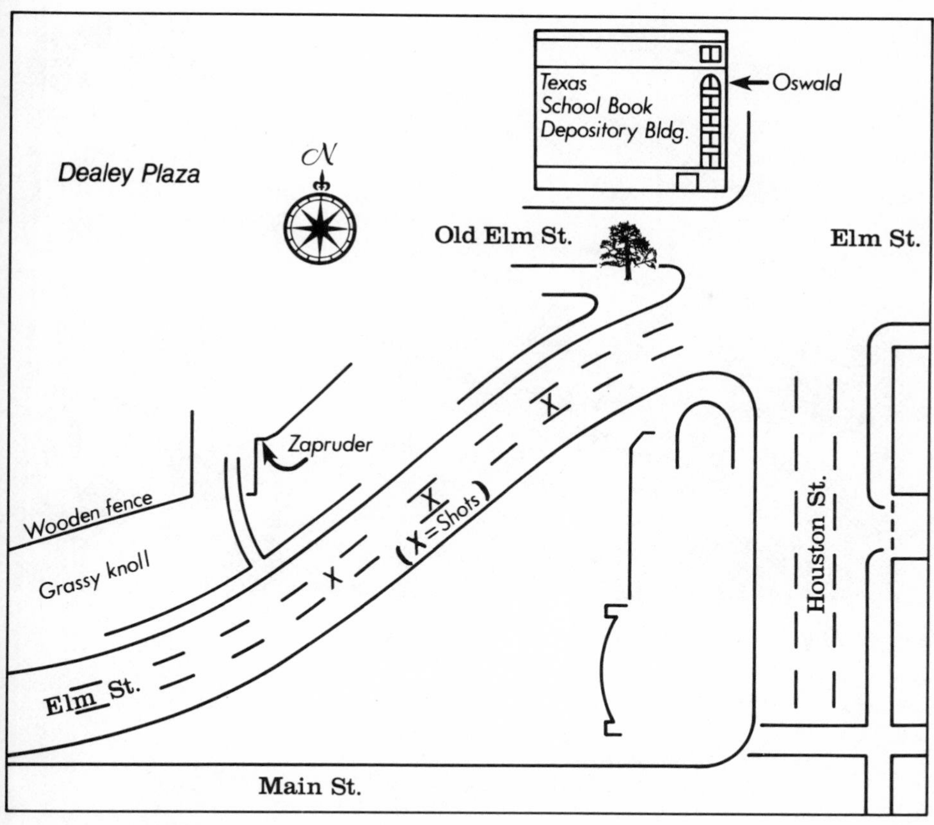

Map 1. Depository Area

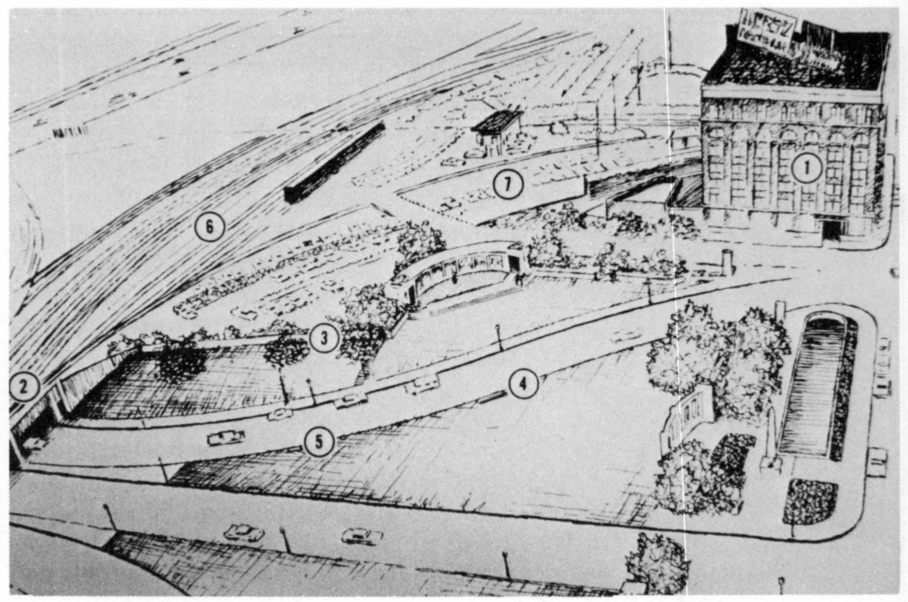

Map 2. Artist's Conception of Depository Area

Legend:

1. Texas School Book Depository building
2. Triple underpass
3. Wooden fence on Grassy Knoll
4. Position of JFK car at time of first shot
5. Position of JFK car at time of head shots
6. Railroad yards behind Grassy Knoll
7. Parking lot behind Grassy Knoll

tain of escape. Then they descended to the first floor and made their way out through the rear door. In the mass confusion following the shooting, they experienced little trouble in finding their getaway vehicle and making good their escape.

Although the evidence about the events in Dealey Plaza is not complete, it does substantiate this version of the assassination. While the House Select Committee on Assassinations asserted that the first shot missed, virtually all other students of the assassination agree that it hit Kennedy in the back. Since the autopsy evidence proved that this shot entered the back at an upward angle, it must have been fired from below the president. Since photographs of the Depository depict open windows on the second floor of the building, and since eyewitness Helen Forrest saw a man with a rifle on the second floor, it is not unreasonable to conclude that the shot came from there. Because of the incline of Elm Street, the first two floors of the Depository were lower than the limousine at the time of the shots. The upward angle of the entrance wound in Kennedy's back precludes that shot as originating from the sixth-floor "Oswald" window.[17]

The second shot, which struck Governor Connally, came from high above him, as the sharp downward angle of the entrance wound in his back proves. That shot could not have first gone through President Kennedy because no bullet exited his neck at a downward angle of 25 degrees. Even though Connally shows no apparent reaction to being struck as early as frame Z208, the House Select Committee's panel of photographic experts did believe that Connally showed signs of reacting to some stimulus as early as frame Z226, immediately after the limousine reappears in the Zapruder film after being hidden from view by the street sign.[18]

Despite the Forensic Pathology Panel's contention that the ovoid shape of the entrance wound in Governor Connally's back indicated that the bullet had first gone through another substance, the evidence attests that the contrary was true. The wound in Connally's back was elongated because it entered at an angle. In other words, the assassin was not directly behind the governor when he shot. The fact that the bullet passed through Connally's chest in a right-to-left trajectory, as well as at a sharp downward slope, fixed the location of the gunman as above, behind, and to the right of the limousine. Since the southeast corner of the Depository's sixth floor would have produced a much flatter trajectory than the 25 degrees measured by Connally's physicians, the assassin must have been at the western end of the building. This would have brought him much closer to the governor, thereby causing a steeper angle for the shot.[19]

The third shot was fired from the Grassy Knoll at frame Z312 and exploded against the right front side of President Kennedy's head. Zapruder frames Z313–321 graphically depict the explosion on the head and the violent backward and leftward movement of the president. The fact that both motorcycle policemen riding to the left rear of the limousine were splattered with brain tissue and the discovery of a piece of the skull over twenty feet behind and to the left of the limousine's location at the instant of the head shot also provide very powerful indications of a shot fired from the right front.[20]

The medical evidence fully supports the knoll shot thesis. After learning of the acoustical evidence of a shot from the knoll, the House Select Committee requested Dr. David O. Davis, an eminent radiologist, to review the Kennedy skull X-rays. Dr. Davis conceded that the X-ray evidence was compatible with a shot from the knoll only if Kennedy's head were "tilted to the left side, that is, with the right ear elevated and the left depressed. . . ." The Zapruder film shows the head in precisely that position in frame Z312, the frame of the shot. The other evidence of a knoll shot—eyewitness, audiovisual, and ballistics—has already been detailed.[21]

The evidence of a shot from the rear at frame Z327 is supplied by eyewitness testimony, the acoustical analysis, the medical evidence, and the Zapruder film. Several witnesses, including trained law enforcement officers, heard a double explosion —"bang, bang"—at the time of the head shots. Assuming its authenticity, the Dallas police tape actually records the double sequence of shots, one from the Grassy Knoll at frame Z312 and another from the Depository at frame Z327, only eight-tenths of a second later.[22]

Eyewitnesses may err, and the findings of the acoustical analysis are subject to revision, but the objective evidence of the Zapruder film cannot be discounted. So preoccupied with the

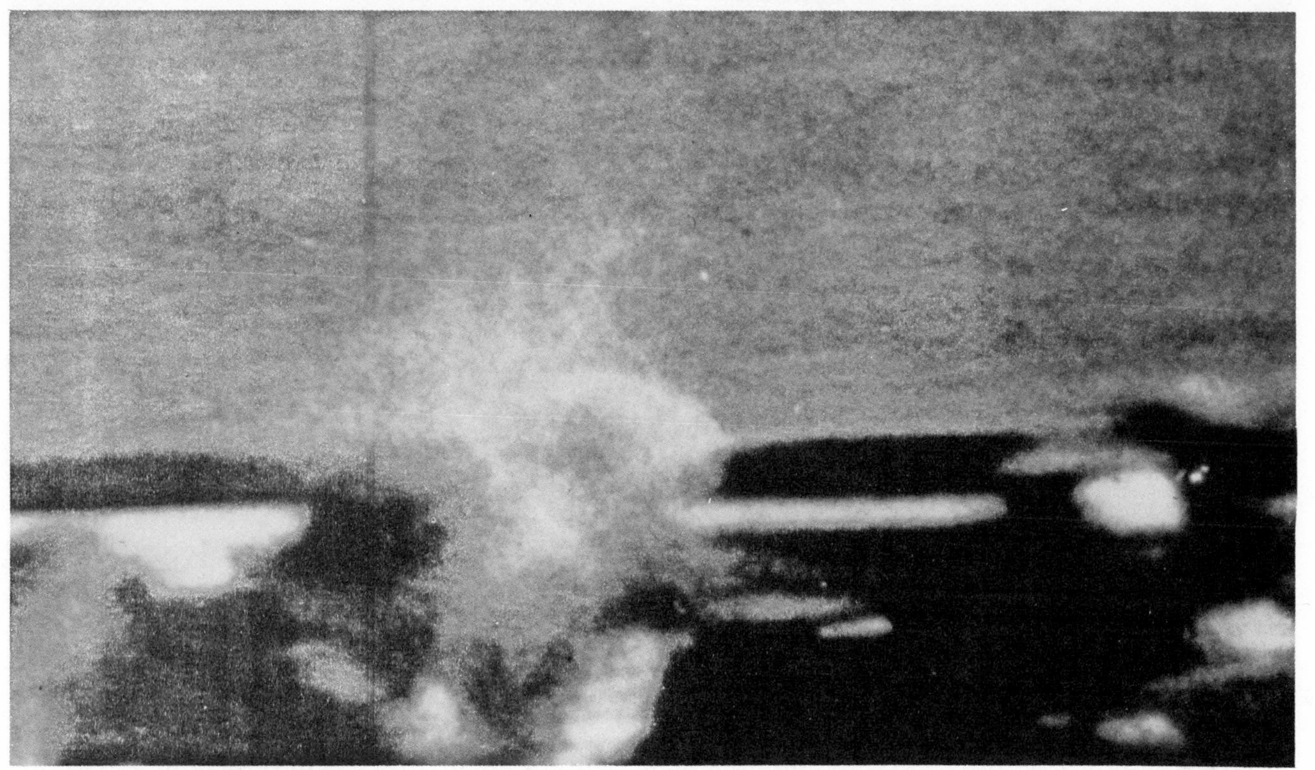

15. *Zapruder Frame Z313*. This frame shows the explosive impact of the Grassy Knoll bullet on JFK's head.

single-bullet frames and with the Z313 head shot have they been that both defenders and critics of the Warren Commission have overlooked the equally significant frames Z321–327 of the film. A careful analysis of those frames reveals positive evidence of a shot's striking President Kennedy in the rear of the head at frame Z327.

After the impact of the Grassy Knoll shot had knocked him against the rear seat of the limousine, President Kennedy bounced back into a sitting position. Frames Z321–327 of the Zapruder film show him leaning forward and to the left in much the same position he was in when the knoll shot struck him. In frame Z327, the large gaping wound on the right side of his head caused by the Grassy Knoll shot is clearly visible. Suddenly, in frame Z328, Kennedy springs rapidly forward. In one-sixth of a second, he was propelled forward over three feet, a velocity almost as great as the backward momentum triggered by the Grassy Knoll shot. The forward movement of the president was so strong that he soon fell face down on the seat with his left foot dangling over the rear door of the vehicle. Since the limousine did not accelerate until after this forward motion, some external force must have caused it. That external force was the bullet entering the rear of the head.[23]

Zapruder frames Z327–335 supply further evidence of this shot. In frames Z314–327, the wound inflicted by the Grassy Knoll shot is visible. That wound extends from above the right ear to the forehead. It is about two and a half inches long and two inches high. Although large and bloody, the wound does not cover the entire right front half of the head. The top of the head is plainly visible, and the skull does not protrude outward. This wound bears all the signs of one caused by an exploding bullet fired from the right front.[24]

Frames Z328–335 reveal a strikingly different picture of the head wound. In those frames, as President Kennedy is driven forward, the head wound visible in the earlier frames suddenly explodes open. Two very large pieces of skull and scalp spring open, revealing a very deep cavity inside the head. By frame Z331 the top of the front half of the head is no longer visible; it is concealed by a huge flap of the scalp. Not visible before frame Z328, the skull becomes plainly visible only one-sixth of a sec-

16. *Zapruder Frame Z327.* JFK at instant of second head shot. Note the wound on the right side of the head. The top of the head above the wound is still visible.

17. *Zapruder Frame Z335.* JFK after being struck by the second head shot, fired from the rear. Note the extent of JFK's forward motion by comparing his position in this frame with his position in the previous photograph, taken less than half a second earlier. Also compare the large, gaping wound in this photograph with that in the previous one. The top of the head above the wound is no longer visible, the two large flaps of scalp now cover much of the front half of the head.

ond later. The 2½-inch-long wound seen in frames Z314–327 expands into an enormous cavity over five inches long and five inches high. The rear of the president's head, intact through frame Z327, is seriously disrupted by frame Z331.[25]

Zapruder frames Z327–331 provide very strong visual evidence of a shot's striking President Kennedy in the rear of the head in frame Z327. The disruption of the rear of the skull was caused by the bullet as it penetrated through the thick cranial bone. The two large flaps of skull and scalp, as well as the huge cranial cavity in the right front side of the head, were caused by the bullet's exploding out of the head. Since the earlier Grassy Knoll shot had already inflicted severe damage to the head, the Z327 rear-entering shot shattered the weakened tissue and bone and, as it exploded out of the head, caused the large wound inflicted by the Z312 knoll shot to mushroom into a massive wound of exit.[26]

This interpretation—that of a knoll shot's striking the right side of the head at frame Z312, followed by a Depository shot's entering the rear of the head and exploding out of the right front at frame Z327—has never been offered before. Yet it is the only scenario that meets the constraints of the medical, ballistics, acoustics, and photographic evidence. The reason the pathologists at the autopsy and the physicians who subsequently examined the autopsy photographs and X-rays did not see evidence of a front-entering shot is that they never looked for it. Superficially, the autopsy materials provide evidence only of a rear-entering shot. A more careful analysis, however, demonstrates that the materials do substantiate the knoll shot thesis. The huge wound on the right front side of the president's head was *both* a wound of entrance and a wound of exit. The knoll shot exploded on the right side of the head, driving a cluster of fragments into the underlying scalp. The Depository shot drove into the rear of the head and left behind a trail of fragments as it blasted out of the already severely damaged right front side of John Kennedy's head.

Immediately after the shooting, numerous eyewitnesses in Dealey Plaza observed events that supply very strong support for the crossfire theory. Right after the shots, Jean Hill saw a man fleeing from Dealey Plaza. About twenty minutes later,

Malcolm Summers saw a car speeding away from the area. Tom Tilson saw a man flee from the Grassy Knoll area right after the shooting. The man ran to a parked car, threw an object into the car, and drove the vehicle away at high speed. J.C. Price observed a man running away from the Grassy Knoll just a few seconds after the shots were fired.[27]

About fifteen minutes after the shots, Earle Brown saw a man run down the stairs on the west side of the Book Depository building. The man ran from the building, but Brown could not tell where he went. Brown's story fully accords with those of Roger Craig, Helen Forrest, and other witnesses who saw Lee Harvey Oswald run from the building at the same time. Numerous eyewitnesses, then, saw gunmen in different floors and windows of the Depository building, saw men trying to escape from Dealey Plaza right after the shooting, and saw Oswald run from the building and get into a station wagon.[28]

It is quite conceivable that Lee Harvey Oswald was a "patsy," as he told newsmen the night of the assassination. Oswald may very well have been eating his lunch when the shots were fired, just as he told the police. After the shooting, Oswald went to the second-floor lunchroom and bought a Coke, as witnessed by Patrolman Baker and Oswald's boss, Roy Truly. Then, he may very well have left the building and caught the bus and cab, just as the Warren Commission claimed. The "Oswald" who ran from the building and entered the station wagon may have been the impersonator we have already encountered calling attention to "Oswald" during the three weeks prior to the assassination. This scenario cannot be demonstrated beyond question, but it does provide an explanation for the curious events that occurred in Dealey Plaza. If true, it would mean that the real Lee Harvey Oswald was innocent, as he claimed, and that the conspirators planted evidence against him.

THE CONSPIRACY: SOME THEORIES

A Hollywood script writer would have been hard pressed to devise a plot as replete with intrigue, suspicion, and mystery as that of the real life story of Lee Harvey Oswald. In his twenty-four years, Oswald lived a life so riddled with contradictions and unexplained events that it continues to mystify assassination researchers. The deeper one delves into the details of Oswald's life, the more ensnared he becomes in mazelike complexity.

Born in New Orleans in October 1939, Lee Harvey Oswald was the product of a broken home. His father died two months before his birth, and Lee spent much of his childhood in orphanages and in the homes of relatives. His grammar school record showed nothing unusual, but when he was thirteen, Lee was placed in a youth home in New York because of repeated truancy violations. When he was fifteen, Oswald and his mother moved to New Orleans, where he attended high school for a few months. But he quit school and went to work, and on his seventeenth birthday, he joined the Marine Corps.[29]

During his three-year tour of duty in the Marines, Oswald learned Russian and served as a radar operator at the Atsugi Base in Japan, whence many U-2 flights originated. In 1959, Oswald was discharged and emigrated to the Soviet Union a week later. After his arrival in Moscow, the twenty-year-old veteran renounced his American citizenship. Little is known about Oswald's two-and-a-half-year stay in the U.S.S.R. Some assassination researchers have suggested that he was a CIA spy and that the KGB recruited him to work for them.[30]

In June 1962, Lee and his Russian wife, Marina, left the Soviet Union and settled in Fort Worth. There they joined the tightly knit Russian emigre community and developed a close friendship with George deMorenschildt, a man with a long history of intelligence work. By April 1963, the Oswalds, experiencing marital and financial difficulties, moved to New Orleans, where Lee got a job at the Reilly Coffee Company. According to the Warren Commission, Oswald's deep attachment to Marxism surfaced during his five-month stay in New Orleans. He organized a pro-Castro Fair Play for Cuba Committee, lectured about Soviet Communism, debated anti-Castro exiles, and corresponded with the national director of the Fair Play for Cuba Committee.[31]

What the Warren Commission failed to disclose is that Oswald led a double life in New Orleans, outwardly posing as a pro-Castro Marxist but secretly associating with such rabidly anti-Communist individuals as Guy Bannister and David Ferrie. Oswald also met with anti-Castro Cuban exiles and developed a close friendship with a prominent leader of the White Citizens' Council and of other segregationist organizations.[32]

Oswald left New Orleans on 25 September 1963 and traveled to Mexico City, where he attempted to obtain a visa from the Cuban embassy. After a brief visit in Mexico, Oswald went to Dallas. In the middle of October, he got a job with the Texas School Book Depository as an order filler and, by all accounts, worked diligently and regularly until the day of the assassination. Other than weekend visits to see Marina and their children at the Paine home, Lee Oswald led a quiet, solitary life.[33]

Oswald's career offers many clues to possible assassination conspiracies. His Fair Play for Cuba Committee in New Orleans used the same address, 544 Camp Street, as the offices of Guy Bannister. The same building had previously been occupied by several militant anti-Castro organizations. According to the FBI, Oswald's Fair Play for Cuba Committee consisted of only one member other than himself, a Tulane University professor well known for his socialist views. Considering Oswald's numerous contacts with right-wing individuals and organizations, the implication is clear. Oswald's committee was a front, a bogus group set up to detract attention from his covert anti-Castro activities in New Orleans.[34]

Oswald's trip to Mexico City in late September 1963 also raises suspicions about his real activities. In 1975, a United States Senate subcommittee investigating the role of intelligence agencies in investigating the Kennedy assassination uncovered evidence of a most curious event. A Latin American informant, code-named "D," stated that on 17 September 1963, he was in the Cuban consulate in Mexico City and saw Lee Harvey Oswald receive a large sum of money from some Cubans after discussing the assassination of the president with them. The Warren Commission discounted "D's" story on the grounds that Oswald was in New Orleans on 17 September and did not leave for Mexico City until 25 September. The commission, however, produced no evidence to substantiate its story. Oswald's whereabouts on 17 September are, in fact, unknown. The fact that records of airlines and buses show no Lee Harvey Oswald registered as a passenger to Mexico City on that day hardly proves that he did not visit there. Oswald may have registered under an assumed name, or he could have used private means of transportation. Also, the Oswald that "D" saw may very well have been the Oswald double. In any event, the Mexico City station of the CIA learned that a "sensitive and reliable source" corroborated "D's" assertion that the Cubans paid Oswald to kill the president.[35]

The CIA knew that the Cuban government employed assassins and that it had actually carried out an assassination in Mexico. On 19 March 1964, the intelligence agency learned that a "Cuban-American" who was somehow "involved in the assassination" crossed the border from Texas to Mexico on 23 November, stayed in Mexico for four days, and flew to Cuba on 27 November. The CIA also received information that on 22 November, a Cubana Airlines flight from Mexico City to Havana was delayed for five hours until a passenger arrived in a private aircraft. The individual boarded the Cubana flight, and it left for Havana shortly before 11:00 P.M.[36]

These occurrences clearly arouse suspicions of an assassination plot engineered by the Cuban government under Fidel Castro. Various items of information gleaned from the recently declassified FBI and CIA assassination files reinforce those suspicions. On 24 November 1963, for example, FBI Director J. Edgar Hoover sent an urgent telegram to the FBI legation in Madrid: "Spanish Intelligence possesses a report that attributes president's assassination to Castro and claims that Oswald was acting as Cuban agent." The CIA also received similar information from several sources. One claimed that the Chinese Communists and Castro had masterminded the assassination. Another source claimed that a "Miss T" heard Cubans talking about having the president killed. Yet another source in Spain told the CIA that local Cuban officials asserted that Oswald "had nothing to do with Kennedy's murder."[37]

In the past six years, evidence of CIA-sponsored assassination plots against Fidel Castro has been made public. Evidently, Castro was aware of these plots, for on 7 September 1963, he warned "United States leaders" that "they themselves would not be safe" if they persisted in their efforts to eliminate the Cuban leader. As we now know, on the very day John Kennedy was assassinated, CIA officials discussed the murder of Castro with a Cuban agent code-named AMLASH. Almost immediately after the assassination, rumors circulated in the Miami Cuban exile community that Quentin Pino Machado, a Cuban diplomat widely known as a dangerous terrorist, had planned to escort Lee Harvey Oswald from Texas to Cuba via Mexico after he shot the president. The plan miscarried because of Oswald's arrest for shooting Officer Tippit.[38]

The House Select Committee on Assassinations concluded that the Cuban government was not involved in the Kennedy assassination. The committee argued that the relaxation of tensions between Cuba and the United States in 1963, the risk of war such an assassination plot would have entailed, the CIA's failure to produce evidence of Cuban complicity, and Castro's cooperation with the committee established that the Cuban government was not involved. However, the committee ignored the fact that Castro was aware of the plots against him, plots concocted with the CIA's approval. Castro also knew that militant anti-Castro exile organizations based in the United States were continuing to launch raids against Cuba. The committee also failed to report the fact that the United States ambassador to Mexico, Thomas Mann, a man very knowledgeable about internal Cuban affairs, reported his suspicions of Cuban complicity right after the assassination. Mann urged the government to investigate what he believed was substantial evidence that Oswald had acted as an agent of the Cuban government. The United States authorities, however, refused to follow Mann's suggestions.[39]

The House Select Committee did not attach any significance to the stories of Clare Boothe Luce and Sylvia Odio, even though both pointed to a possible Cuban conspiracy. In light of the fact that several sources of the FBI and CIA reported that individuals with connections to the Cuban government revealed foreknowledge of the assassination, the committee's discounting of the Cuban complicity theory appears unwarranted. Even the committee itself conceded that to resolve the matter of a Cuban conspiracy, "a definitive answer" could have been reached only in 1963 and 1964, when the leads were still fresh.[40]

A second conspiracy theory revolves around Lee Harvey Oswald's well-documented associations with anti-Castro exile organizations and individuals in 1963. Oswald's contacts with Guy Bannister and David Ferrie, his frequent associations with Cubans, the right-wing sympathies he expressed on numerous occasions during his sojourn in New Orleans in the summer of 1963, and his presence at meetings of anti-Castro groups shortly before the assassination all raise obvious questions of a possible right-wing conspiracy. On 21 November 1963, a Secret Service informant met with a Chicago-based anti-Castro activist, Homer S. Echevarria. Echevarria told the informant that his organization had "plenty of money" and would conduct an illegal arms sale "as soon as we take care of Kennedy." After Kennedy was killed the following day, the Chicago office of the Secret Service recommended a thorough investigation into the Echevarria case. The matter was turned over to the FBI, since President Johnson had designated the bureau as the federal agency responsible for probing the assassination. Incredibly, the FBI dropped the Echevarria case.[41]

The facts that Echevarria spoke of taking "care of Kennedy" only a day before the assassination, that certain Cuban exile groups deeply resented Kennedy's Cuban policies, and that Lee Harvey Oswald frequented the company of Cuban and American anti-Castro activists led the House Select Committee on Assassinations to conclude that "anti-Castro groups, as groups, were not involved in the assassination," but the committee "could not preclude the possibility that individual members may have been involved." Since the identity of the conspirators remains unknown, one can hardly disagree with the committee's conclusion. It should be kept in mind, however, that the committee failed to uncover any concrete evidence that the anti-Castro groups or individuals were involved in the assassination.[42]

The third main conspiracy theory is that organized crime was responsible for Kennedy's murder. Jack Ruby's long-time ties with the Mafia, the Kennedy brothers' attack on organized crime, and the threats against the Kennedys privately voiced by certain Mafia bosses provide the only serious support for this theory. Whatever Ruby's past, there exists no positive evidence linking his murder of Oswald to the mob. It is true, as the House Select Committee stated, that reputed mob bosses Carlos Marcello and Santos Trafficante disliked President Kennedy and voiced their hostility many times. The fact that Ruby visited a Havana jail in 1959, when Trafficante was an inmate there, and the allegation that Oswald's uncle was a bookie working for Marcello hardly constitute evidence of a mob-inspired assassination conspiracy.[43]

Such are the main theories about the assassination of President Kennedy. All three, especially that of the involvement of the Cuban government, are supported by some evidence. That evidence, however, is not substantial enough to identify either the organization or the individual conspirators. Nor is that evidence sufficient to demonstrate that Lee Harvey Oswald was a member of the conspiracy. Despite certain leads developed by the House Select Committee on Assassinations, those responsible for the murder of John Kennedy got away with it. Their successful escape from arrest and prosecution was aided and abetted by the incompetence of the Warren Commission and by the vigorous efforts of the executive branch of the government and by the House of Representatives to suppress the evidence in the case. Today, some eighteen years after John Kennedy was gunned down in Dallas, the American people are still not permitted to review all the evidence their government possesses about the crime of the century.

GUIDE TO ABBREVIATIONS

Appendix to HSCA Hearings — U.S. House of Representatives. *Investigation of the Assassination of President John F. Kennedy: Appendix to Hearings Before the Select Committee on Assassinations of the U.S. House of Representatives.* 7 vols. 95th Cong., 2nd Sess. Washington, D.C.: U.S. GPO, 1979.

CIA Papers — Central Intelligence Agency. Papers on the Assassination of President Kennedy. 15 vols., 3847 pp. Linus A. Sims Memorial Library, Southeastern Louisiana University, Hammond, La.

Clark Panel Report — "1968 Panel Review of Photographs, X-ray Films, Documents and Other Evidence Pertaining to the Fatal Wounding of President John F. Kennedy on November 22, 1963 in Dallas, Texas." Undated report. National Archives, Washington, D.C.

FBI Papers — Federal Bureau of Investigation. Papers on the JFK Assassination, Lee Harvey Oswald, Jack Ruby, and the Warren Commission. 125,000 pp. Linus A.

Sims Memorial Library, Southeastern University, Hammond, La.

GPO — Government Printing Office

HSCA Hearings — U.S. House of Representatives. *Investigation of the Assassination of President John F. Kennedy: Hearings Before the Select Committee on Assassinations.* 5 vols. 95th Cong., 2nd Sess. Washington, D.C.: U.S. GPO, 1978–79.

HSCA Report — U.S. House of Representatives. *Report of the Select Committee on Assassinations.* 95th Cong., 2nd Sess. Washington, D.C.: U.S. GPO, 1979.

Rockefeller Commission Report — *Report of the Commission on CIA Activities Within the United States.* Washington, D.C.: U.S. GPO, 1975.

Sibert-O'Neill Report — FBI Special Agents Francis X. O'Neill, Jr., and James W. Sibert, "Autopsy of Body of President John Fitzgerald Kennedy," Warren Commission Document No. 7, WC Records, NA.

SS Reports — U.S. Treasury Department, Protective Research Division (U.S. Secret Service), Reports of Agent Richard Johnsen and Chief James Rowley, 23–24 November, 1963, WC Records, NA.

WC Hearings — *Hearings Before the President's Commission on the Assassination of President Kennedy.* 26 vols. Washington, D.C.: U.S. GPO, 1964.

WC Records, NA — Records of the President's Commission on the Assassination of

President Kennedy. Record Group 272. National Archives and Records Service, Washington, D.C.

WC Report — *Report of the President's Commission on the Assassination of President Kennedy.* Washington, D.C.: U.S. GPO, 1964.

NOTES

NOTES FOR CHAPTER ONE

1. *Dallas Times-Herald,* 22 Nov. 1963.

2. Testimony of John B. Connally, *Investigation of the Assassination of President John F. Kennedy: Hearings Before the Select Committee on Assassinations of the U.S. House of Representatives,* 95th Cong., 2nd Sess., 5 vols. (Washington, D.C.: U.S. GPO, 1978–79), I, 11–16. Hereafter cited as *HSCA Hearings.*

3. "The Motorcade," *Investigation of the Assassination of President John F. Kennedy: Appendix to Hearings Before the Select Committee on Assassinations of the U.S. House of Representatives,* 95th Cong., 2nd Sess., 7 vols. (Washington, D.C.: U.S. GPO, 1979), XI, 528–29. Hereafter cited as *Appendix to HSCA Hearings.*

4. *Report of the Select Committee on Assassinations: U.S. House of Representatives,* 95th Cong., 2nd Sess. (Washington, D.C.: U.S. GPO, 1979), 38–39. Hereafter cited as *HSCA Report.*

5. Abraham Zapruder, Orville Nix, and Robert Hughes assassination films, copies in author's personal possession.

6. Zapruder film, frames Z153–454; Secret Service account of interview with Abraham Zapruder, 24 Nov. 1963, Records of the President's Commission on the Assassination of President Kennedy, National Archives and Records Service, Washington, D.C., Record Group 272. Hereafter cited as WC Records, NA.

7. Testimony of Howard Brennan, *Hearings Before the President's Commission on the Assassination of President Kennedy,* 26 vols. (Washington, D.C.: U.S. GPO, 1964), III, 141–57. Hereafter cited as *WC Hearings.*

8. *Report of the President's Commission on the Assassination of President Kennedy* (Washington, D.C.: U.S. GPO, 1964), 64–65. Hereafter cited as *WC Report.*

9. Testimony of Arnold Rowland, *WC Hearings,* II, 167–76.

10. Affadavit of Julia Ann Mercer, 22 Nov. 1963, ibid., XIX, 483–84.

11. Testimony of Lee Bowers, ibid., VI, 288–89; Affadavit of J.C. Price, 22 Nov. 1963, ibid., XIX, 492; *Texas Observer,* 13 Dec. 1963.
12. Testimony of Marrion Baker, *WC Hearings,* III, 244–57.
13. *HSCA Report,* 40.
14. Testimony of Drs. Carrico and Perry, *WC Hearings,* III, 348–50, 368–70.
15. Perry testimony, ibid., 372–75.
16. Ibid.
17. *WC Report,* 54.
18. Ibid., 57–59.
19. Smith testimony, *WC Hearings,* VII, 535.
20. Report of Roger Craig to Dallas County Sheriff's Department, 23 Nov. 1963, WC Records, NA.
21. Testimony of Howard L. Brennan, *WC Hearings,* III, 142–49; Tape of Dallas Police Department, ibid., 401.
22. Mooney and Boone testimony, ibid., 293–98; Weitzman testimony, ibid., VII, 107.
23. *WC Report,* 79.
24. Ibid., 79–80.
25. Ibid., 92–94.
26. Ibid., 80–81; U.S. Treasury Department, Protective Research Section (U.S. Secret Service) Reports of Agent Richard Johnsen and Chief James Rowley, 23–24 Nov. 1963, WC Records, NA. Hereafter cited as SS Reports.
27. Report of Agent Berger, *WC Hearings,* XVIII, 795.
28. Kantor and Tice testimony, ibid., XV, 79–81, 388–96.
29. UPI Bulletin, 22 Nov. 1963; CBS News Special, 22 Nov. 1963.
30. See "Life: John F. Kennedy Memorial Edition," *Life* 29 Nov. 1963, n.p.
31. See *Four Dark Days in History* (Los Angeles: Special Publications, 1963), entire issue, for a good description of the crowd response.
32. Reid testimony, *WC Hearings,* III, 273–78.
33. *WC Report,* 157–59.
34. Whaley testimony, *WC Hearings,* II, 254–73.
35. *WC Report,* 163–65.
36. Ibid., 166–69.
37. Ibid., 166.
38. Ibid., 176–81.
39. Ibid., 181–82.
40. Ibid., 130–31.
41. Ibid., 40.
42. Ibid., 86.

43. Humes testimony, *WC Hearings,* II, 352–59.

44. FBI Special Agents Francis X. O'Neill, Jr., and James W. Sibert, "Autopsy of Body of President John Fitzgerald Kennedy," Warren Commission Document No. 7, WC Records, NA. Hereafter cited as Sibert-O'Neill Report.

45. Humes testimony, *WC Hearings,* II, 351–71.

46. Sibert-O'Neill Report: Testimony of Dr. Pierre A. Finck, 24 Feb. 1969, *State of Louisiana v. Clay L. Shaw,* X, 115.

47. Sibert-O'Neill Report.

48. Testimony of James J. Humes, *HSCA Hearings,* I, 330–31.

49. Craig Report, WC Records, NA; Dallas police account of Oswald arrest and interrogation, WC Records, NA.

50. Transcript of Oswald press conference, 22 Nov. 1963, WC Records, NA.

51. Ibid.

52. Author's interview with Jerry R. Herald, 17 April 1978.

53. *WC Report,* 196–206.

54. Ibid., 89.

55. Ibid., 89–90.

56. James J. Humes, Handwritten Autopsy Notes, WC Records, NA.

57. Ibid.

58. *WC Report,* 209.

59. Ibid., 209–13.

60. Ibid., 214–16.

61. *Life,* JFK Memorial Edition, 29 Nov. 1963.

NOTES FOR CHAPTER TWO

1. Hoover to Johnson, 23 Nov. 1963; Katzenbach deposition, 4 Aug. 1978, *Appendix to HSCA Hearings,* XI, 325–26.

2. Ibid., 5.

3. Katzenbach to Moyers, 25 Nov. 1963, Papers of the Federal Bureau of Investigation on the Assassination of President Kennedy. Collection in Linus A. Sims Memorial Library, Southeastern Louisiana University, Hammond, La. Hereafter cited as FBI Papers.

4. Memorandum, Hoover to Clyde Tolson, et al., 29 Nov. 1963, ibid.; Lyndon B. Johnson, *The Vantage Point* (New York: Popular Library, 1972), 26–27; Earl Warren, *The Memoirs of Chief Justice Warren* (Garden City, N.Y.: Doubleday, 1977), 356–58.

5. Executive Order No. 11130, *WC Report,* 471.

6. Johnson, *Vantage Point,* 26; Eisenberg Memorandum, 17 Feb. 1964, WC Records, NA.

7. Rankin testimony, 17 Aug. 1978, *Appendix to HSCA Hearings,* XI, 348–50, 353–54, 360–63.

8. Rankin, "Tentative Outline for the Work of the President's Commission," 11 Jan. 1964, WC Records, NA; Specter's testimony, 8 Nov. 1977, *Appendix to HSCA Hearings,* XI, 331.

9. FBI Report, 9 Dec. 1963, FBI Papers.

10. "Monthly Progress of the Warren Commission Investigation," *Appendix to HSCA Hearings,* XI, 75–77.

11. *WC Report,* 18.

12. Brennan testimony, *WC Hearings,* III, 142–44.

13. Euins and Jackson testimony, ibid., II, 157–59, 204; Couch testimony, ibid., VI, 156–57; Cabell testimony, ibid., VII, 485–86.

14. *WC Report,* 71–76.

15. Ibid., 76–81.

16. Ibid., 81–85.

17. Dr. Robert H. Shaw testimony, *WC Hearings,* IV, 109; Dr. G. Thomas Shires interview, *Appendix to HSCA Hearings,* VII, 341–42.

18. Kennedy Autopsy, *WC Report,* 540–43.

19. Ibid., 96–117.

20. Abraham Zapruder film, special optically enhanced version in personal possession of author.

21. *WC Report,* 98–109; Specter testimony, 8 Nov. 1977, *Appendix to HSCA Hearings,* XI, 87–88, 96–100.

22. *WC Report,* 98–103.

23. For examples of critical views of the theory, see Harold Weisberg, *Whitewash* (New York: Dell, 1965), I, 304–14, and Mark Lane, *Rush to Judgment* (New York: Dell Reprint, 1975), 69–80.

24. Olivier testimony, *WC Hearings,* V, 75–80; *WC Report,* 102.

25. Connally testimony, *WC Hearings,* IV, 132–33; *HSCA Hearings,* I, 40–41, 43–46.

26. Secret Service Report, 3 Dec. 1963, File CO-2-34000, p. 15, SS Reports; FBI Supplemental Report of 9 Dec. 1963, pp. 6–12, FBI Papers; Eisenberg memo, 22 April 1964; Belin to Rankin, 30 Jan. 1964, WC Records, NA.

27. *WC Report,* 19.

28. Ibid., 118–22.

29. Ibid., 123–25; Stombaugh testimony, *WC Hearings,* IV, 83–88.

30. *WC Report,* 125–28.

31. Marina Oswald testimony, *WC Hearings,* I, 119.

32. *WC Report,* 129.

33. Ibid., 129–33.

34. Ibid., 129–37.

35. Ibid., 138–43.
36. Brennan testimony, *WC Hearings,* III, 148.
37. *WC Report,* 148–54.
38. Ibid., 157–60.
39. Ibid., 161–63.
40. Roberts testimony, *WC Hearings,* VII, 439–40.
41. Belin Report, Commission Exhibit 1119-A, WC Records, NA.
42. *WC Report,* 163–65; Markham testimony, *WC Hearings,* III, 306–16.
43. *WC Report,* 165–71.
44. Ibid., 170–74.
45. Ibid., 176.
46. Ibid., 20.

NOTES FOR CHAPTER THREE

1. *WC Report,* 18.
2. Ibid., 64–65.
3. Ibid., 143–44.
4. Ibid., 144–45.
5. Brennan testimony, *WC Hearings,* III, 145.
6. Curry testimony, ibid., IV, 150–76; Hargis testimony, ibid., VI, 293–96; Weitzman testimony, ibid., VII, 105–9, XXIV, 228; Sorrels testimony, ibid., VII, 345. For a list of the Dealey Plaza witnesses and their observations as to the source of the shots, see Josiah M. Thompson, *Six Seconds in Dallas* (Philadelphia: Bernard Geis, 1967), 254–70.
7. Rowland testimony, *WC Hearings,* II, 169–72; *WC Report,* 251.
8. Barbara Rowland testimony, *WC Hearings,* VI, 185–90.
9. *WC Report,* 145–46; Brennan testimony, *WC Hearings,* III, 154.
10. Price affadavit, *WC Hearings,* XIX, 483–84.
11. Smith testimony, ibid., VII, 535; Weitzman testimony, ibid., 107–9; *WC Report,* 52.
12. Worrell interview, 23 Nov. 1963, FBI Papers, Section 21, Document 89-43; Carr affadavit, 23 Nov. 1963, Commission Document 385, WC Records, NA; Robinson interview, 23 Nov. 1963, Commission Document 5, ibid.; Craig Report, WC Records, NA, Craig testimony, ibid., VI, 266–67.
13. Robert Hughes film, WC Records, NA; Thompson, *Six Seconds in Dallas,* 245–48; CBS News, "The American Assassins: Part One," 25 Nov. 1975.
14. *WC Report,* 644.
15. Ibid., 18.

16. Ibid., 80–81.
17. Ibid., 81.
18. Tomlinson testimony, *WC Hearings,* VI, 130.
19. Ibid., II, 368.
20. Tomlinson testimony, ibid., VI, 130–34; Thompson, *Six Seconds in Dallas,* 205–6; *WC Report,* 81.
21. Thompson, *Six Seconds in Dallas,* 175–76.
22. Bullet 399 contained no blood, clothing fibers, nor any other markings associating it with the wounds on either man. See the testimony of FBI ballistics expert Robert Frazier, *WC Hearings,* III, 428–31.
23. Report of Secret Service Agent Richard Johnsen, 22 Nov. 1963, ibid., XVIII, 799–800.
24. Tomlinson and Wright interviews, ibid., XXIV, 412.
25. *WC Report,* 76–77.
26. FBI Spectrographic Analysis Report, J. Edgar Hoover to Jesse Curry, 23 Nov. 1963, FBI Papers.
27. Jesse Curry, *JFK Assassination File* (Dallas: American Poster, 1969), 34, 36.
28. Kantor testimony, *WC Hearings,* XV, 88; *WC Report,* 336.
29. Berger Report, 23 Nov. 1963, *WC Hearings,* XVIII, 795.
30. Rowley to Rankin, 17 March 1964, WC Records, NA.
31. See *WC Report,* 555–58.
32. Ibid., 18, 555–56.
33. *WC Hearings,* XXVI, 449–50.
34. *WC Report,* 110.
35. *WC Hearings,* XXVI, 449.
36. Hoover to Rankin, 2 June 1964, WC Records, NA; FBI Ballistics Report, 25 Dec. 1964, ibid.
37. Alan Stang, "They Killed the President: Lee Harvey Oswald Wasn't Alone," *American Opinion* 19 (Feb 1976), 5–9.
38. Ibid.
39. See Ch. 6 for an accounting of Oswald's movements.
40. Hoover to Rankin, 2 June 1964, WC Records, NA.
41. Author's interview with ballistics expert Fred Bouchard, 18 May 1978.
42. *WC Report,* 555–57.

NOTES FOR CHAPTER FOUR

1. *WC Report,* 18–19.
2. *WC Hearings,* XVII, 1–48.

3. *WC Report,* 19.

4. See David W. Belin, *November 22, 1963* (New York: Quadrangle, 1973), 302–7.

5. Zapruder film, frames Z312–321.

6. Ibid., frames Z153–225.

7. *WC Report,* 98–105.

8. Ibid., 103–5.

9. U.S. Secret Service, memorandum, 28 Nov. 1963, SS Reports; FBI Report, 23 Nov. 1963, p. 2, FBI Papers; Belin to Rankin, 30 Jan. 1964, pp. 1–2, Eisenberg memorandum, 22 April 1964, WC Records, NA.

10. Frazier testimony, *WC Hearings,* III, 407; ibid., V, 153–54.

11. *WC Report,* 97–105; FBI Report of Firing Tests, 26 May 1964, FBI Papers; U.S. National Weather Service, Records for Dallas, Texas, 22 Nov. 1963 and for 24 May 1964.

12. *WC Report,* 98–99.

13. Commission Exhibits 509, 511, 724, 733, *WC Hearings,* XVII, 220, 222, 505, 509; *Life,* JFK Memorial Edition, 29 Nov. 1963, n.p.; the photograph appears in J. Gary Shaw and Larry R. Harris, *Cover-Up* (Cleburne, Tex.: J. Gary Shaw, 1976), 31.

14. Even the Warren Commission conceded that Oswald may have been "sitting or kneeling" by the window. *WC Report,* 144.

15. Philip A. Willis Slide no. 5, copy in author's possession; Willis testimony, *WC Hearings,* XXI, 773; Robert F. Groden and F. Peter Model, *JFK: The Case for Conspiracy* (New York: Manor, 1976): 143–46.

16. *WC Report,* 540–46.

17. Ibid.

18. "1968 Panel Review of Photographs, X-Ray Films, Documents and Other Evidence Pertaining to the Fatal Wounding of President John F. Kennedy on November 22, 1963 in Dallas, Texas," 8–10, 13; Hereafter cited as Clark Panel Report; John K. Lattimer, "Observations Based on a Review of the Autopsy Photographs, X-Rays, and Related Materials of the Late President John F. Kennedy," *Resident and Staff Physician Medical Times* 34 (May 1972), 46; Cyril H. Wecht and Robert P. Smith, "The Medical Evidence in the Assassination of President John F. Kennedy," *Forensic Science* 3 (1974), 113–14.

19. Clark Panel Report, 15; Sibert-O'Neill Report, 3.

20. Willis slide no. 5; FBI Exhibit no. 60, FBI Papers.

21. Willis slide no. 5; Zapruder film, frames Z166–225.

22. See FBI Exhibit no. 60, FBI Papers, for a closeup view of the clothing.

23. Hill testimony, *WC Hearings,* II, 143; XVIII, 744; Sibert-O'Neill Report, 2; confidential interview.

24. Commission Exhibit 379; Theran Ward, Death Certificate, John F. Kennedy, 3 Dec. 1963, WC Records, NA.

25. George Burkeley, Certificate of Death, John F. Kennedy, 22 Nov. 1963, ibid.

26. Transcript of Warren Commission Executive Session, 27 Jan. 1964, p. 193 (declassified 1976); Transcript of Commission Session of 20 Jan. 1964, p. 13, ibid.

27. Perry testimony, *WC Hearings,* VI, 11–14; Carrico testimony, ibid., 5–6; other Dallas doctors also present(ed) corroborating descriptions of the hole as one of entrance, ibid., 33, 35, 42, 55–56, 65, 67.

28. See *New York Times,* 27 Nov. 1963; *St. Louis Post-Dispatch,* 1 Dec. 1963.

29. *WC Report,* 88–92, 541.

30. *WC Report,* 88–89; Finck testimony, Shaw trial, X, 113–18.

31. *WC Report,* 543.

32. Clark Panel Report, 15; Lattimer, "Observations," 51.

33. *WC Report,* 91; *WC Hearings,* V, 76–78; Commission Exhibit no. 850, WC Records, NA.

34. Harold Weisberg, *Post-Mortem* (Frederick, Md.: Harold Weisberg, 1975), 376–78.

35. *WC Report,* 545; Cyril H. Wecht, "JFK Assassination: A Prolonged and Willful Cover-Up," *Modern Medicine* 42 (28 Oct. 1974), 40CC–40DD.

36. John K. Lattimer, John Lattimer, and Gary Lattimer, "The Kennedy-Connally One Bullet Theory: Further Circumstantial and Experimental Evidence," *Medical Times* 36 (Nov. 1974), 44–48.

37. FBI Exhibit 60, FBI Papers; J. Edgar Hoover to J. Lee Rankin, 16 April 1964, WC Records, NA; FBI expert Robert Frazier contradicted Hoover and said the slits were *not* characteristic of bullet exit wounds, *WC Hearings,* V, 59–62.

38. *WC Report,* 91–109.

39. Commission Exhibit 399, WC Records, NA.

40. See Lane, *Rush to Judgment,* 56–66; Thompson, *Six Seconds in Dallas,* 146–54.

41. Commission Exhibits 853 and 856, WC Records, NA.

42. "Wounds Ballistics of 6.5 mm. Mannlicher-Carcano Ammunition," March 1965, Technical Report CRDLR3264 of the Chemical Research and Development Laboratories, Edgewood Arsenal, U.S. Army, National Archives, Washington, D.C.

43. Ibid., 6–10.

44. Melvin A. Eisenberg, Memorandum for the Record, 22 April 1964, p. 2, WC Records, NA.

45. Lattimer, "The Kennedy-Connally One Bullet Theory," 49–53.

46. Commission Exhibit 846, WC Records, NA.

47. Dr. Charles Gregory, Operative Record for Governor John B. Connally, 22 Nov. 1963, p. 1, ibid.

48. Lattimer, "The Kennedy-Connally One Bullet Theory," 33–56.

49. FBI Report of interview with Dr. Jack Reynolds, 29 Nov. 1963, Commission Document no. 5, p. 157, WC Records, NA; Frazier testimony, Shaw Trial, IX, 21 Feb. 1969, pp. 148–49.

50. Tangipahoa Parish (La.) Sheriff's Department, Case 76-2913, 3 June 1976, autopsy photographs and bullet in author's possession.

51. Wecht, "Medical Evidence," 120–28.

52. Zapruder film, frames Z224–228.

NOTES FOR CHAPTER FIVE

1. *WC Report,* 18, 543.

2. Ibid., 540–43.

3. Commission Exhibit 397, p. 16; Commission Exhibit 385, WC Records, NA.

4. Clark Panel Report, 9–13; Humes testimony, *WC Hearings,* II, 364.

5. Clark Panel Report, 5–6, 9–10.

6. JFK skull X-rays, *HSCA Hearings,* I, 239–44.

7. Clark Panel Report, 7.

8. Ibid., 8; Lattimer, "Observations," 37; Spitz interview, Citizens Commission of Inquiry *Newsletter,* no. 1 (Feb. 1976), 4.

9. Clark Panel Report, 8; Lattimer, letter to author, 10 July 1977, p. 3; Cyril H. Wecht, "Pathologist's View of JFK Autopsy: An Unsolved Case," *Modern Medicine* 40 (27 Nov. 1972), 29.

10. Clark Panel Report, 8; Robert Frazier testimony, *WC Hearings,* III, 414.

11. *HSCA Hearings,* I, 239–44; *WC Hearings,* XVII, 843–44.

12. Clark Panel Report, 590; interview with Ballistics Expert Fred Bouchard, 3 May 1978.

13. Bouchard interview; *WC Report,* 543; Clark Panel Report, 11.

14. Lattimer, "Observations," 37.

15. Ibid., 39.

16. Ibid., 42–45.

17. *WC Report,* 76–77.
18. Lattimer, "Observations," 44–48.
19. Ibid.
20. Ibid., 51.
21. Ibid., 51–52.
22. Olivier testimony, *WC Hearings,* V, 87–89; John K. Lattimer, John Lattimer, and Gary Lattimer, "An Experimental Study of the Backward Movement of President Kennedy's Head," *Surgery, Gynecology and Obstetrics* 142 (1976), 246–54.
23. Lattimer, "Experimental Study," 246–54; Wecht letter to author, 9 Sept. 1977.
24. Ibid.; *HSCA Hearings,* I, 239–44.
25. Wecht and Smith, "Medical Evidence," 111–20.
26. Ibid., 121.
27. Stang, "They Killed the President," 8; Weston remarks, CBS News, "American Assassins: Part One," 25 Nov. 1975.
28. Wecht and Smith, "Medical Evidence," 123; Thompson, *Six Seconds in Dallas,* viii–ix.
29. *WC Report,* 540–43.
30. Wecht, "Pathologist's View," 21–24.
31. Zapruder film, frames Z153–312.
32. Ibid., frames Z313–321.
33. Lane, *Rush to Judgment,* 44–45.
34. Itek Report, cited in CBS News, "American Assassins," 25 Nov. 1975.
35. Luis Alvarez, "A Physicist Examines the Kennedy Assassination Film," *American Journal of Physics* 44 (1976), 813–27.
36. Lattimer, "Experimental Study," 246–54.
37. Ibid.; Alvarez, "Physicist," 815.
38. *Report of the Commission on CIA Activities Within the United States* (Washington, D.C.: U.S. GPO, 1975), 251–60. Hereafter cited as Rockefeller Commission Report.
39. Numerous interviews, 1967–80.
40. See, for example, World War II films of the Italian 8th Army in action on the Russian Front.
41. Fred Wahl and Joseph Kramer, "Neutron Activation Analysis," *Scientific American* 216 (April 1967), 68–86.
42. FBI Results of Neutron Activation Analysis, 72-page report, 6 May 1964, FBI Papers.
43. Ibid.
44. Ibid.
45. Ibid.

NOTES FOR CHAPTER SIX

1. *WC Report,*, 19.
2. Ibid.
3. Ibid., 118–22.
4. Day testimony, *WC Hearings,* IV, 260–61; FBI expert Sebastian Latona testimony, ibid., 24–28.
5. *WC Report,* 124–25.
6. Ibid., 126.
7. Marina Oswald testimony, *WC Hearings,* I, 114.
8. Ibid.; Ruth Paine testimony, ibid., III, 21–25; Michael Paine testimony, ibid., II, 414–16, IX, 437–40; Wesley J. Liebler, "Memorandum re Galley Proofs of Chapter IV of the Report," 6 Sept. 1964, pp. 20–25, WC Records, NA.
9. Hoover to Rankin, 30 April 1964, p. 15, Commission Exhibit 2562, WC Records, NA; Lattimer, "Kennedy-Connally One Bullet Theory," 45.
10. *American Rifleman,* 76, Feb. 1963, p. 58.
11. *WC Report,* 128–31.
12. Ibid., 19, 129–30.
13. Ibid., 129–37.
14. Curry, *JFK Assassination File,* 63; Howard Roffman, *Presumed Guilty* (Cranbury, N.J.: Associated Univ. Presses, 1975), 160; Jerry Herald interview; Rankin to Hoover, 31 Aug. 1964, WC Records, NA.
15. *WC Report,* 131–34.
16. Ibid., 134–35; Frazier testimony, *WC Hearings,* II, 226–29.
17. Frazier testimony, ibid., 239–41; Randle testimony, ibid., 248–50.
18. Frazier and Randle testimony, ibid., 227, 231, 239, 248, 249.
19. *WC Report,* 135–37.
20. Ibid., 135; Craig interview, 6 Oct. 1972.
21. *WC Report,* 135.
22. Ibid., 136; Curry, *JFK Assassination File,* 88.
23. *WC Hearings,* XVII, 329–30.
24. Cadigan testimony, ibid., IV, 97; *WC Report,* 137.
25. *WC Report,* 19.
26. Ibid., 138–39.
27. Ibid., 140.
28. Ibid., 141.
29. Ibid., 566.
30. Ibid., 143.

31. Piper affadavit, 22 Nov. 1963, WC Records, NA; Givens interview, 22 Nov. 1963, FBI Papers.

32. FBI Report of Arnold interview, 23 Nov. 1963, FBI Papers; FBI Report, 8 Dec. 1964, ibid.

33. Williams deposition, Commission Exhibit 2003, p. 229; Testimony, *WC Hearings,* III, 167–72.

34. *WC Report,* 143–45.

35. Euins testimony, *WC Hearings,* II, 203–7; Fisher testimony, ibid., VI, 193–94; Edwards testimony, ibid., 203–5.

36. Baker interview, 22 Nov. 1963, FBI Papers; Testimony, *WC Hearings,* III, 245–50; Truly testimony, ibid., 221–28.

37. *WC Hearings,* VII, 593.

38. *WC Report,* 152–53.

39. Howlett testimony, *WC Hearings,* VII, 592.

40. Ibid.; Mooney testimony, ibid., III, 285; Craig interview.

41. Ibid.; Boone testimony, *WC Hearings,* III, 293.

42. Roffman, *Presumed Guilty,* 210–23.

43. *WC Report,* 19; Zapruder film, frames Z189–312.

44. *WC Report,* 189–95; *WC Hearings,* XVII, 260–63; CBS News, "The Warren Report," 26 June 1967; Sylvia Meagher, *Accessories After the Fact* (New York: Vintage, 1976), 106–10.

45. *WC Report,* 598–636.

46. Ibid., 20.

NOTES FOR CHAPTER SEVEN

1. McWatters testimony, *WC Hearings,* II, 275–83.

2. *WC Report,* 158.

3. *WC Hearings,* II, 270; XXIV, 347; XXV, 899–901; Bledsoe testimony, ibid., VI, 401–3.

4. Craig interview; Baker testimony, *WC Hearings,* III, 248–54; Whaley testimony, ibid., II, 254–60; *WC Report,* 159–60.

5. *WC Report,* 160–62.

6. Whaley testimony, *WC Hearings,* II, 261–94.

7. Ibid., VI, 430.

8. *WC Report,* 163–65.

9. Ibid., 162–63, 335–37; Whaley testimony, *WC Hearings,* II, 259–61, VI, 434.

10. *WC Hearings,* VI, 433–34; *WC Report,* 163.

11. *WC Report,* 161; Craig testimony, *WC Hearings,* VI, 266–70.

12. *WC Report,* 158; Whaley testimony, *WC Hearings,* II, 254–73.

13. Craig testimony, *WC Hearings,* VI, 266–70.

14. Ibid.; *WC Report,* 160.

15. Walther interview, *WC Hearings,* XXIV, 522; Worrell affadavit, ibid., XVI, 959; Testimony, ibid., II, 196.

16. Carr interview, 22 Nov. 1963, Commission Document 385, WC Records, NA; Robinson interview, 23 Nov. 1963, Commission Document 5, ibid.

17. Helen Forrest interview, 17 May 1974.

18. Shaw and Harris, *Cover-Up,* 14–18, 27, 101.

19. Whaley testimony, *WC Hearings,* II, 256.

20. *WC Report,* 161, 649; Whaley logbook, FBI Papers.

21. *WC Report,* 160–63.

22. Roberts testimony, *WC Hearings,* VI, 434–44; *WC Report,* 164; *WC Hearings,* XXV, 170–71, 914, XII, 341–47.

23. *WC Report,* 163–65, 175; Roberts testimony, *WC Hearings,* VI, 443–44.

24. *WC Hearings,* VI, 439.

25. Ibid., 434; Meagher, *Accessories,* 255.

26. Bowley testimony, *WC Hearings,* XXIV, 202; Markham affadavit, *WC Report,* 651.

27. Bowley affadavit, *WC Hearings,* XXIV, 202.

28. Benavides testimony, ibid., VI, 448.

29. *WC Report,* 165.

30. Markham testimony, *WC Hearings,* III, 310.

31. Ibid., 307, 315, 320, XX, 590; XXIV, 225; VI, 468; VII, 273–74.

32. *WC Report,* 165.

33. Benavides testimony, *WC Hearings,* VI, 444–54; CBS News, "The Warren Report," 27 June 1967.

34. Acquila Clemmons statement, "Rush to Judgment," film (New York: Mark Lane-Emilio de Antonio, 1967).

35. Wright interview, *The New Leader* (12 Oct. 1964); FBI Report, 16 March 1964, FBI Papers; FBI Report of interview of William Arthur Smith, 13 Dec. 1963, ibid.; Hoover to Gordon Shanklin, Head, Dallas FBI office, 1 Oct. 1964, Lee Harvey Oswald, Section 216, Document no. 5102, FBI Papers.

36. *WC Report,* 165–69.

37. Ibid.

38. *WC Hearings,* XXIV, 415, III, 474; Dallas Police Oswald Evidence Sheet. The original of this document, in WC Records, NA, says that only two cartridge cases were found in the Depository building. A copy says that three were found.

39. Cunningham testimony, *WC Hearings,* III, 475.

40. Ibid.; Nicol testimony, ibid., 512.
41. Ibid.
42. *WC Report,* 175–76; *WC Hearings,* III, 308, 327, 343, 352; VI, 448; VII, 397; XIX, 181–82.
43. *WC Report,* 176–78.

NOTES FOR CHAPTER EIGHT

1. FBI Supplement Report, 9 Dec. 1963, FBI Papers.
2. Katzenbach to Moyers, 25 Nov. 1963, ibid.
3. *WC Report,* 86–90.
4. Humes statement, *WC Hearings,* II, 373; Helpern quote, Marshall Houts, *Where Death Delights* (New York: Coward-McCann, 1967), 55–57.
5. Transcript of 27 Jan. 1964 Commission Meeting, 193, WC Records, NA.
6. Rankin Memorandum, 23 Jan. 1964; Specter to Rankin, 12 March 1964; Specter to Rankin, 12 March 1964, all in WC Records, NA.
7. Specter to Rankin, 30 April 1964, pp. 1–2, ibid.
8. Sibert-O'Neill Report.
9. FBI Receipt, 22 Nov. 1963, FBI Papers; Secret Service Receipt, 23 Nov. 1963, SS Reports.
10. Jerry Herald interview, 17 April 1978.
11. Ibid.
12. Ibid.
13. Ibid.
14. *WC Report,* 315–18.
15. Ibid., 316; Herald interview.
16. Herald interview.
17. Ibid.; *WC Report,* 321; FBI Documents no. 273, 284, 295, FBI Papers.
18. Odio testimony, *WC Hearings,* XI, 368–85.
19. *WC report,* 321–24.
20. Ibid., 324–25; FBI Report, 11 Oct. 1964, FBI Papers.
21. *WC Report,* 169.
22. Ibid., 122–23.
23. FBI expert Sebastian Latona testimony, *WC Hearings,* IV, 24–25.
24. *WC Report,* 139.
25. Ibid., 208–25.
26. Harris and Shaw, *Cover-Up,* 83–84.

27. *Dallas Times-Herald,* 10 Dec. 1963; FBI Report, 23 Nov. 1963, FBI Papers.

28. See *WC Hearings,* XIX, 523.

29. J. Lee Rankin, "Memorandum to Warren Commission Members," 11 Jan. 1964, pp. 1–5, WC Records, NA.

30. Transcript of 27 Jan. 1964 Commission Meeting, 171, WC Records, NA.

31. Norman Redlich, "Proposed Outline of Report of the Commission," 14 March 1964, pp. 1-6, WC Records, NA. Emphasis added.

32. Slawson to Rankin, 27 Jan. 1964, p. 2, WC Records, NA; Redlich to Rankin, 21 Jan. 1964, p. 1, ibid. Emphasis added.

33. *WC Hearings,* I–XV.

34. See XVII, 329–30; XXII, 395.

NOTES FOR CHAPTER NINE

1. See *New York Times,* 29 Sept. 1964; *Washington Post,* 29 Sept. 1964; Gerald R. Ford, "Piecing Together the Evidence," *Life,* 2 Oct. 1964, pp. 42–50b; CBS News, "November 22 and the Warren Report," 27 Sept. 1964.

2. Lane, *Rush to Judgment;* for reactions to Lane's book, see *New York Times,* 24 Nov. 1966; "A Primer of Assassination theories;" *Esquire* 66 (Dec. 1966), 51–62, 206–11; Fred J. Cook, "The Warren Report," *Nation,* 200, Oct. 1966, pp. 38–54; Fletcher Knebel, "A New Wave of Doubt," *Look,* 30, 12 July 1966, pp. 31–43.

3. William Manchester, *The Death of a President* (New York: Harper and Row, 1967); James A. Bishop, *The Day Kennedy Was Shot* (New York: Funk and Wagnalls, 1968); CBS News Inquiry, "The Warren Report," 4 parts, 25–28 June 1967; NBC News, "The JFK Conspiracy: The Case of Jim Garrison," 19 June 1967; Fred Powledge, "Is Garrison Faking?" *New Republic* 156 (17 June 1967), 14–18.

4. ABC, "Goodnight America: Mark Lane," 27 March 1975.

5. Tape Recording of "Politics of Conspiracy" Conference, Boston University, 31 Jan.–2 Feb. 1975; Robert Sam Anson, "The Greatest Cover-Up of Them All? *New Times* 4 (18 April 1975), 16–29; George O'Toole, "The Oswald-FBI Cover-Up," *Penthouse,* Aug. 1975, pp. 44–47, 112–14; CBS News Inquiry, "The American Assassins," pts. I and II, 25–26 Nov. 1975; ABC News, "Assassination: An American Nightmare," 14 Nov. 1975.

6. Rockefeller Commission Report, 251–69, U.S. Senate, *The Investigation of the Assassination of President John F. Kennedy: The Performance*

of the Intelligence Agencies; Book V, *Final Report of the Select Committee to Study Governmental Operations Within the United States With Respect to Intelligence Activities,* 94th Cong., S. Report 94-755. (Washington, D.C.: U.S. GPO, 1976).

7. U.S. House of Representatives, *House Resolution 1540,* 15 Sept. 1976; *House Resolution 9,* 4 Jan. 1977; *House Resolution 222,* 2 Feb. 1977; *House Resolution 430,* 30 March 1977.

8. *HSCA Report,* p. 11; Jerry Policoff and William Scott Malone, "A Great Show, A Lousy Investigation," *New Times* 8 (4 Sept. 1978), 5–6, 8, 12; Tracy Kidder, "The Assassination Tangle," *Atlantic Monthly* 227 March 1979, 4, 6–8, 10, 13–16, 24, 26, 28.

9. *HSCA Report,* 513–14.

10. Ibid., 11, 18–19.

11. Ibid., 19.

12. *Appendix to HSCA Hearings,* VII, 43–71.

13. Ibid., 73–198.

14. Ibid., 80–89.

15. Ibid., 89–95.

16. Ibid., 95–102.

17. Ibid., 106–7.

18. Ibid., 246, 254–55, 260–63.

19. Ibid., 117–35.

20. Ibid., 138–63.

21. Ibid., 199–210; *HSCA Hearings,* I, 332–73.

22. *HSCA Hearings,* I, 383–427.

23. Wahl and Kramer, "Neutron Activation Analysis," 68–86.

24. *HSCA Hearings,* I, 490–567.

25. *HSCA Report,* 47; *WC Report,* 18.

26. *HSCA Hearings,* II, 154–203; *Appendix to HSCA Hearings,* VI, 32–62.

27. *Appendix to HSCA Hearings,* VI, 63–107; VIII, 223–388.

28. *HSCA Report,* 56–63.

29. Ibid., 65.

30. Ibid., 67.

31. Dallas police tape, copy in author's possession.

32. *HSCA Report,* 66–67.

33. *Appendix to HSCA Hearings,* VIII, 44–45.

34. Ibid., 47–48.

35. *HSCA Report,* 72.

36. *HSCA Hearings,* V, 556.

37. *HSCA Report,* vi–ix.

38. Ibid., 130–31.

39. *Appendix to HSCA Hearings,* X, 1-160.

40. Secret Service Memorandum, 27 Nov. 1963, Secret Service no. 2-1-611.0, p. 1, SS Reports.

41. *HSCA Report,* 129, 139–47.

42. Ibid., 154–55.

NOTES FOR CHAPTER TEN

1. *WC Report,* 541; *Appendix to HSCA Hearings,* VII, 85.
2. *Appendix to HSCA Hearings,* VII, 175.
3. Ibid., 179.
4. Ibid., VI, 47.
5. *HSCA Hearings,* I, 231.
6. Ibid., *Appendix to HSCA Hearings,* VI, 44–45, 51, 53.
7. *Appendix to HSCA Hearings,* VII, 93.
8. Ibid., 93, 270, 302.
9. Ibid., 104–5, 115.
10. Ibid., 118–23, 131.
11. Ibid., 134, 176–77.
12. Ibid., 144, 166–67, 142–43, 104.
13. *HSCA Hearings,* I, 393–401.
14. Ibid., 401; *Appendix to HSCA Hearings,* VII, 131, 119; *WC Report,* 543.
15. *HSCA Hearings,* I, 415–17.
16. *HSCA Report,* 509.
17. Ibid., 290–91; BBC-TV, *The World At War,* "The Battle of Stalingrad," shows several scenes of soldiers shot in the head.
18. *HSCA Report,* 48.
19. *Appendix to HSCA Hearings,* VII, 168–69; VI, 43–56.
20. *HSCA Hearings,* I, 528–33.
21. Ibid., 538.
22. Ibid., 547–49.
23. Ibid., 538.
24. *HSCA Report,* 52–56.
25. Ibid., 57.
26. Williams testimony, *WC Hearings,* III, 167–72; Marrion Baker testimony, ibid., 245–50; Roy Truly testimony, ibid., 221–28.
27. *HSCA Report,* 59–60.
28. See ch. 7 for details.
29. *HSCA Report,* 63.
30. Ibid., 65–76.
31. *HSCA Hearings,* II, 108–10; V, 556–684.

32. Ibid., II, 105–6.
33. *HSCA Report,* 80.
34. Ibid., 81.
35. Ibid., 95–225.
36. Ibid., 129–78.
37. Ibid., 9–20.
38. Ibid., 54–56; *Appendix to HSCA Hearings,* VI, 138–225.

NOTES FOR CHAPTER ELEVEN

1. Secret Service Agents Edward E. Moore and Forrest C. Sorrels, Report of 11 Dec. 1963, SS Reports; Dallas Police Homicide Report, 22 Nov. 1963, WC Records, NA; Dallas County Medical Examiner's Office, Report on Autopsy of Officer J.D. Tippit, 22 Nov. 1963, Autopsy Protocol No. M63-352, WC Records, NA; Hoover to Rankin, 27 March 1964, FBI Papers.
2. Ruby interrogation, *WC Hearings,* V, 194; *WC Report,* 373.
3. See *HSCA Report,* 156–59.
4. Jerry Herald interview; FBI reports of interviews with Carrol Jarnigan and Lawhill Wade, FBI Papers.
5. FBI Report, 12 Dec. 1964, FBI Papers; FBI Report, 11 Dec. 1964, ibid.
6. Jerry Herald interview.
7. See Michael L. Kurtz, "Lee Harvey Oswald in New Orleans: A Reappraisal," *Louisiana History* 21 (1980), 7–22.
8. Ibid., 18–19; *HSCA Report,* 143–46.
9. Kurtz, "Oswald in New Orleans," 18–20; *HSCA Report,* 143–46.
10. Author's interview, George Wilcox, 9 Sept. 1979.
11. *HSCA Report,* 143–46; FBI interviews of David Ferrie, 26 Nov. 1963, 27 Nov. 1963, FBI Papers.
12. *Appendix to HSCA Hearings,* vol. X.
13. Sullivan testimony, U.S. Senate, *Investigation of the Kennedy Assassination,* 32–43; Katzenbach deposition, 4 Aug. 1978, *Appendix to HSCA Hearings,* XI, 76.
14. CIA Papers, miscellaneous documents.

NOTES FOR CHAPTER THIRTEEN

1. *HSCA Report,* 230–34; *HSCA Hearings,* III, 447; Commission Documents 137, 1347, WC Records, NA.
2. *HSCA Report,* 230–34; *WC Hearings,* XXVI, 441.
3. *Appendix to HSCA Hearings,* X, 199.

4. FBI Report, 26 Nov. 1963, FBI Papers.

5. FBI Documents 535, 1643, 1762, FBI Papers; CIA Documents 288-692, 347-115, 370-727B, Papers of the Central Intelligence Agency on the Assassination of President Kennedy. Linus A. Sims Memorial Library, Southeastern Louisiana University, Hammond, La. Hereafter cited as CIA Papers.

6. *HSCA Report,* 137–39.

7. *Appendix to HSCA Hearings,* X, 83.

8. *Dallas Morning News,* 10 June 1979.

9. *WC Hearings,* XXIV, 704; XXVI, 450, 682, 702–4; Commission Documents 950, 385, WC Records, NA.

10. *WC Hearings,* X, 386; XXIII, 403; XXVI, 368.

11. *WC Report,* 330–38.

12. Mercer affadavit, *WC Hearings,* XIX, 483–84; Rowland testimony, ibid., II, 167–76; Helen Forrest interview; *Dallas Morning News,* 19 Dec. 1978; Anthony Summers, *Conspiracy* (New York: McGraw-Hill, 1980), 73–74.

13. Sibert-O'Neill Report, 4.

14. Zapruder film, frames Z189–208.

15. Ibid., Z312–313.

16. Ibid., Z327–335.

17. *Appendix to HSCA Hearings,* VII, 175.

18. Ibid., VI, 54–56.

19. Ibid. This contains the trajectory analysis, which distorted the true position of Governor Connally. The angle from the "Oswald" window to the limousine was 17 degrees. *WC Report,* 106–7.

20. *WC Hearings,* VI, 294–95; VII, 107.

21. *Appendix to HSCA Hearings,* VII, 226–27.

22. *WC Hearings,* II, 132–34; *HSCA Report,* 81.

23. Zapruder film, frames Z321–331.

24. Ibid., Z314–327.

25. Ibid., Z328–331.

26. Ibid., Z327–331.

27. *Appendix to HSCA Hearings,* VII, 103–34.

28. Ibid., XII, 18–19.

29. *WC Report,* 669–80; FBI Report, Section EBF, Document no. 377, FBI Papers.

30. *WC Report,* 690–702; see Edward Jay Epstein, *Legend: The Secret World of Lee Harvey Oswald* (New York: Reader's Digest, 1978).

31. FBI Report, sec. 53, no. NO-100-16601, 85 pp., FBI Papers.

32. Summers, *Conspiracy,* 297–343, 362–66.

33. *WC Report,* 730–40.

34. FBI Report, sec. 53, no. NO-100-16601, FBI Papers.

35. U.S. Senate, *Investigation of the Assassination,* 28–31; Cable, Mexico City Station to CIA Headquarters, 26 Nov. 1963, CIA Papers.

36. U.S. Senate, *Investigation of the Assassination,* 60–61.

37. Hoover to FBI Legation, Madrid, 24 Nov. 1963, sec. 26, Document 1643, FBI Papers; CIA Document 412-76, 27 Nov. 1963, CIA Document 347-115, 7 Dec. 1963, CIA Document 370-727B, 10 Dec. 1963, CIA Papers.

38. U.S. Senate, *Investigation of the Assassination,* 14–21.

39. *HSCA Report,* 127–29.

40. Ibid., 133–34.

41. Ibid.

42. Ibid., 147.

43. Ibid., 147–80.

BIBLIOGRAPHY

BIBLIOGRAPHICAL NOTE

The following selective bibliography includes all the main sources consulted for this work. It is not comprehensive. Numerous works about the assassination are worthless as source materials, for they rely on sensationalism and speculation rather than scholarship. The bibliography provides a representative sampling of these materials to give the reader an idea of the innumerable varieties of works the assassination has generated.

Other sources remain unavailable to the researcher. The working papers and unpublished documents of the House Select Committee on Assassinations, for example, are filed with the Clerk of the House and are placed under a fifty year time seal. A large number of the papers of the Warren Commission, the FBI, and the CIA are either censored or classified and thus beyond the scrutiny of the scholar.

A. UNPUBLISHED PRIMARY SOURCES

I. U.S. Government Documents

Central Intelligence Agency. Papers on the Assassination of President Kennedy. 15 vols., 3847 pp. Linus A. Sims Memorial Library, Southeastern Louisiana Univ., Hammond, La.

Federal Bureau of Investigation. Papers on the JFK Assassination, Lee Harvey Oswald, Jack Ruby, and the Warren Commission. 125,000 pp. Linus A. Sims Memorial Library, Southeastern Louisiana Univ., Hammond, La.

National Archives and Records Services, General Services Administration. Records of the Government Printing Office Relating to the *Report* of the Commission, 8 April–4 Dec. 1964. National Archives, Washington, D.C.

National Archives and Records Services, General Services Administration. Records of the President's Commission on the Assassination of President Kennedy. Record Group 272. National Archives, Washington, D.C.

National Archives and Records Services, General Services Administration. National Archives Gift Collection on the Assassination of President Kennedy. Record Group 200. National Archives, Washington, D.C.

National Archives and Records Services, General Services Administration. Related Materials Received From the Secret Service, 1963 and 1965. National Archives, Washington, D.C.

II. Unpublished Reports

"1968 Panel Review of Photographs, X-Ray Films, Documents and Other Evidence Pertaining to the Fatal Wounding of President John F. Kennedy on November 22, 1963 in Dallas, Texas." Undated report. National Archives, Washington, D.C.

"Report of Inspector by Naval Medical Staff on November 1, 1966 at National Archives of X-Rays and Photographs of Autopsy of President John F. Kennedy." Undated report. National Archives, Washington, D.C.

"Wounds Ballistics of 6.5 mm. Mannlicher-Carcano Ammunition." March 1965. Technical Report CRDLR3264, Chemical Research and Development Laboratories, Edgewood Arsenal, United States Army. National Archives, Washington, D.C.

III. Unpublished State Documents

Carr, Waggoner. Texas Supplemental Report on the Assassination of President John Kennedy and the Serious Wounding of Governor John B. Connally, November 22, 1963. 24 vols. Austin: State of Texas, 1964.

Jaworski, Leon. Files of Evidence Connected With the Investigation of the Assassination of President John F. Kennedy. Texas Court of Inquiry. 21 vols. Washington, D.C.: Microcard Editions, 1967.

State of Louisiana v. Clay L. Shaw. Preliminary Hearings No. M-703. Criminal District Court: New Orleans, 1967. 5 vols. Linus A. Sims Memorial Library, Southeastern Louisiana Univ., Hammond, La.

State of Louisiana v. Clay L. Shaw. Case 198-059, 1426 (30), Section "C,"

Criminal District Court, New Orleans. 40 vols. Linus A. Sims Memorial Library, Southeastern Louisiana Univ., Hammond, La.

B. PUBLISHED PRIMARY SOURCES

Commission on CIA Activities Within the United States. *Report of the Commission on CIA Activities Within the United States.* Washington, D.C.: U.S. GPO, 1975.

National Archives and Records Services. *Inventory of the Records of the President's Commission on the Assassination of President Kennedy: Record Group 272.* Compiled by Marion M. Johnson, National Archives and Records Services. Washington, D.C.: U.S. GPO, 1973.

President's Commission on the Assassination of President Kennedy. *Hearings Before the President's Commission on the Assassination of President Kennedy.* 26 vols. Washington, D.C.: U.S. GPO, 1964.

President's Commission on the Assassination of President Kennedy. *Report of the President's Commission on the Assassination of President Kennedy.* Washington, D.C.: U.S. GPO, 1964.

House of Representatives. Government Information and Individual Rights Subcommittee on Governmental Operations. *National Archives-Security Classification Problem Involving Warren Commission Files and Other Records.* 94th Cong., 1st Session. Washington, D.C.: U.S. GPO, 1976.

House of Representatives. Select Committee on Assassinations. *Investigation of the Assassination of President John F. Kennedy: Appendix to Hearings Before the Select Committee on Assassinations of the U.S. House of Representatives.* 7 vols. 95th Cong., 2nd Session. Washington, D.C.: U.S. GPO, 1979.

House of Representatives. Select Committee on Assassinations. *Investigation of the Assassination of President John F. Kennedy: Hearings Before the Select Committee on Assassinations of the U.S. House of Representatives.* 5 vols. 95th Cong., 2nd Session. Washington, D.C.: U.S. GPO, 1978–79.

House of Representatives. Select Committee on Assassinations. *Report of the Select Committee on Assassinations.* 95th Cong., 2nd Session. Washington, D.C.: U.S. GPO, 1979.

Senate. Select Committee to Study Governmental Operations With Respect to Intelligence Activities. *The Investigation of the Assassination of President John F. Kennedy: The Performance of the Intelligence Agencies.* Book V, *Final Report of the Select Committee to Study Governmental Operations With Respect to Intelligence Activities.* 94th Cong., 2nd Session. Senate Report 94-755. Washington, D.C.: U.S. GPO, 1976.

Wrone, David R., ed. *The Freedom of Information Act and Political Assassinations.* Vol. I. *The Legal Proceedings of Harold Weisberg v. General Services Administration, Civil Action 2052-73: Together With the January 22 and 27 Warren Commission Transcripts.* Stevens Point, Wis.: Foundation Press, 1978.

C. OTHER PRIMARY SOURCES

I. *Films and Photographs*

Robert Hughes film. National Archives, Washington, D.C.

Mary Muchmore film. National Archives, Washington, D.C.

Orville Nix film. National Archives, Washington, D.C.

"Rush to Judgment." Produced by Mark Lane and Emilio deAntonio. New York: 1967.

Visual Materials on the Kennedy Assassination Collection. Linus A. Sims Memorial Library, Southeastern Louisiana Univ., Hammond, La.

Visual Materials on the Kennedy Assassination Private Collection. In author's possession.

Abraham Zapruder film. National Archives, Washington, D.C.

II. *Records and Tapes*

"The Actual Voices and Events of Four Days that Shocked the World." Colpix Records, 1967.

"Dallas Police Tapes." In author's possession.

"Kennedy Assassination Conference Tapes." 12 cassettes. Georgetown Univ., 1975.

"Lee Harvey Oswald Speaks." Truth Records, 1967.

"The Oswald Case." Broadside, 1964.

Tapes and Records Collection. Linus A. Sims Memorial Library, Southeastern Louisiana Univ., Hammond, La.

Tapes and Records Private Collection. In author's possession.

D. SECONDARY SOURCES

I. *Books*

Adler, Bill, comp. *The Weight of the Evidence: The Warren Report and Its Critics.* Edited by Jay David. New York: Meredith, 1968.

Anson, Robert Sam. *They've Killed the President: The Search For the Murderers of John F. Kennedy.* New York: Bantam, 1975.

Ashman, Charles. *The CIA-Mafia Link.* New York: Manor, 1975.

Associated Press. *The Torch Is Passed: The Associated Press Story of the Death of a President.* New York: Associated Press, 1963.

Baker, Dean C. *The Assassination of President Kennedy: A Study of the Press Coverage.* Ann Arbor: Univ. of Michigan Press, 1965.

Belin, David W. *November 22, 1963: You Are the Jury.* New York: Quadrangle, 1973.

Belli, Melvin M., and Carroll, M.C. *Dallas Justice: The Real Story of Jack Ruby and His Trial.* New York: McKay, 1964.

Bishop, James A. *The Day Kennedy Was Shot.* New York: Funk and Wagnalls, 1968.

Bloomgarden, Henry S. *The Gun: A Biography of the Gun That Killed John F. Kennedy.* New York: Grossman, 1975.

Blumenthal, Sid, and Yazijian, Harvey, eds. *Government by Gunplay: Assassination Conspiracies from Dallas to Today.* New York: New American Library, 1976.

Bonner, Judy W. *Investigation of a Homicide: The Murder of John F. Kennedy.* Anderson, S.C.: Droke House, 1969.

Brener, Milton E. *The Garrison Case: A Study in the Abuse of Power.* New York: Potter, 1969.

Bringuier, Carlos, *Red Friday: Nov. 22nd, 1963.* Chicago: C. Hallberg, 1969.

Buchanan, Thomas G. *Who Killed Kennedy?* New York: Putnam, 1964.

Canfield, Michael, and Weberman, Alan. *Coup d'Etat in America: The CIA and the Assassination of John F. Kennedy.* New York: Third Press, 1975.

Curry, Jesse E. *JFK Assassination File.* Dallas: American Poster, 1969.

Cutler, Robert B. *Crossfire: Evidence of a Conspiracy.* Danvers, Mass.: Mirror Press, 1975.

______. *The Flight of CE399: Evidence of Conspiracy.* Beverly, Mass.: R.B. Cutler, 1969.

______. *The Umbrella Man: Evidence of Conspiracy.* Danvers, Mass.: Mirror Press, 1975.

Demaris, Ovid, and Willis, Gary B. *Jack Ruby.* New York: New American, 1968.

Eddowes, Michael. *November 22: How They Killed Kennedy.* London: Spearman, 1976.

______. *The Oswald File.* New York: Crown, 1977.

Epstein, Edward Jay. *Counterplot.* New York: Viking, 1969.

______. *Inquest: The Warren Commission and the Establishment of Truth.* New York: Viking, 1966.

______. *Legend: The Secret World of Lee Harvey Oswald.* New York: Reader's Digest, 1978.

Evica, George Michael. *And We Are All Mortal: New Evidence and Analysis in the Assassination of John F. Kennedy.* West Hartford, Conn.: Univ. of Hartford, 1978.

Fensterwald, Bernard, Jr., ed. *Coincidence or Conspiracy?* New York: Zebra Books, 1977.

Ford, Gerald R., and Stiles, John M. *Portrait of an Assassin.* New York: Simon and Schuster, 1965.

Garrison, Jim. *A Heritage of Stone.* New York: Putnam. 1970.

Gertz, Elmer. *Moments of Madness: The People v. Jack Ruby.* Chicago Follett, 1968.

Greenberg, Bradley S., and Parker, Edwin B., eds. *The Kennedy Assassination and the American Public: Social Communication in Crisis.* Stanford: Stanford Univ. Press, 1965.

Groden, Robert F., and Model, F. Peter. *JFK: The Case For Conspiracy.* New York: Manor, 1976.

Hanson, William H. *The Shooting of John F. Kennedy: One Assassin, Three Shots, Three Hits, No Misses.* San Antonio: Naylor, 1969.

Harris, Larry R., and Shaw, J. Gary. *Cover-Up: The Governmental Conspiracy to Conceal the Facts About the Public Execution of John Kennedy.* Cleburne, Tex.: J. Gary Shaw, 1976.

Hepburn, James. *Farewell America.* Vaduz, Cal.: Frontiers, 1968.

Hoch, Paul L., Scott, Peter Dale, and Stetler, Russell, eds. *The Assassinations; Dallas and Beyond: A Guide to Cover-Ups and Investigations.* New York: Vintage, 1976.

Houts, Marshall. *Where Death Delights: The Story of Dr. Milton Helpern and Forensic Medicine.* New York: Coward-McCann, 1967.

Itek Corporation. *Life-Itek Kennedy Assassination Film Analysis.* Lexington, Mass.: Itek, 1967.

James, Rosemary, and Wardlaw, Jack. *Plot or Politics? The Garrison Case and Its Cast.* New Orleans: Pelican, 1967.

Joesten, Joachim. *Oswald: Assassin or Fall Guy?* New York: Morzani, 1964.

Jones, Penn. *Forgive My Grief.* 4 vols. Midlothian, Tex.: Midlothian Mirror, 1966–74.

Kantor, Seth. *Who Was Jack Ruby?* New York: Everest House, 1978.

Kaplan, John, and Waltz, Jon R. *The Trial of Jack Ruby.* New York: Macmillan, 1965.

Kilgallen, Dorothy. *Murder One.* New York: Random, 1967.

Kirkwood, James. *American Grotesque: An Account of the Clay Shaw-Jim Garrison Affair in the City of New Orleans.* New York: Simon and Schuster, 1970.

Lane, Mark. *A Citizen's Dissent.* New York: Holt, Rinehart, 1968.

______. *Rush to Judgment.* New York: Holt, Rinehart, 1966.

Lewis, Richard Warren. *The Scavengers and Critics of the Warren Report.* New York: Delacorte, 1967.

Lifton, David. *Best Evidence: Disguise and Deception in the Assassination of John F. Kennedy.* New York: Macmillan, 1980.

McDonald, Hugh C. *Appointment in Dallas: The Final Solution to the Assassination of JFK.* New York: Hugh McDonald, 1975.

McMillan, Priscilla Johnson. *Marina and Lee.* New York: Harper and Row, 1977.

MacParlane, Ian Colin. *Proof of Conspiracy in the Assassination of President Kennedy.* Melbourne, Australia: Book Distributors, 1975.

Manchester, William R. *The Death of a President: November 20–November 25, 1963.* New York: Harper and Row, 1967.

Marchetti, Victor, and Marks, John D. *The CIA and the Cult of Intelligence.* New York: Knopf, 1974.

Meagher, Sylvia. *Accessories After the Fact: The Warren Commission, the Authorities, and the Report.* New York: Vintage, 1976.

______. *Subject Index to the Warren Report and Hearings and Exhibits.* New York: Scarecrow, 1966.

Miller, Tom. *The Assassination Please Almanac.* Chicago: Regency, 1977.

Morin, Relman. *Assassination: The Death of President John F. Kennedy.* New York: New American Library, 1968.

Newman, Albert H. *The Assassination of John F. Kennedy: The Reasons Why.* New York: Potter, 1970.

Noyes, Peter. *Legacy of Doubt.* New York: Pinnacle, 1973.

Oglesby, Carl. *The Yankee and Cowboy War: Conspiracies from Dallas to Watergate.* Mission Kan.: Andrews and McMeel, 1976.

O'Toole, George. *The Assassination Tapes: An Electronic Probe Into the Murder of John F. Kennedy and the Dallas Cover-Up.* New York: Penthouse Press, 1975.

Popkin, Richard H. *The Second Oswald.* New York: Avon, 1966.

Roberts, Charles. *The Truth About the Assassination.* New York: Grosset and Dunlap, 1967.

Roffman, Howard. *Presumed Guilty: Lee Harvey Oswald in the Assassination of President Kennedy.* Cranbury, N.J.: Associated University Press, 1975.

Sparrow, John Hanbury Anges. *After the Assassination: A Positive Appraisal of the Warren Report.* New York: Chilmark, 1967.

Summers, Anthony. *Conspiracy.* New York: McGraw-Hill, 1980.

Thompson, Josiah. *Six Seconds in Dallas: A Micro-Study of the Kennedy Assassination.* New York: Bernard Geis, 1967.

Thornley, Kerry W. *Oswald.* Chicago: New Classics, 1965.

Weisberg, Harold. *Oswald in New Orleans.* New York: Canyon, 1967.

______. *Post-Mortem: JFK Assassination Cover-Up Smashed.* Frederick, Md.: H. Weisberg, 1975.

______. *Whitewash.* 4 vols. Hyattstown-Frederick, Md.: H. Weisberg, 1965–75.

White, Stephen. *Should We Believe the Warren Report?* New York: Macmillan, 1968.

II. Journal Articles

Alvarez, Luis W. "A Physicist Examines the Kennedy Assassination Film." *American Journal of Physics* 44 (1976), 813–27.

Ansbacher, Heinz and Rowena R., and Shiverick, David and Kathleen. "Lee Harvey Oswald: An Alderian Interpretation." *Psychoanalytic Review* 53 (Fall 1966), 55–68.

Appelbaum, Stephen A. "The Kennedy Assassination." *Psychoanalytic Review* 53 (Fall 1966), 69–80.

Back, Kurt, and Sarvary, Judith. "From Bright Ideas to Social Research: The Studies of the Kennedy Assassination." *Public Opinion Quarterly* 31 (1967), 253–64.

Bonjean, Charles M., Hill, Richard J., and Martin, Harry W. "Reactions to the Assassination by Sex and Social Class." *Southwest Sociology Association* 15 (1965), 21–37.

Brogan, Dennis W. "Death in Dallas: Myths After Kennedy." *Encounter* 23 (1964), 20–26.

Cole, Alwyn. "Assassin Forger." *Journal of Forensic Sciences* 11 (1966), 272–88.

Cushman, Robert F. "Why the Warren Commission?" *New York University Law Review* 40 (1965), 477–503.

Feldman, Jacob J., and Sheatsley, Paul B. "The Assassination of President Kennedy: A Preliminary Report on Public Reactions and Behavior." *Public Opinion Quarterly* 28 (1964), 189–215.

Freese, Paul L. "The Warren Commission and the Fourth Shot: A Reflection on the Fundamentals of Forensic Fact Finding." *New York University Law Review* 40 (1965), 424–65.

Gales, Robert Robinson. "The Assassination of the President: Jurisdictional Problems." *Syracuse Law Review* 16 (1964), 69–81.

Gallup Poll. "Were Kennedy, King Conspiracy Victims?" *Gallup Opinion Index* 139 (Feb. 1977), 1–4.

Goodhart, Arthur L. "The Mysteries of the Kennedy Assassination and the English Press." *Law Quarterly Review* 83 (1967), 23–63.

______. "The Warren Commission From A Procedural Standpoint." *New York University Law Review* 40 (1965), 404–23.

Kaplan, John. "Controversy: The Assassins." *American Scholar* 36 (1967), 271-308.

Kurtz, Michael L. "Lee Harvey Oswald in New Orleans: A Reappraisal." *Louisiana History* 21 (1980), 7-22.

Lattimer, John K. "Factors in the Death of President Kennedy." *Journal of The American Medical Association* 198 (24 Oct. 1966), 327-33.

______. "Observations Based on a Review of the Autopsy Photographs, X-Rays, and Related Materials of the Late President John F. Kennedy." *Resident and Staff Physician Medical Times* 34 (May 1972), 34-63.

Lattimer, John K., Gary, and Jon. "Could Oswald Have Shot President Kennedy? Further Ballistics Studies." *Bulletin of the New York Academy of Medicine* 48 (1972), 513-24.

______. "An Experimental Study of the Backward Movement of President Kennedy's Head." *Surgery, Gynecology and Obstetrics* 142 (1976), 246-54.

______. "The Kennedy-Connally One Bullet Theory: Further Circumstantial and Experimental Evidence." *Medical Times* 36 (Nov. 1974), 33-56.

Lattimer, John K., and Jon. "The Kennedy-Connally Single Bullet Theory: A Feasibility Study." *International Surgery* 50 (1968), 524-32.

MacDonald, Neil. "Confidential and Secret Documents of the Warren Commission Deposited in U.S. Archives." *Computers and Automation* 19 (Nov. 1970), 44-47.

Olson, Don, and Turner, Ralph. "Photographic Evidence and the Assassination of President John F. Kennedy." *Journal of Forensic Sciences* 16 (1971), 399-419.

Orren, Karen, and Peterson, Paul. "The Kennedy Assassination: A Case Study in the Dynamics of Political Socialization." *Journal of Politics* 29 (1967), 388-404.

O'Toole, James K. "Mourning A President." *Psychiatric Quarterly* 40 (1966), 737-55.

Raskin, Marcus. "Rush to Judgment." *Yale Law Journal* 75 (1967), 581-97.

Roffman, Howard. "Freedom of Information: Judicial Review of Executive Security Classification." *University of Florida Law Review* 28 (1976), 551-68.

Schonfeld, Maurice W. "The Shadow of a Gunman." *Columbia Journalism Review* 14 (1975), 46-50.

Scobey, Alfredda. "A Lawyer's Notes on the Warren Commission Report." *American Bar Association Journal* 51 (1965), 39-43.

Tinder, Glenn. "The Death of a President and the Problem of Meaning." *Review of Politics* 29 (1967), 407–15.

Wecht, Cyril H. "A Critique of the Medical Aspects of the Investigation Into the Assassination of President Kennedy." *Journal of Forensic Sciences* 11 (1966), 300–317.

______. "JFK Assassination: A Prolonged and Willful Cover-Up." *Modern Medicine* 42 (28 Oct. 1974), 40x–40z.

______. "Pathologist's View of JFK Autopsy: An Unsolved Case." *Modern Medicine* 40 (27 Nov. 1972), 28–32.

Wecht, Cyril H., and Smith, Robert P. "The Medical Evidence in the Assassination of President John F. Kennedy." *Forensic Science* 3 (1974), 105–28.

Wickey, John, and Saltz, Eli. "Resolutions of the Liberal Dilemma in the Assassination of President Kennedy." *Journal of Personality* 33 (1965), 636–48.

Wrone, David R. "The Assassination of John Fitzgerald Kennedy: An Annotated Bibliography." *Wisconsin Magazine of History* 56 (1972), 21–36.

III. Unsigned Magazine Articles

"Accused." *Time* 82 (27 Nov. 1963), 27–28.

"Again the Assassination." *Newsweek* 68 (15 Aug. 1966), 30–33.

"Are There New Leads?" *Newsweek* 89 (11 April 1977), 32–33.

"As Warren Inquiry Starts: Latest on the Assassination." *U.S. News and World Report* 55 (30 Dec. 1963), 28–30.

"Assassination." *Newsweek* 64 (5 Oct. 1964), 32–40, 45–52, 57–60, 62–64.

"Assassination: Behind Moves to Reopen JFK Case." *U.S. News and World Report* 78 (2 Jan. 1975), 30–33.

"Assassination of President Kennedy." *Life* 55 (29 Nov. 1963), 22–32.

"Autopsy." *Time* 82 (27 Dec. 1963), 18.

"Awful Interval." *Newsweek* 63 (6 Jan. 1964), 19–20.

"Bourbon Street Rococo: J. Garrison's Investigation." *Time* 89 (3 March 1967), 26.

"Carnival in New Orleans: Jim Garrison's Investigation." *Newsweek* 69 (6 March 1967), 32.

"Charge of Conspiracy." *Newsweek* 69 (3 April 1967), 36–37.

"Charged: A Cover-Up in the Kennedy Killing." *U.S. News and World Report* 81 (5 July 1976), 21.

"The Cloak Comes Off." *Newsweek* 85 (23 June 1975), 16–27.

"Confusion Compounded." *National Review* 18 (18 Oct. 1966), 1032–33.

"Curtains for the DA: Physicians Examine Photographs and X-Rays." *Newsweek* 73 (27 Jan. 1969), 27.
"DA Wins a Round." *Time* 89 (24 March 1967), 17–18.
"Dallas: Late Casualty." *Newsweek* 67 (28 Feb. 1966), 31–32.
"Dallas: New Questions and Answers." *Newsweek* 85 (28 April 1975), 36–38.
"Dallas Revisited." *Time* 93 (21 Feb. 1969), 18–19.
"The Day Kennedy Died." *Newsweek* 62 (2 Dec. 1963), 20–26.
"Death in Dallas." *Reader's Digest* 84 (Jan. 1964), 39–44.
"Death of a President: The Established Facts." *Atlantic Monthly* 215 (March 1965), 112–18.
"Disclose the Evidence: Call for New Investigation." *Nation* 221 (13 Dec. 1975), 611–12.
"The Documents." *New Republic* 173 (27 Sept. 1975), 12–48.
"Fresh Doubts on JFK Assassination: Forensic Experts Call for a New Investigation on All the Evidence." *Medical World News* 16 (2 June 1975), 25–28.
"Friends of Lee Oswald." *National Review* 16 (10 March 1964), 183–85.
"The Ghost Will Not Rest." *New Republic* 173 (27 Sept. 1975), 7.
"The Government Still Lives." *Times* 82 (29 Nov. 1963), 21–32.
"How JFK Died." *Newsweek* 62 (30 Dec. 1963), 55.
"Into the Archives: X-Rays and Photographs of Body of JFK." *Time* 88 (11 Nov. 1966), 33.
"JFK Assassination: Justice Department Publishes a Report by Doctors." *New Republic* 160 (1 Feb. 1969), 9–10.
"JFK Censored?" *Newsweek* 68 (3 Oct. 1966), 65–66.
"JFK: Clean Bill for CIA." *Newsweek* 87 (23 June 1976), 21.
"JFK: The Death and the Doubt." *Newsweek* 68 (5 Dec. 1966), 25–26.
"JFK's Murder: Sowers of Doubt." *Newsweek* 63 (6 April 1964), 22–24.
"LBJ on the Assassination." *Newsweek* 75 (11 May 1970), 41.
"Life: John F. Kennedy Memorial Edition." *Life* (29 Nov. 1963), entire issue.
"Mark Lane Interview." *Playboy* 14 (Feb. 1967), 41–42, 44–64, 66–68.
"A Matter of Reasonable Doubt." *Life* 61 (25 Nov. 1966), 38–48B, 53.
"More than a Man in the Dock." *Time* 93 (14 Feb. 1969), 26–29.
"New Wave of Doubt." *Look* 30 (12 July 1966), 60–72.
"November 22, 1963: Photos by Nine Bystanders." *Life* 63 (25 Nov. 1967), 87–97.
"Opening the JFK File." *Newsweek* 90 (12 Dec. 1977), 34–35.
"Oswald and the Weight of the Evidence." *Newsweek* 62 (9 Dec. 1963), 36, 41–42.
"A Primer of Assassination Theories." *Esquire* 66 (Dec. 1966), 205–10.

"Questions that Won't Go Away." *Saturday Evening Post* 247 (Dec. 1975), 38–39.

"A Second Primer of Assassination Theories." *Esquire* 67 (May 1967), 104–7.

"Tracking Down Kennedy's Killers." *Newsreal* (July 1977), entire issue.

"Truth About Kennedy Assasination: Questions Raised and Answered." *U.S. News and World Report* 61 (10 Oct. 1966), 44–50.

"Warren Commission Report." *Time* 84 (2 Oct. 1964), 45–50.

"Who Killed JFK?" *Skeptic Forum* (Sept.–Oct. 1975), entire issue.

"Who Killed JFK? Just One Assassin." *Time* 106 (24 Nov. 1975), 32–34, 37–38.

"Who Killed Kennedy?" *National Review* 20 (2 July 1968), 642.

"Why Is the Assassinations Committee Killing Itself? Anatomy of a Murder Inquest." *Rolling Stone* 184 (7 April 1977), 42–45.

"Why the JFK Case Is Coming Back to Life." *U.S. News and World Report* 82 (17 Jan. 1977), 28–30.

IV. Signed Magazine Articles

Anson, Robert Sam. "The Greatest Cover-Up of All?" *New Times* 4 (18 April 1975), 16–29.

______. "The Man Who Never Was." *New Times* 5 (19 Sept. 1975), 14–16, 21–25.

Autry, James A. "The Garrison Investigation: How and Why It Began." *New Orleans* 1 (April 1967), 8, 50–51.

Aynesworth, Hugh. "JFK Conspiracy: J. Garrison's Investigation of a Plot to Kill J.F. Kennedy." *Newsweek* 69 (15 May 1967), 36, 38, 40.

Belin, David W. "The Second Gunman Syndrome." *National Review* 31 (27 April 1979), 534–55.

______. "They've Killed the President." *National Review* 28 (6 Feb. 1976), 81–85, 88–90.

Bickel, Alexander M. "CBS on the Warren Report." *New Republic* 157 (15 July 1967), 29–30.

______. "Failure of the Warren Report." *Commentary* 43 (April 1967), 23–26.

______. "Reexamining the Warren Report." *New Republic* 156 (7 Jan. 1967), 25–28.

Boyle, Richard. "The Strange Death of Clay Shaw." *True* 56 (April 1975), 54–57, 86–89.

Branch, Taylor, and Crile, George III. "The Kennedy Vendetta." *Harper's* 251 (Aug. 1975), 49–63.

Butterfield, Roger. "Assassination: Some Serious Exceptions to the Warren Report." *Harper's* 233 (Oct. 1966), 122, 124–26.

Callahan, John W. "Did Jack Ruby Kill the Wrong Man?" *Argosy* 365 (Sept. 1967), 29, 96–101.

Cohen, Jacob. "Conspiracy Fever." *Commentary* 60 (Oct. 1975), 33–42.

______. "What the Warren Report Omits: Vital Documents." *Nation* 203 (11 July 1966), 43–49.

Condon, Richard. "Manchurian Candidate in Dallas." *Nation* 197 (28 Dec. 1963), 449–51.

Cook, Fred. J. "Irregulars Take the Field." *Nation* 213 (19 July 1971), 40–46.

______. "The Warren Report." *Nation* 200 (Oct. 1966), 38–54.

Cooper, Paulette. "President Kennedy's Brain Is Missing." *True* 54 (May 1973), 45, 116, 119–20.

Dreifus, Claudia. "Who Stole John Kennedy's Brains and Other Questions on the Assassination of the President." *Playgirl* 3 (Aug. 1975), 50–51, 58–59, 80–81, 92, 100–101, 140–41.

Epstein, Edward Jay. "Final Chapter in the Assassination Controversy." *New York Times Magazine* (20 April 1969), 30–31, 115–20.

______. "Garrison." *New Yorker* 44 (13 July 1968), 35–40, 42, 49–52, 54–56, 58–60, 62–76, 79–81.

______. "Who's Afraid of the Warren Report?" *Esquire* 66 (Dec. 1966), 204, 330–32, 334.

Evans, M. Stanton. "Cover-Up Proved in JFK Murder Probe." *Human Events* 36 (24 July 1976), 13, 15.

Groden, Robert. "A New Look at the Zapruder Film." *Rolling Stone* 185 (24 April 1975), 35–36.

Grosvenor, Melville Bell. "The Last Full Measure." *National Geographic* 125 (March 1964), 307–55.

Hammer, Richard. "Playboy's History of Organized Crime: Part XII, the American Nightmare." *Playboy* 21 (July 1974), 123–26, 148, 204–15.

Houts, Marshall. "Warren Commission One-Bullet Theory Exploded." *Argosy* 365 (July 1967), 108–16.

Jackson, Donald. "The Evolution of an Assassination." *Life* 58 (21 Feb. 1964), 68A–80.

Joling, Robert J. "JFK Assassination: Still an Unsolved Murder Mystery." *Saturday Evening Post* 247 (Dec. 1975), 44–46.

Kaiser, Robert Blair. "The JFK Assassination: Why Congress Should Reopen the Investigation." *Rolling Stone* 185 (24 April 1975), 27–28, 30–31, 33, 37–38.

Kempton, Murray. "The Disposable Jack Ruby." *Spectator* 218 (13 Jan. 1967), 35.

______. "Warren Report: Case for the Prosecution." *New Republic* 151 (10 Oct. 1964), 13–17.

Kidder, Tracy. "The Assassination Tangle." *Atlantic Monthly* 227 (March 1979), 4, 6–8, 10, 13–16, 24, 26, 28.

Lardner, George, Jr. "Congress and the Assassinations." *Saturday Review* 4 (19 Feb. 1977), 14–18.

Linn, Edward. "The Untold Story of Jack Ruby." *Saturday Evening Post* 237 (25 July 1964), 24–26, 28, 33, 36–37, 40, 48–49.

Lowenstein, Allard. "The Kennedy Killings." *Argosy* 383 (Feb. 1976), 28–33, 86.

Lynd, Straughton, and Minnis, Jack. "Seeds of Doubt: Some Questions About the Assassination." *New Republic* 149 (21 Dec. 1963), 14–17.

Macdonald, Dwight. "A Critique of the Warren Report." *Esquire* 63 (March 1965), 59–63, 127–38.

McKinley, James. "Cries of Conspiracy." *Playboy* 23 (May 1976), 122–27, 130, 132, 200–208.

______. "The End of Camelot." *Playboy* 23 (April 1976), 125, 127–30, 142, 193, 196, 198–200, 202–4, 206, 208.

McMillan, Priscilla Johnson. "Why Oswald Really Killed Kennedy." *Ladies Home Journal* 94 (Nov. 1977), 122–43.

Maddox, Henry. "The Plot According to Garrison." *New Orleans* 1 (July 1967), 18–19, 52–53.

Malone, William Scott. "The Secret Life of Jack Ruby." *New Times* 10 (23 Jan. 1978), 46–51.

Mills, Andrew. "Who Killed Kennedy? The Warren Report Is Right." *True* 48 (Dec. 1967), 32, 72, 75–77.

Model, F. Peter. "Killing the Kennedys: The Case for Conspiracy." *Argosy* 382 (July 1975), 34–41, 64–66.

Nash, George and Patricia. "The Other Witnesses." *New Leader* 47 (12 Oct. 1964), 6–9.

Norden, Eric. "Jim Garrison: A Candid Conversation With the Embattled District Attorney of New Orleans." *Playboy* 14 (Oct. 1967), 59–60, 62, 64, 66, 68, 70, 72, 74, 156–63, 165–68, 170–72, 174–76, 178.

O'Toole, George. "The Assassination Probe." *Saturday Evening Post* 247 (Nov. 1975), 45–48, 112.

______. "Assassination Tapes." *Penthouse* 4 (July 1973), 44–47, 112–14, 124–26.

______. "Lee Harvey Oswald Was Innocent." *Penthouse* 6 (April 1975), 48–51, 62, 89–90, 123.

O'Toole, George, and Hoch, Paul. "Dallas: The Cuban Connection." *Saturday Evening Post* 248 (March 1976), 44–45, 96.

O'Toole, George, and Whalen, Richard J., and Lane, Mark. "The Unsolved J.F.K. Murder Mystery." *Saturday Evening Post* 247 (Sept. 1975), 45–53, 100–102, 107, 110, 119.

Phelan, James. "The Assassination that Will Not Die." *New York Times Magazine* (23 Nov. 1975), 27–28, 109–11, 119–23, 126, 132–33.

______. "Plot to Kill Kennedy? Rush to Judgment in New Orleans." *Saturday Evening Post* 240 (6 May 1967), 21–25.

______. "The Vice Man Cometh." *Saturday Evening Post* 236 (8 June 1963), 67–71.

Policoff, Jerry. "The Media and the Murder of John Kennedy." *New Times* 5 (8 Aug. 1975), 29–32, 34–36.

Policoff, Jerry, and Malone, William Scott. "A Great Show, A Lousy Investigation." *New Times* 8 (4 Sept. 1978), 5–6, 8, 12.

Powledge, Fred. "Is Garrison Faking?" *New Republic* 156 (17 June 1967), 13–18.

Prouty, L. Fletcher. "The Guns of Dallas." *Gallery* (May 1976), 19–22.

Reynolds, Ruth. "The Oswald Riddle." *Coronet* 5 (March 1967), 122–27.

Richler, Mordecai. "It's a Plot." *Playboy* 22 (May 1975), 132–33, 179–85, 188–90.

Roberts, Charles. "Eyewitness in Dallas." *Newsweek* 68 (5 Dec. 1966), 26–29.

Roberts, Gene. "The Case of Jim Garrison and Lee Oswald." *New York Times Magazine* (21 May 1967), 32–35.

Rogers, Warren. "The Persecution of Clay Shaw." *Look* 33 (26 Aug. 1969), 53–56, 58–60.

Russell, Francis. "Doubts About Dallas." *National Review* 18 (6 Sept 1966), 887–88, 890–93.

Salandria, Vincent J. "The Warren Report?" *Liberation* 10 (March 1965), 14–32.

Salisbury, Harrison. "Who Killed President Kennedy?" *Progressive Magazine* 30 (Nov. 1966), 36–39.

Schorr, Daniel. "The Assassins." *New York Review of Books* 24 (3 Oct. 1977), 14–22.

Snyder, Le Moyne. "Lee Oswald's Guilt: How Science Nailed Kennedy's Killer." *Popular Science* 186 (April 1965), 68–73.

Stang, Alan. "They Killed the President." *American Opinion* 19 (Feb. 1976), 1–8, 59–61, 63, 65, 67, 69, 71–72.

Stolley, Richard B. "What Happened Next: Film of John Kennedy's Assassination." *Esquire* 80 (Nov. 1973), 134–35, 262–63.

Thompson, Josiah. "The Cross Fire that Killed President Kennedy." *Saturday Evening Post* 240 (2 Dec. 1967), 27–31.
Trillin, Calvin. "The Buffs." *New Yorker* 43 (10 June 1974), 41–46, 48, 50, 53–54, 56, 59–60, 62, 65–66, 68, 71.
Turner, William W. "The Garrison Commission of the Assassination of President Kennedy." *Ramparts* 6 (Jan. 1968), 43–68.
Wahl, Fred, and Kramer, Joseph. "Neutron Activation Analysis." *Scientific American* 216 (April 1967), 68–86.
Weisberg, Harold. "Kennedy Murder: Buried Proof of a Conspiracy." *Saga* 34 (April 1967), 28–31, 89–90, 92, 94–96.
Welsh, Dan, and Turner, William. "In the Shadow of Dallas." *Ramparts* 7 (25 Jan. 1969), 61–71.
Whalen, Richard J. "The Kennedy Assassination." *Saturday Evening Post* 240 (14 Jan. 1967), 19–25.
Wheeler, Keith. "Cursed Gun: The Track of C2766." *Life* 59 (27 Aug. 1965), 62–65.
Wise, David. "Secret Evidence on the Kennedy Assassination." *Saturday Evening Post* 241 (6 April 1968), 70–73.
Young, Roger. "The Investigation: Where It Stands Today." *New Orleans* 1 (July 1967), 16–17, 54–59.

V. Television Programs and Documentaries

American Broadcasting Company
"Assassination: An American Nightmare." 14 Nov. 1975.
"Fidel Castro Speaks: Barbara Walters Interview." 9 June 1977.
"Friday Night: Mark Lane." 5 Jan. 1979.
"Goodnight America: Dick Gregory." 9 June 1977.
"Goodnight America: Mark Lane." 27 March 1975.
"Goodnight America: Marguerite Oswald." 23 Aug. 1976.
"Issues and Answers: Jim Garrison." 28 May 1967.
"The Trial of Lee Harvey Oswald." 30 Sept.–2 Oct. 1977.
British Broadcasting Corporation
"The Kennedy Cover-Up." 6 March 1978.
Canadian Broadcasting Corporation
"The JFK Assassination." 31 Dec. 1978; 2, 4, 5, 16 Jan. 1979.
Columbia Broadcasting System
"The American Assassins." Pts. I and II. 25–26 Nov. 1975.
"Face the Nation: David Belin." 23 Nov. 1975.
"Face the Nation: Richard Schweiker." 27 June 1976.
"Face the Nation: Louis Stokes." 31 Dec. 1978.
"November 22 and the Warren Report." 27 Sept. 1964.
"Walter Cronkite Interviews Lyndon Johnson." 4 May 1970.

"The Warren Report." 25–28 June 1967.
National Broadcasting Company
"The JFK Conspiracy: The Case of Jim Garrison." 19 June 1967.
"Tomorrow: Robert Groden." 1 April 1975.
"Tomorrow: Arlen Specter." 2 April 1975.
"Tonight: Johnny Carson Interviews Jim Garrison." 31 Jan. 1968.
Public Broadcasting System
David Susskind. "Who Was Lee Harvey Oswald?" 21 Jan. 1978.

VI. Newspapers

Dallas Morning News, 1963–80.
Dallas Times-Herald, 1963–80.
New Orleans States-Item, 1963–80.
New Orleans Times-Picayune, 1963–80.
New York Times, 1963–80.
Washington Post, 1963–80.
Texas Observer, 1963–67.

VII. Interviews

Bouchard, Fred. 18 May 1978
Burns, Van. 1 Sept. 1980
Craig, Roger. 18 Aug. 1972
Forrest, Helen. 17 May 1974
Herald, Jerry. 17 April 1978
Wilcox, George. 9 Sept. 1979
Numerous other interviews, the transcripts of which are in the author's possession.

VIII. Tabloids

Anderson, Dave. "JFK Assassination Still Mystery." *Bald Eagle,* 18–19 April 1975, pp. 14–24.

Branch, Sandy. "Where Were You When the Shots Rang Out? The Loss of Innocence in Louisiana." *Gris-Gris,* 13–19 Nov. 1978, pp. 33–43.

Carter, Philip D. "Eyewitness to the Autopsy: 15 Years Later, Richard Lipsey Can Finally Speak." *Gris-Gris,* 13–19 Nov. 1978, pp. 27–32.

"The Cover-Up of the Conspiracy That Assassinated JFK Is About to End." *National Tattler,* 8 June 1975, pp. 16–20.

Dick, William, and Dworken, Art. "JFK Was Killed By a Russian Agent." *National Enquirer,* 4 May 1976, p. 4.

Evans, Medford. "Why Was JFK's Body Reburied?" *Review of the News,* 15 Oct. 1975, pp. 31–40.
Gibson, Rod. "Warren Report on JFK Autopsy Was Wrong." *National Enquirer,* 7 Oct. 1975, p. 41.
"JFK Murder Solved." *Los Angeles Free Press,* 14 Feb. 1978, entire issue.
"Kennedy Murder Solved." *National Tattler,* Sept. 1975, entire issue.
"The Kennedy Tragedy: A Decade of Doubt." *National Tattler,* Nov. 1973, entire issue.
"Oswald May Have Been Cointelpro Agent: Evidence Assembled Indicates Mysterious Connections." *The Councilor,* 7 May 1975, pp. 8–11.

IX. Fiction

a. NOVELS

Condon, Richard. *Winter Kills.* New York: Dial, 1974.
Dimona, Joseph. *Last Man at Arlington.* New York: Arthur Fields, 1973.
Garrison, Jim. *The Star Spangled Contract.* New York: McGraw-Hill, 1976.
Fox, Victor J. (pseud.). *The White House Case.* Pleasantville, N.Y.: Fargo, 1968.
Lane, Mark, and Freed, Donald. *Executive Action.* New York: Dell, 1973.
Malzberg, Barry N. *The Destruction of the Temple.* New York: Pocket Books, 1974.
Singer, Loren. *The Parallax View.* Garden City, N.Y.: Doubleday, 1970.
Thurston, Wesley S. *Trumpets of November.* New York: Bernard Geis, 1966.

b. POETRY

Of Poetry and Power: Poems Occasioned by the Presidency and Death of John Kennedy. New York: Basic, 1964.

c. PLAYS (with place and date of opening performance)

DNA Collective. *Sparky and Truth Detector.* San Francisco, 1975.
Ducovney, Anram, and Friendman, Leon. *The Trial of Lee Harvey Oswald.* New York, 1967.
Garson, Barbara. *MacBird!* New York, 1967.

Gevirtzman, Bruce. *The Trial of Lee Harvey Oswald.* Hammond, La., 1979.

Hastings, Michael. *Lee Harvey Oswald: A Far Mean Streak of Independence Brought On By Negleck.* Atlanta, 1968.

Logan, John. *Jack Ruby: All-American Boy.* Dallas: 1974.

McIntyre, Mark. *J.F.K. Lives.* San Francisco, 1977.

INDEX